The Precarity of Masculinity

The Precarity of Masculinity
Football, Pentecostalism, and
Transnational Aspirations in Cameroon

Uroš Kovač

berghahn
NEW YORK • OXFORD
www.berghahnbooks.com

First published in 2022 by
Berghahn Books
www.berghahnbooks.com

© 2022, 2024 Uroš Kovač
First paperback edition published in 2024

All rights reserved. Except for the quotation of short passages
for the purposes of criticism and review, no part of this book
may be reproduced in any form or by any means, electronic or
mechanical, including photocopying, recording, or any information
storage and retrieval system now known or to be invented,
without written permission of the publisher.

Library of Congress Cataloging-in-Publication Data

Names: Kovač, Uroš, author.
Title: The precarity of masculinity: football, Pentecostalism, and transnational aspirations in Cameroon / Uroš Kovač.
Description: New York: Berghahn Books, 2022. | Includes bibliographical references and index.
Identifiers: LCCN 2021062580 (print) | LCCN 2021062581 (ebook) | ISBN 9781789209273 (hardback) | ISBN 9781789209280 (ebook)
Subjects: LCSH: Soccer—Cameroon. | Soccer players—Selection and appointment—Cameroon. | Soccer—Religious aspects—Christianity. | Pentecostalism—Cameroon. | Masculinity in sports—Cameroon. | Cameroon—Emigration and immigration.
Classification: LCC GV944.C17 K68 2022 (print) | LCC GV944.C17 (ebook) | DDC 796.334096711—dc23/eng/20220104
LC record available at https://lccn.loc.gov/2021062580
LC ebook record available at https://lccn.loc.gov/2021062581

British Library Cataloguing in Publication Data

A catalogue record for this book is available from the British Library

ISBN 978-1-78920-927-3 hardback
ISBN 978-1-80539-330-6 paperback
ISBN 978-1-80539-441-9 epub
ISBN 978-1-78920-928-0 web pdf

https://doi.org/10.3167/9781789209273

Contents

List of Illustrations		vi
Preface		viii
Acknowledgments		x
Introduction.	Precarity, Spirituality, and Masculinities	1
Chapter 1.	Dreams of Mobility: Football between Politics, Economy, Spirituality, and Transnational Markets	23
Chapter 2.	"This Is a Business, Not a Charity": Political and Moral Economy of Football and the Production of the Suffering Subject	49
Chapter 3.	Becoming Useful and Humble: Moral Masculinities in Uncertain Times	71
Chapter 4.	"Tapping the Power": Ruptures and Continuities in the Spiritual World of Football	96
Chapter 5.	Anxious Athletes, Spiritual Wives: Football, Pentecostalism, and the Body	120
Conclusion.	Masculinities, Faith, and the Production of Aspiration	143
References		154
Index		169

Illustrations

Maps

Map 0.1. The Southwest and Northwest Regions of Cameroon. United Nations map, public domain.   xiii

Figures

Figure 0.1. Half-time rest during a friendly match. Buea, Cameroon, October 2014. Photo by the author.   17

Figure 1.1. Almost every training session starts and ends with a collective prayer. Buea, Cameroon, September 2014. Photo by the author.   36

Figure 1.2. A billboard in downtown Buea announcing the beginning of the selection process for the most prominent football academy in Cameroon. June 2015. Photo by the author.   44

Figure 3.1. Interquarter match on a muddy field in Buea Town. Buea, Cameroon, July 2015. Photo by the author.   77

Figure 3.2. A Nigerian footballer and his Cameroonian teammate (in the background), recent arrivals on a third-division club in a village in Slovakia. June 2016. Photo by the author.   87

Figure 4.1. Pentecostal stickers, ubiquitous in cars and homes. Buea, Cameroon, May 2015. Photos by the author.   112

Figure 5.1. Whoever forces his opponent to touch the ground with his back or belly wins. The *sanja* or "wrapper" that one of the wrestlers is wearing around his waist indicates that he is

representing his village Bokwai, the standing champions. Bova,
Cameroon, May 2015. Photo by the author. 130

Figure 5.2. A Cameroonian footballer in deep prayer before a
training session with his new team in Southern Poland. May 2016.
Photo by the author. 137

Figure 6.1. Taking a selfie: the author with the famous
Cameroonian midfielder Eyong Enoh. Amsterdam, the
Netherlands, June 2016. Photo by the author. 143

Figure 6.2. Three generations of family members gathered in
a kitchen around a three-stone cooking fire. Fundong, Cameroon,
January 2015. Photo by the author. 152

Preface

In October 2016 teachers and lawyers from Cameroon's Anglophone Northwest and Southwest Regions protested against government officials, demanding them to stop appointing Francophone magistrates to preside over Anglophone courts and Francophone teachers to teach subjects other than French. The protest was one dramatic moment in a long history of Cameroon's "Anglophone problem," i.e., Anglophone Cameroonians' claim of being marginalized by an authoritarian state apparatus located in the French-speaking capital Yaoundé. Government security forces violently shut down the 2016 protest, arrested some of the organizers and trade union members, charged them with terrorism, and kept them imprisoned for months. Further protests soon followed. Some demanded a return to a federal state, but as the government continued to refuse to meaningfully negotiate with the protesters, a separatist movement formed, and in October 2017 unilaterally declared the region's independence from the Republic of Cameroon and established the independent state of "Ambazonia." The government responded by sending military forces, who used tear gas and shot and killed approximately forty people. In December 2017 the octogenarian president Paul Biya declared war on the separatists. Since then, the crisis has devolved into a full-blown armed conflict, with separatist militias killing security force members and kidnapping officials and government security forces terrorizing the region. Civilians have been caught in the crossfire. By 2021 anywhere between 3,000 and 12,000 civilians have been killed, at least 750,000 have been displaced, more than 200 villages have been burnt, schools have been closed, and numerous instances of rape, kidnappings, torture, and unlawful imprisonment have been reported. Atrocities have been committed by both sides, but evidence indicates that most of the indiscriminate violence has been committed by the government security forces. In 2021 the armed conflict continues, with no clear prospect for resolution (Kewir et al. 2021).

In the face of such immense suffering, a book about Cameroon that focuses on football, spirituality, and migration may sound trivial. Most ethnographic materials for this book have been collected in 2014 and 2015, more than a year before the violence escalated, at a time when, despite the long-standing tensions, an armed conflict of such magnitude seemed unlikely. And yet, the topics and arguments of this book are still relevant.

Firstly, this book provides a perspective on youth and masculinity beyond accounts of "problematic" young men who take part in violence, illicit activities, or armed conflicts. As Cameroonian scholars (for instance, Jude Fokwang and Divine Fuh) have been arguing for more than a decade, there is a need for detailed accounts of young men that move beyond simplistic narratives of poverty, abjection, and violence, but also emphasize the structural conditions that limit their prospects for a stable future. A focus on football, migratory disposition, and the spiritual life of young Cameroonians shows how young men seek to fashion themselves as moral subjects, primarily by seeking to fulfill their desires and obligations to provide for their kin, in the midst of socioeconomic conditions that make their futures profoundly uncertain.

Moreover, this book follows a perspective that critically approaches the discourse of crisis as a starting point for studying the African continent and its people. As many African and Africanist scholars have long argued (for instance, Achille Mbembe, Janet Roitman, and Francis Nyamnjoh), crisis as an exclusive starting point to think about the continent is inevitably limited. Even though the Southwest and Northwest Regions are suffering tremendously from the recent shocking and exceptional political crisis, a prolonged and routinized "crisis" in Cameroon, as both a discourse and reality, has shaped the region and the entire country ever since the 1980s and the imposed neoliberal structural adjustment programs. Both young Cameroonians' disposition to migrate overseas (nowadays also through football) as well as their protests against the Cameroonian government are a result of a long-term socioeconomic stalemate and young people's dwindling opportunities for a stable future in their own country. These issues have been prevalent long before the armed conflict and plague the entire country, not only its Anglophone regions.

The book therefore highlights the structural conditions that continue to shape and limit lives of young Cameroonians beyond the current conflict. Just like the roots of the conflict can be traced back to European colonial powers' demarcation of boundaries in West and Central Africa, to controversial interventions by an outgoing colonial British acting commissioner and the United Nations who denied the region the option of secession in the dawn of independence (Willis et al. 2019), or to an aging authoritarian president who emanates power from his residence in the Francophone capital (or a luxurious hotel suite in Switzerland), so are the future prospects of the region's young people shaped and limited by economic and political decisions taken elsewhere and by others, often by powers beyond their reach.

In general, I hope that this book provides a perspective on the region that moves beyond the inevitable future academic and expert accounts of "war-torn," "conflict-ridden," or "postconflict" Anglophone Cameroon, accounts that will likely tie people's lives and perspectives to a single tragedy or crisis.

Acknowledgments

My deepest gratitude goes to the Cameroonian footballers and their families in Buea, Limbe, Bamenda, and the countryside for their hospitality, patience, friendship, and knowledge. Unfortunately, in order to safeguard their anonymity, I cannot thank them individually. In this book I tried my best to do justice to their experiences and perspectives. I thank them for sharing with me their lives, dreams, struggles, and triumphs and for accepting me as a friend and researcher. I am also indebted to the football coaches, managers, and team staff members who facilitated my fieldwork in their clubs and academies. I thank them for allowing me to train in their clubs, ask countless questions, and probe their personal lives.

At the University of Amsterdam, where this project started, I was privileged to be mentored by very generous scholars. Niko Besnier assembled and led an outstanding research team on sports and globalization and was very generous with his feedback and critique. Peter Geschiere offered invaluable and detailed comments on the book, illuminated exciting new perspectives on my ethnography, and provided endless inspiration. I thank them both for guidance and support. The Department of Anthropology provided me with a dynamic academic home, and I greatly profited from the support from my colleagues. Apostolos Andrikopoulos, Dina Zbeidy, Arsenii Alenichev, Jordi Halfman, Anita Hardon, Rachel Spronk, Robert Pool, Amisah Zenabu Bakuri, Tanja Ahlin, Natashe Lemos Dekker, Julie McBrien, Eileen Moyer, Carla Rodrigues, Megan Raschig, Marten Boekelo, colleagues from the "Chemical Youth" and "Long Term Care" research groups—I thank them all for challenging workshops and encouraging conversations.

The research reported herein has received funding from the European Research Council under Grant Agreement 295769 for a project entitled "Globalization, Sport and the Precarity of Masculinity" (GLOBALSPORT). I owe to this project far more than simply a book title: the people involved in it profoundly shaped my work. I wish to thank the GLOBALSPORT team—Adnan Hossain, Daniel Guinness, Márk Hann, Domenica Gisella Calabrò, Sebastián Fuentes, Paweł Banaś, Michael K. Peters, Minke Nouwens, and Douglas K.

Thompson—for their friendship, inspiration, work, and support. I thank Susan Brownell for reading my early drafts and helping me formulate arguments more explicitly. Leo Hopkinson, Romit Chowdhury, and Mariane da Silva Pisani provided invaluable critical feedback.

My fieldwork in Cameroon would have been impossible without the help and guidance of my Cameroonian elders and friends. I thank Robert Mbe Akoko of the University of Buea and coach John Mayebi for guidance. I thank Akebegho Kingsley Akoh, Ravenstein Awuh (Crespo), and Mokom Njang (Abu) for their friendship and for welcoming me into their homes. I thank Emmanuel Mwambo for sharing with me his house in Limbe. At the University of Buea, Emmanuel Yenshu Vubo assisted me in obtaining the ethical clearance for this research.

I was also lucky to receive valuable support from a number of scholars all over the world. Walter Gam Nkwi, Rogers Tabe Egbe Orock, Francis Nyamnjoh, Basile Ndjio, Carmen Rial, Katrien Pype, Jarrett Zigon, James Esson, Paul Darby, Richard Giulianotti, John McManus, Sine Agergaard, Christian Ungruhe, Joseph Alter, Cheikh Tidiane Wane, William Kelly, Susana Narotzky, Tarminder Kaur, Dorothea E. Schulz, and Souleymane Diallo—I thank them all for their critical feedback. Elements from this book have been presented at various conferences and colloquiums: European Association for Social Anthropologists (EASA) Conference 2016 and 2018; American Anthropological Association (AAA) Annual Meeting 2016; African Studies Association of the United Kingdom (ASAUK) Conference 2018; University of Münster Department of Social and Cultural Anthropology Colloquium 2019; and African Studies Association (ASA) Virtual Annual Meeting 2021. I thank all the participants, panelists, and discussants for their constructive feedback. I also thank the two reviewers of this book who provided critical and encouraging comments. Thanks to Tom Bonnington, Marion Berghahn, and Lizzie Martinez at Berghahn Books for a smooth production process, and to Louise Chapman at Lex Academic for indexing.

I am grateful to the following publishers for permissions to republish revised selections from previous publications. Elements from "Becoming Useful and Humble: Masculinity, Morality, and Association Football in Cameroon," *Anthropological Quarterly* 94(3): 411–42 (2021) are reprinted with the permission of George Washington University Institute for Ethnographic Research. Parts of "'This Is a Business, Not a Charity': Football Academies, Political Economy, and Masculinity in Cameroon," in *Sport, Migration, and Gender in the Neoliberal Age*, edited by N. Besnier, D. G. Calabrò, and D. Guinness, 213–30 (London: Routledge, 2021) are reprinted with the permission of Taylor & Francis Group. Finally, elements from "Rethinking Masculinity in the Neoliberal Order: Cameroonian Footballers, Fijian Rugby Players, and Senegalese Wrestlers" (coauthored with N. Besnier, D. Guinness, and M. Hann), *Comparative Studies in Society and History* 60(4): 839–72 (2018) are reprinted with the permission of Cambridge University Press.

Much of this book was written in Utrecht (The Netherlands), a town that has over the years become my second (third? fourth?) home. My gratitude goes to the "De Kasko" living community that accepted me as a member and housemate. Ton Robben's early input was paramount in my decision to pursue anthropology. Between Utrecht and Amsterdam, Ana Poças Ribeiro, Uwe Thümmel, and Elke Linders have always been fabulous friends and housemates.

Back in Belgrade (Serbia), my family and friends have been very supportive and patient throughout my long absences. Nikola and Tamara Milenković inspired me with their love, and in the meantime Iskra was born. I always looked up to my aunt, Dragana Zečević-Saveski, who instilled in me a sense for drama and a joyful perspective on life. I thank my cousin, Aleksa Saveski, for making me fall in love with Belgrade once again. Nothing would have been possible without the support of my parents, Branislava and Radivoj Kovač, who brought me up to appreciate others and always seek new challenges.

Finally, Joska Ottjes was there when the first phone call came that started this research project, and she stuck around despite the long-distance travels and long working hours. We shared the joys of travel and discovery, and she allowed me to pull through in difficult moments. Her family—Lia, Jan, and Jesse—have accepted me as their own. In the last stages of revision of this book our daughter Nina was born, launching us into a new stage of family life. I am grateful for her unwavering support during this journey, and I look forward to the adventures and challenges coming our way.

Map 0.1. The Southwest and Northwest Regions of Cameroon. United Nations map, public domain.

Introduction
Precarity, Spirituality, and Masculinities

"It is time for me to reap the fruits of my labor!"

Ayuk was clearly frustrated. It was September 2014. I was walking with him and our friend Emil up the main road in Buea, a mountainous town in the Southwest Region of Cameroon, listening to them vent about their football agent. They were in their mid-twenties and they trained at a football academy, Buea Young Star FC. They dreamed of migrating abroad and playing football for a living with a foreign club.

Ayuk had already acquired a "football age" passport showing that he was nineteen—European football clubs could legally hire only players over eighteen, and they demanded young men no older than twenty-one. Ayuk had even managed to acquire a three-month tourist visa to enter the European Union. But his "football age" was already on the high side—soon it would be twenty, which would significantly reduce his chances of landing a position—and his visa would expire in a month and a half. Time was running out, but here he was, still in Cameroon, with his agent seemingly no longer interested in making the necessary arrangements to send him to Europe. "Why should I train every day if I am getting nothing from it?" he vented.

Emil, the captain of Buea Young Star FC, listened intently. Among aspiring footballers he was known as "MOG," short for "man of God," a nickname that reflected his fluency in Bible verses and dedication to Pentecostal Christianity, an increasingly influential spiritual movement. According to the visions of the future that God had revealed to Emil during his fervent prayers, Ayuk would leave Cameroon and play football abroad for a living only if he managed to resist giving in to numerous temptations of the devil and follow the path of God. "Right now, the devil is playing with you," Emil repeated several times. "The devil is making you consider departing from the path that God intended for you, the path of football." After a lengthy fit of rage, Ayuk calmed down and seemed less likely to lash out at the agent who held the key to his geographical and social mobility.

Ayuk's story illustrates how playing football for a living is an attractive but highly elusive opportunity for both livelihood and fame—a contemporary form of precarity that is central to this book. He was first spotted at age fourteen by coaches from the Ecole de Football Brasseries du Cameroun, the most prominent football academy in the country. He left school and Buea to begin training there, in Douala, the country's largest city and economic hub, with the goal of playing professionally. Some of his academy teammates were picked up by European youth clubs and developed international careers and superstar status, and the entire nation watched their performances on television. Ayuk, however, after four years at the academy, returned to Buea without a professional contract.

He was discouraged but refused to give up. Over the next few years he played and trained with local clubs and went "footing"—i.e., running—on Buea's hilly streets, alone, every morning at 5:00 A.M. before the sun rose. At that hour nightclubs were closing, and late-night partiers were returning from a night of drinking and dancing. One morning an expensive car stopped next to him, and out popped a young man who was most likely returning from a spending spree in Dream Lounge or some other popular nightclub or drinking joint. "I saw you on the field the other day," he said, "and I liked how you play. I like that you train so diligently. I want to help you in your football career. I want to help you play abroad." Ayuk accepted, and the man became his agent.

The agent seemed to keep his promise. He arranged for Ayuk to train with the junior national team—foreign clubs hired players based on their CVs, and tenure with the national team, however short, was a significant boost to Ayuk's list of accomplishments. The agent arranged for his doctored passport. He even arranged a trip to Europe, where Ayuk trained with a youth club in Germany for a few months, but then returned to Cameroon without a contract.

Meanwhile, his family obligations mounted. He needed to pay school fees and medical bills for his six-year-old daughter. He could barely pay the rent. His family elders were impatient, as they expected him to begin earning a living. Ayuk counted on playing for a wealthy European club, but now his agent appeared to be ignoring him. He did not disappear—the agent was not a *feyman*, i.e., a scammer, a dangerous type that young footballers are vigilant about—but he no longer seemed interested in financing his trips to Europe. Hence Ayuk's frustration in September 2014.

Emil was also bent on playing football and leaving Cameroon. His intervention in Ayuk's life illustrates the central role of spirituality among young men whose futures are plagued by uncertainty, a key analytical focus in this book. Emil was among the increasing number of young footballers who found Pentecostal denominations attractive, but he also stood out with his dedication to, as Pentecostals say, "filling himself with the Holy Spirit" by praying and reading the Bible. On numerous occasions he told me the details of visions he had during extensive prayer sessions when the Holy Spirit revealed to him each of his teammates' destinies. Ayuk had the "brightest star" of all, he said, the highest potential to prosper. But his success was conditional: Ayuk was surrounded by "bad men," "quarter boys" who drove him to gambling, drinking, and smoking marijuana. Ayuk needed to resist the temptations that surrounded him, Emil insisted; only then would the devil stop "blocking his star," and he would be free to migrate and prosper.

The agent eventually found an opportunity for Ayuk, who for the second time left Cameroon for Europe, in February 2015. I visited him in May 2016, over a year later, in his small rental apartment in Slovakia. His uncertain situation had not ended with his departure. He had encountered many challenges in his new setting—physical and verbal attacks by racist football fans, horrid living conditions, difficulties in obtaining documents, and an exploitative football club director who sought to profit from reselling players from Africa to other European clubs. But he was determined to continue playing in Europe for two reasons. The first had to do with his individual ambition—despite the difficulties and uncertainties, he loved playing football, and, as he said, "in life, you need to do what brings you happiness." The second was his obligations as a migrant: he was afraid to return to Cameroon without enough money to support his daughter, elder siblings, and parents. He had to stay in Europe and earn more before returning to Cameroon. "Otherwise, they will call me a useless man," incapable of providing and caring for others.

The stories of Ayuk and Emil, to which I will return several times, highlight problems that are central to this book. For many young men in Cameroon, as in many other places, the future is uncertain. This has become increasingly so since the economic crisis in the 1980s and the subsequent neoliberal structural adjustment programs that failed to reboot the economy and hampered young people's transition to adulthood. The expansion of the global market for football players beginning in the 1990s—a global market that exemplified neoliberal principles of deregulation and free enterprise—has offered young men the hope of not only achieving adulthood but also doing so in style, by playing "the beautiful game" and enjoying the superstar status that comes with it. Yet flashy football "careers" are elusive, and new forms of uncertainty have emerged. With the new opportunities of transnational sporting careers come new opportunities to fail.

Pentecostal spirituality emerges as a way for young men to both deal with the crippling uncertainty and actively engage with it. Many footballers sought the advice of Pentecostal pastors and prophets, often referred to as "men of God," and joined Pentecostal Christian denominations. Some used Pentecostal paraphernalia, such as anointed oil and holy water, to help them win matches and score goals. Others looked to churches for support in a fickle industry in which many fail. Yet others prayed with Pentecostal men of God to be granted a visa, leave the country, and compete for positions at foreign clubs. In all instances, Pentecostalism allowed players to deal with uncertainty.

In Cameroonian football, the emergence of Pentecostal spirituality is striking for two reasons. First, Cameroonians largely associate the game of football with sorcery and occult practices commonly referred to as "witchcraft." Cameroonians often speculate that when football coaches and managers want to prepare their teams for important matches, they seek help from traditional healers who perform rituals in order to increase the chance of winning. When football players want to stand out on the team, they may consult traditional healers who provide them with substances that can poison opponents or even teammates who are competing for the same position. The use of sorcery is highly secretive and difficult to pin down, but it is quite common in football. Recently, however, young footballers seem to be more inclined to seek advice from Pentecostal men of God, who are unapologetic in their calls that all practices that resemble "traditional" spirituality constitute the devil's work and need to be eliminated from football and all social life. In this sense, it is not entirely surprising that Pentecostal Christian men of God would wish to intervene in the "witchcraft-ridden" space of football, but it is striking that young footballers themselves, without any real pressure from coaches or managers or Christian pastors, gravitate toward Pentecostal men of God.

The emergence of Pentecostal Christianity among footballers is also striking because many Cameroonians consider footballers prime examples of virile youthful masculinity characterized by enthusiasm for nightlife, flirtatiousness with women, a promiscuous lifestyle, and frequent enjoyment of beer and whiskey. The image of young men who gladly enjoy the visibility that comes with football is not entirely unfounded. And yet a considerable number of aspiring footballers are willing to distance themselves from the perks of masculine popularity and subscribe to Pentecostal Christian denominations that scorn hypermasculine performances that they deem sinful and seek to transform sinners into good Christians and responsible men. The convergence of football aspirations and Pentecostal spirituality produces a performance of masculinity that is very different from the reductive stereotypes of "African" and "hegemonic" masculinity.

Ayuk's fear of being labeled a "useless man," a morally charged trope that describes those who fail to provide financially, reflects young men's growing fear of being seen as superfluous in the eyes of their kin. Relations with and obligations to kin figure centrally in young men's everyday experiences of training, migration aspirations, and migration itself. Cameroonian parents have long considered football an activity that distracts young men from education and social mobility, and many still do; however, since the turn of the millennium, football has emerged as an opportunity to migrate and begin earning a living, and parents have begun supporting young footballers' aspirations and helping finance their migration projects. On the surface, football stardom is emblematic of spectacular individual success, an ambition driven by a need to realize one's "God-given" talent, and young aspiring athletes are prime examples of entrepreneurs of the self whose success relies on individual focus, dedication to the sport, and deploying bodily capital to achieve material ends. As will become clear, the transformation of football into a global industry has amplified the drive to fulfill individual dreams of success. Yet at the same time, young athletes' migration projects are strewn with responsibilities for others, especially moral obligations to provide for their kin. The danger of becoming "useless" in the eyes of others can drive young athletes to embark on journeys strewn with obstacles and uncertainty.

This book focuses on these young men in precarious conditions, who increasingly harbor anxieties of being seen as superfluous, anxieties that are not exclusive to Cameroon but commonplace among young men throughout the world. Instead of taking at face value common assumptions of idleness of young men in Africa whose agency is limited to domains of criminality, trickery, or playful performance of cosmopolitan style, this book shows how young men struggle to construct alternative versions of masculinity that are built on moral values of self-discipline and care for their kin. I argue that attention to globalized sport is central to understanding how young men imagine and shape their future and seek to overcome the difficulties they face in the post-structural-adjustment period. Moreover, I aim to unpack the role of Pentecostal spirituality in areas of social life that are influenced by neoliberal transformations, a spirituality that allows young men to fashion themselves as gendered and moral subjects and reconfigure notions of masculinity, and yet remains inextricable from the stifling economic uncertainty that characterizes much of structurally adjusted West Africa.

Young Men, Precarity, and Cruel Optimism

In many parts of the world young men find it increasingly difficult to provide for themselves and their families, and transnational economic processes are central to these dynamics. The turn of the millennium has arguably produced a "contemporary predicament of youth" (Comaroff and Comaroff 2000: 306), by which young people struggle to reach adulthood in contexts of deepening social, economic, and political insecurity. More specifically, austerity measures and structural adjustment programs that have been implemented since the 1980s have increasingly excluded young men from ways of becoming and performing as men, especially through economic productivity (Cole and Durham 2007; Mains 2007; Weiss 2009). Many are forced to devise novel strategies to overcome economic uncertainty, including petty trade, informal work, and scam artistry (Newell 2012; Ndjio 2008b). At the same time, many young men seek to overcome local socioeconomic structures, which are often gerontocratic and driven by relations of patronage, and become fascinated by cosmopolitan imagery, such as hip-hop music and style (Weiss 2009), conspicuous performances of foreign elegance and wealth (Newell 2012), and, perhaps most strikingly, transnational migration.

For young men in many places, transcontinental migration has become a key strategy for securing an income, looking for opportunities lacking at home, and meeting older generations' growing expectations. Young men are eager to migrate at all costs and participate in processes of globalization and modernization from which they feel excluded (Ferguson 2006; Piot 2010). At the same time, regular routes to the global North have become strewn with obstacles, and migration for many has become increasingly "illegal" and risky (Andersson 2014; de Genova 2002). As a result, social networks and entire industries that focus on obtaining travel and migration documents have proliferated (Gaibazzi 2014; Piot with Batema 2019).

One of the avenues for migration that has gained considerable visibility over the last two decades is the transnational market for football players, as teams and clubs have been increasingly recruiting players from West Africa (Alegi 2010; Darby, Akindes, and Kirwin 2007). Much of this recruiting takes place through academies that proliferated since the 1990s in countries such as Ghana, Nigeria, Ivory Coast, Senegal, and Cameroon, many with the specific focus of identifying talented young men and preparing them for the transnational market (Darby 2013; Esson 2015b). Images of superstar athletes such as the Cameroonian Samuel Eto'o and the Ivorian Didier Drogba have spread all over the world in the past two decades, fueling young people's hopes of global recognition. Driven by a passion for the beautiful game, the star status of elite athletes, and economic and social anxieties, many young men dream of opportunities abroad and enroll in academies and clubs in the hope of launching a coveted career in professional sports.

In Cameroon, the idea of playing football for a living has increasingly appealed to young men since the mid-1990s, mainly (but not exclusively) those from poorer backgrounds who found themselves navigating increasing economic uncertainty that resulted from the economic crises in the 1980s and the failures of the structural adjustment programs that followed. In this context, the commercialization of football as a global sport and the expanding market for players that increasingly looked to West African countries for talented young men seemingly provided new and attractive opportunities for Cameroon's young men.

In reality, despite the perceived opportunities, it is extraordinarily difficult to stand out as an exceptional footballer in a very narrow window of time:

Cameroonian footballers need to be between eighteen and twenty-one years old—at least on paper, as Ayuk's case shows—if they hope to launch a career and travel abroad in order to earn a living by playing. Large numbers of boys and young men train and pursue the dream of a transnational football career, but only very few sign professional contracts. Even those who manage to leave Cameroon are often forced to take "irregular" migration trajectories, leaving them susceptible to exploitation by profit-seeking football agents. The hope and dream that the life project of becoming a transnational footballer provides are not in line with the precarious realities of actually "making it." Many projects of becoming a migrant athlete amount to "cruel optimism" (Berlant 2011), by which faraway dreams appear close, achievable, meaningful, and worthy of labor yet are beyond one's grasp and very difficult to attain. Thus young aspiring footballers in Cameroon experience precarity, i.e., the uncertainty of life in the globalized context of labor uncertainty (Allison 2013; Tsing 2015; Millar 2018), in two ways: first, through difficulties stemming from the country's post-structural-adjustment era, and second, through the attractive but precarious life project of "making it" as a professional footballer.

As will become clear in the following chapters, major transnational processes anchored in neoliberal ideologies of deregulation and free enterprise are crucial to these dynamics. In particular, the increasing corporatization and commoditization of the global business of sport, including football, in the 1990s (Andrews and Silk 2012; Besnier, Brownell, and Carter 2018; Besnier, Calabrò, and Guinness 2021) and the consequences of neoliberal structural adjustment programs imposed the world over by the International Monetary Fund, the World Bank, and international donors in the late 1980s shape the lives and experiences of young Cameroonian aspiring footballers.

This book will unpack the differing scales of the global and of the local—specifically that of the globalized football market and that of small football academies—and show how they are becoming critical in shaping young men in Cameroon. For instance: young Cameroonians flock to football academies that promise to sell them to clubs abroad. The academies in turn seek to inculcate young men with values of suffering and perseverance in the face of adversity and limited opportunities. The academies frame these values as cornerstones of adulthood. But in the context of commercialized global football, they are also values that allow the young men to internalize the precarity intrinsic to the competitive industry. Football in Cameroon is thus a fertile and concrete field for examining how people both deal with and actively seek to submit to neoliberal governmentality, i.e., the process of making self-reliant subjects on whose shoulders rests the responsibility for both success and failure (Foucault 2008: 229–33; Gershon 2011; McGuigan 2014).

Spirituality, Uncertainty, and the Gendered Subject

Despite the commonly held idea that modernity will reduce the role of religious and spiritual movements, people at the turn of the century are increasingly inclined to engage with the supernatural in order to deal with and actively participate in new economic and social circumstances. The global South in particular has seen the rise of what Jean and John L. Comaroff (2000) dubbed the "occult economies." Occult economies stand for an increasing number of occult interpretations of sudden and unexpected accumulations of wealth: if one manages to accumulate wealth with seemingly few resources and despite unlikely odds, people often consider that person's efforts as assisted by forces beyond practical explanation, such as magic and witchcraft (Geschiere 1997). The proliferation of occult economies throughout the world is an indicator that people recognize the accumulation of wealth in globalized "millennial capitalism" (Comaroff and Comaroff 2000) as having less to do with practical reason, rational decision-making, and work and more to do with speculation, risk-taking, and luck.

According to this vision, contemporary forms of Pentecostal Christianity are "holy-owned subsidiaries" (Comaroff and Comaroff 2000: 314) of occult economies. Contemporary Pentecostal denominations that promote the "prosperity gospel," i.e., the notion that prayers and dedication to the Holy Spirit will bring material wealth to dedicated Christians, have spread all over the world (Meyer 2004; Robbins 2004). Prayer meetings and healing sessions in "prosperity gospel" denominations respond to people's desire for miraculously quick solutions to economic hardship. As with occult economies, the prosperity gospel of Pentecostal Christianity allegedly relies on the "instant efficacy of the magical and the millennial" (Comaroff and Comaroff 2000: 314–15). The Pentecostal prosperity gospel also embodies a contradiction: on the one hand Pentecostal Christians condemn those who enrich themselves in seemingly magical ways, and on the other they pursue instant material gains through novel spiritual means in prayer meetings and healing sessions (Meyer 1999). From this point of view, despite its different iterations across the world, Pentecostal Christianity is not much different from occult economies.

Critics of the notion of "occult economies" have argued that the global expansion of spiritual practices, whether linked to the occult or to the Holy Spirit, is not simply a response to the expansion of global markets and the increased uncertainty that characterizes twenty-first-century capitalism. Spiritual practices are not merely otherworldly reflections of deregulated markets or allegorical images of modernity's contradictions. For example, in Ghanaian Akan shrines in Detroit, young priests use discourses of witchcraft not only to criticize excessive consumerism but also to develop an alternative "American dream" rooted in old-style Fordist capitalism (Parish 2015). In another example, one more globally visible, an increasing number of people throughout the post-structural-adjustment global South join Pentecostal Christian denominations in order to construct new social relations at a time when neoliberal austerity programs have eroded old ones (Haynes 2012; Haynes 2013; Robbins 2009). For some followers of Pentecostal Christianity, prayers and congregations can lead to a long-term process of self-transformation that can fuel ambitions of large-scale social and political change (Marshall 2009). All of these examples are of people for whom spiritual practices are not only celestial reflections of material processes, such as market dynamics, but also a form of action, with tangible consequences in the material world.

As the following chapters will make clear, Pentecostal spirituality for young footballers is a way of dealing with the cruel optimism of competitive transnational football industries. It is also a way of imagining a future elsewhere, outside of Cameroon, and actively dealing with barriers that limit geographical and social mobility, such as the need for passports and visas. Moreover, for young aspiring footballers, involvement with Pentecostal spirituality acquires a particularly relevant material dimension. Like athletes everywhere, young footballers are focused on training and maintaining their athletic bodies. Aspiring athletes are perfect examples of people who use their bodily capital as a source of action—a way to fulfill life ambitions or find a way out of poverty. But before athletic bodies can be put to use, they need to become "docile" (Foucault 1995 [1979]), that is, subject to manipulation, training, and discipline (Brownell 1995). For young Cameroonian footballers this is most clearly articulated in their anxieties concerning sexual behavior. As will become clear in chapter 5, a "common piece of knowledge" among footballers and their coaches is that excessive sexual activity results in diminished athletic performance. Pentecostal spirituality emerges as one way of articulating and controlling fears over the loss of bodily capital.

Looking "beyond the body proper" (Farquhar and Lock 2007), i.e., beyond the material body extracted from its social context, Pentecostal spirituality is crucial for young Cameroonian footballers in their efforts to challenge and transform common notions of youthful masculinity that are grounded in performances of virility. Pentecostalism in different parts of the world often leads to the "domestication of men," by which people measure men's moral standing based on their attention to the household and confinement of sexual practices to marriage (Brusco 1995; Soothill 2007). It also inspires novel projects of nation building based on the idea that masculinity is in dire need of transformation (van Klinken 2016). But the attraction of Pentecostalism among young men who aspire to move abroad and who harbor dreams of transnational careers reveals a key role of Pentecostal spirituality in the making of gendered subjects in conditions of globalized uncertainty.

Football is thus a fertile and concrete field for investigating the wide-ranging issues that the Comaroffs and their critics have raised. For one, what is the role of spirituality, especially Pentecostal Christianity, for people who deal with new and old forms of uncertainty? Second, what is the role of spirituality in the making and maintenance of gendered bodies? And finally, what is the role of spirituality in the making of gendered—in this case masculine—subjects? Rather than asking whether spirituality, Pentecostal or otherwise, reflects large-scale processes of contemporary capitalism, I seek to investigate exactly why Pentecostalism is attractive to young Cameroonians and why they seem to increasingly gravitate toward Pentecostal men of God rather than traditional healers, and I endeavor to determine the consequences of their spiritual practices. This book will show that Pentecostalism is very much intertwined with the "global production of desire" (Trouillot 2001: 129) of the contemporary moment and clearly provides the "instant efficacy of the magical and the millennial" (Comaroff and Comaroff 2000: 315) that resembles occult practices. However, it will also show that Pentecostalism offers young men a disciplinary and moral regime that converges with the demands of their coaches and helps them deal and engage with new forms of precarity.

In order to do justice to the perspectives and everyday practices of my research participants, I prefer to analyze Pentecostal Christianity in terms of "spirituality" and "spiritual practice" rather than as a "religion." The main reason for this is grounded in my ethnographic observations. My Pentecostal Christian friends rarely speak about Pentecostalism as a religion. Quite the opposite: they refer to their way of practicing Christianity as a "way of life," one not bounded by a religious canon or an institution but instead depending on their individual experience of the Holy Spirit that defies institutional boundaries. Rather than referring to themselves as "religious," they consider themselves "spiritual" in the sense of investing considerable energy and time in relating to entities beyond the material world.

Another reason for a focus on "spiritual" rather than "religious" is an anthropological critique that demonstrates how defining and objectifying the religious as an isolated domain of social life is a product of a unique post-Protestant reformation history in Europe when Christian churches sought to achieve coherence in doctrines, practices, and rules (Asad 1993). More often than not, religion does not have an autonomous essence that is separate from politics, law, science, or sport but instead infuses different domains of social life. This is certainly true of Pentecostal Christianity (despite its historical origins in Evangelical Protestantism), a worldwide spiritual movement that seeks to infuse the Holy Spirit in domains commonly considered profane, such as markets and politics (Comaroff 2009; Marshall 2009).

The goal of shifting attention from "religious" to "spiritual" is not to argue that Pentecostal Christianity is not a religion. After all, its denominations rely on literal interpretations of the Bible, Pentecostal pastors closely follow the book as the word of God, and their main activities take place in churches. The goal is rather to recognize ruptures and continuities between different kinds of spiritual practices, such as sorcery, Pentecostal Christianity, and other forms of Christianity, as well as to consider the role of spiritual practices in other forms of everyday life not necessarily linked to the church, such as football and aspirations for mobility.[1]

Beyond the Crisis of Masculinity

Masculinity, the enactment and embodiment of being a man, has occasionally come to be regarded as being in crisis in the contemporary world. The notion of "crisis of masculinity" has been used by analysts to highlight how recent transformations on a global scale threaten the previously more predictable ways men used to realize their masculinity and to demonstrate men's difficulties in dealing with neoliberal structural adjustments and socioeconomic change in general (Comaroff and Comaroff 2000: 307; Perry 2005; see also Silberschmidt 2001). All over the world women have been deeply affected by structural adjustment programs, at least as deeply as men, yet they seem to have been more capable in adapting to new conditions, through avenues such as entrepreneurship and the informal economy, strategic marriages, or participation in industries that are traditionally female preserves, such as caregiving and domestic work (Cole 2010; Freeman 2014; Niger-Thomas 2000). In contrast, young men faced with the consequences of austerity measures seem to have become particularly anxious of being seen as superfluous, especially by their kin, and being labeled as "useless" by women and the elderly (Cornwall 2002; Lin 2016; Perry 2005). Many have been relegated to experiences of "boredom" and "waithood" (Honwana 2012; Jeffrey 2010; Masquelier 2013; O'Neill 2014) or have found precarious livelihoods in male-dominated fields marked by violence and illegality, such as "gangs," drug trafficking circuits, and militias (Van Stapele 2021; Vigh 2015; Vigh 2017).

But while the notion of "crisis of masculinity" captures some of the challenges that men face in the contemporary world, it does not address the variety of ways in which men in difficult economic or political circumstances struggle to overcome hardships and attempt to make themselves into moral and gendered subjects. Taking "crisis" as an exclusive starting point of inquiry is problematic, as it has come to be a "place from which one claims access to and knowledge of history" (Roitman 2017: 24), especially about Africa and Africans. The Anglophone Southwest and Northwest Regions of Cameroon have been affected by a political crisis that started in 2016 and has since escalated into a shocking and unprecedented armed conflict (Kewir et al. 2021). And yet, in the years before the conflict, when the bulk of the fieldwork for this book was conducted, "crisis" was nothing new in Anglophone Cameroon. Like elsewhere in West Africa (Piot 2010), the discourse and reality of crisis has shaped everyday life here since the neoliberal structural adjustments of the late 1980s (Fokwang 2008; Johnson-Hanks 2005; Konings 2011). After the initial profound shock of austerity measures, the socioeconomic life settled into a routinized state of crisis (Mbembe and Roitman 1995) or "crisis ordinariness" (Berlant 2011: 10), an experience quite different from the rupturing experience of crisis as an interception of stable life. Moreover, the notion of "crisis of masculinity" has been subjected to loaded interpretations. In some cases, the notion attributes social problems to men and masculinity and its use can result in pathologizing them (Smith 2017; Enria 2016). In other (quite different) interpretations, it is used to indicate that men's economic and political power in relation to women has decreased; yet men still hold positions of power, continue to benefit from the patriarchal dividend, and dominate most domains of life (see Morrell 2002). Finally, the idea that masculinity is in crisis often emerges as an ideological construct that overemphasizes gendered identity while obscuring underlying structural conditions, such as the restructuring of the economy (Cornwall, Karioris, and Lindisfarne 2016: 8–9; Yang 2010). As a number of analysts have recently noted (Ammann and Staudacher 2021; Little 2016; McLean 2021; Musariri and Moyer 2021; Schultz 2021), the notion of "crisis of masculinity" obscures more than it reveals.

Another common way in which masculinity has been discussed is by focusing on how people assert some forms of masculinity as "hegemonic" by way of subordinating other, less dominant forms of masculinity. The core of the notion of "hegemonic masculinity" (Connell 1987; Connell and Messerschmidt 2005) is useful because it not only reasserts the widely accepted idea that people construct masculinities differently in various contexts and histories (Cornwall and Lindisfarne 1994; Gutmann 1996; Hodgson 1999) but also reveals a hierarchy of forms of masculinity, some emerging as more dominant than others. Yet the notion of "hegemonic masculinity" is less useful when it suggests that a hierarchy is so clearly defined and that a single notion of masculinity emerges as hegemonic in any particular context (Dawley and Thornton 2018: 16; Miescher 2005; Ocobock 2017; Osella and Osella 2006; Ratele 2016). Moreover, masculinities, despite being considered in specific contexts, become in this way extracted and objectified as clearly definable categories of social life. In reality, masculinities emerge at the intersections of different domains of social life, such as economic and political activities, and it is not always clear what kind of masculinity emerges as hegemonic.

When considering constructions of masculinity in situations in which different kinds of uncertainty intersect, I suggest instead to discuss the "precarity of masculinity."[2] The term is useful for two reasons. First, it emphasizes that all types of masculinity, even those that appear sovereign, are unstable and subject to contestation. For instance, many young Cameroonians defy the idea that "African masculinity" is based on performances of virility. Even though most contemporary studies of masculinities in Africa have concluded that masculinities on the continent are diverse and cannot be reduced to a singular notion of "African" (Lindsay and Miescher 2003; Ouzgane and Morell 2005), there still exists an "idea of African men" (Spronk 2014), held and reproduced by both Africans and outside observers (such as public health professionals who focus on issues of HIV/AIDS), that assumes virility as a cornerstone of African masculinity. The social invention of a virile African man has permeated different spheres of life of men on the continent, from street culture (Aterianus-Owanga 2013; Pype 2007) to state building (Ndjio 2012). It remains at the heart of the idea of African masculinity as a problem, both among outside researchers and women in Africa (Igonya and Moyer 2013; Smith 2009). "*Man pikin* [young man] likes cheating too much," Cameroonian women often complain, and the men who brag about their sexual exploits and their ability to "keep" many women invoke traditions of polygyny as explanations and excuses. However, many young men challenge this notion of masculinity, and even though Cameroonians often mark footballers as yet another instance of youthful virile masculinity, many footballers seek to stay away from these models, seeing them as key problems that prevent young men from using their athletic talents and advancing in life. Both football training and Pentecostal Christian churches are crucial to this "emergence" (Inhorn and Wentzell 2011) of alternative forms of manhood and renegotiation of masculinity. Thus, even the most seemingly dominant modes of masculinity, and perhaps especially those, are prone to contestation.

Another good reason to refer to masculinity as precarious is that the term "precarity," in the sense of a contemporary mode of uncertainty of labor and income characteristic of globalized neoliberal capitalism (Allison 2013; Tsing 2015; Millar 2018), suggests that performances of masculinity cannot be separated from structural conditions that limit and shape men's possibilities for economic reproduction (see also Cornwall, Karioris, and Lindisfarne 2016). Masculinity is a production inextricable from the political economy and is grounded in gendered aspirations and disciplining regimes specific to a given political and economic moment. In the contemporary post-structural-adjustment time in West Africa, this means that performances of masculinity are intertwined with the economic uncertainty that haunts young men as well as with the increasing perception that opportunities for a livelihood and social adulthood lie in participation in unpredictable globalized markets. The former is particularly clear when one considers that young men risk becoming labeled "useless men" by their elders, a condemnation that is closely tied to their inability to financially provide for their families. The latter is especially clear when one considers that an increasing number of young men see their chances in a competitive and intrinsically precarious transnational football industry.

The damning label "useless man" reflects another simple fact: that men are constantly faced with moral judgments from their social surroundings and struggle to live up to others' expectations. Like people everywhere (Robbins 2013), young Cameroonians struggle to make themselves into moral subjects. In poor urban settings, young men seek to "fight social ills" like sexual promiscuity, urban violence, and consumption of alcohol and to gain respectability and recognition as social adults in the context of what they perceive as contemporary Cameroon's moral bankruptcy (Fokwang 2008: chapter 7; Fuh 2012). The young men respond to moralized discourses that label them "useless" and orient themselves to moral values by striving to become "humble." These moralized gendered discourses need to be taken seriously and not conflated with issues of power, hierarchy, or politics (Khan 2018; Spall 2020).

Sport is a particularly fertile social realm to analyze the construction of moral and gendered subjects. It rarely concerns only the construction of athletic bodies. Sports are a key site for the construction of gender ideologies (Besnier, Brownell, and Carter 2018: chapter 5; Klein 1993), and athletes are frequently subjected to moral evaluations, often perceiving their athletic endeavors as development of moral subjectivity. For instance, wrestlers in India see their athletic endeavors as development of individual character as well as a public critique of what they see as the modern Indian state's morally bankrupt practices (Alter 1992). In China people compel athletes to embody state-promoted values such as "civilization" and "discipline" (Brownell 1995). Cricket in the West Indies (James 2005 [1963]) and surfing in South Africa (Laderman 2014) serve as platforms to challenge colonial subjugation and racism on moral grounds.

I suggest that the term "moral masculinities" can account for ways in which men struggle to negotiate a variety of gendered moral evaluations and judgments and fashion themselves as moral and gendered subjects. If, according to Didier Fassin, moral economies consist of the "production, distribution, circulation, and use of moral sentiments, emotions and values, and norms and obligations in social space" (Fassin 2009: 1257), then moral masculinities are oriented toward how these aspects of the moral shape masculine subjects. Moral masculinities are ways of being a man that emerge from men's attempts to deal with others' moral judgments (Meiu 2009), from their attempts to orient themselves to moral values (Baral 2016; Simoni 2015; Thornton 2018; Wignall 2016), and from their struggles to do and be good (Smith 2017). Like all people, young Cameroonian footballers evaluate what is the right path to take and what is the right thing to do and reflect on their own actions and the actions of others. They act in relation to the judgments of others (e.g., their peers and elders), institutions (e.g., religious institutions), and large-scale processes (e.g., transnational markets). As Lila Abu-Lughod writes, "For individuals . . . conformity to the code of honor and embodying the cultural ideals set by that code for the individual are not empty acts of impression management but the stuff of morality" (Abu-Lughod 1986: 238). Cameroonian footballers are not conforming to a clearly outlined moral code, but, rather, they navigate evaluations articulated on both global and local levels, from transnational markets to family relations. Still, however, their activities are not reducible to either fulfilling unavoidable social obligations or calculated pragmatic actions motivated by self-interest (see Lambek 2010). Their actions are also not reducible to simple responses to neoliberal restructuring of the economy, even when they formulate dispositions that help them participate in globalized neoliberalism (see Zigon 2011). Rather, it is the "stuff of morality" that shapes young men as gendered subjects. Focusing on morality helps with moving beyond limited approaches to masculinities that rely on representations of men as either victims of contemporary transformations and crises or powerful agents who reproduce the hegemony of certain forms of masculinity.

However, it is not enough to consider men as moral subjects. Anthropologists need to be attentive to how moralized discourses become central when people invoke masculinity as a problem and an obstacle, a reason for a lack of progress (see also Smith 2017: chapter 5). As Masquelier (2019) shows in her analysis of accusations of idleness aimed toward young men in Niger, "the discourse of idleness is often fraught with moral implications: to be idle is to be lazy. . . . Rather than seeing idleness as a by-product of structural inequality, many elders associate it with thievery and delinquency" (Masquelier 2019: 3–4). In Cameron, the "useless man" trope is freely deployed by Cameroonians young and old when referring to young men who supposedly waste their time in urban quarters and avoid the struggle to provide for their family elders and juniors. Cameroonians discuss how social problems will be solved only after young men manage to change: if they would only stop taking part in time-wasting local football matches, spending too much time socializing with "bad friends" in their neighborhoods, having a lack of focus due to "distractions" such as drinking and gambling, or having too many sexual partners, they would manage to avoid becoming "useless." Footballers are not excluded from these discourses: for many Cameroonians, all of these issues diminish footballers' possibilities to not only perform well on the field but also to obtain visas and passports and sign contracts with international football clubs, despite the fact that opportunities to do so are scarce. Thus, young men are navigating a range of gendered moral judgments and evaluations that can effectively obscure the uncertainties of transnational markets and the elusiveness of adulthood in times of economic hardship. Anthropologists need to critically assess how different forms of precarity become translated into issues of morality and masculinity and how gendered notions of morality can obscure the consequences of economic and political processes that shape and limit young men.

Athletes, Academies, and the *Waytman* Researcher: Fieldwork in the Southwest Region

My ethnographic research on masculinities and globalizing sports was based in football fields and academies in the Southwest Region of Cameroon. Very soon after my first arrival in 2014 in Buea, the regional capital home to some 130,000 inhabitants, I was immersed in the world of football. A well-known coach, who became famous for being the first to guide a team from Anglophone Cameroon to a national championship title, offered me the "lay of the land" of football in the region and the country and introduced me to key stakeholders and institutions. Two clubs struck me as the most interesting.[3]

One was Unisport Limbe FC, a well-established football academy and club in Limbe, a coastal town of around 90,000 inhabitants, less than one hour's drive from Buea. The club was founded by a very prominent figure who managed a large parastatal company, was close to the region's chiefs and traditional authorities, and built his reputation as a "big man" who spearheaded regional development. The club competed in the Cameroonian elite national division. The other was Buea Young Star FC, a small, recently founded club in Buea, almost ad hoc in appearance and practice, run by a young Cameroonian entrepreneur. The club competed in the lower rungs of Cameroonian football, but its real goal was not national promotion: the club president focused on discovering and training young talented footballers and selling them to clubs abroad. The contrast between the two clubs was striking: one was large and "local," i.e., an established institution widely recognized in the country and firmly grounded in the region's history and politics, while the other was small and "transnational," i.e., a one-man show oriented toward establishing connections in Europe and selling players abroad.

I settled in Buea, moving between two quarters (Molyko and Great Soppo) during my twelve-month stay, and trained with Buea Young Star FC for the first four months. On odd days I made trips to Limbe, where I followed the footballers and coaches of Unisport Limbe FC in preparations for key matches as well as in their private lives in their homes and quarters. My home base in Limbe was the house of a well-known footballer in the region, one of four houses he had built using his salary from the club he played for in France. I stayed there with his brother and nephews, also footballers, aspiring or accomplished.

A key part of my fieldwork was focused on establishing and cultivating relationships with young footballers such as Emil and Ayuk, whose conversation helped introduce this book. As will become clear, much of my ethnographic materials came from my everyday engagements with teammates and young men who became my friends. Like the opening story above, most of the materials in this book acquire depth only when placed in the appropriate social context, as stories of specific individuals. During my stay in Cameroon, I trained and spent time with them and their friends in Buea and Limbe quarters, on and around football fields (figure 0.1), in their homes, and in my rented rooms. I attended family funerals and weddings and traveled to home villages in the Northwest and Southwest Regions to visit parents and grandparents. I accompanied them to churches and prayer meetings. I was only a few years older than most of the footballers, and in most cases I was able to take part in their social lives. Establishing relationships based on trust also allowed me to inquire about details of more intimate issues, like sexuality. As in every social anthropological study, information and analysis emerged through an intersubjective exchange of knowledge between the people whose stories appear in these pages and me.

Buea, Limbe, and the Southwest Region were perfect locations to conduct research on sports and all the social dynamics that surround them. In addition to football and the expected craze for it, all kinds of sports and physical activities were an integral part of the region's social life. Buea is located at the foot of Mount Cameroon, and a major annual event in the town is the "Race of Hope," a stunning forty-kilometer competition in which athletes run up the slopes

Figure 0.1. Half-time rest during a friendly match. Buea, Cameroon, October 2014. Photo by the author.

of the highest peak in West Africa and back down it in a remarkable display of athleticism and endurance. More important for this book, the Southwest Region is home to the popular *wesua* or *pala-pala*, a form of traditional wrestling practiced by the Bakweri, an ethnic group indigenous to the coast of the Southwest Region. Wrestling tournaments are organized in villages and quarters during the dry season, between February and June. Interviews with young wrestlers, and especially with retired wrestling champions (*ngumu*), were crucial in understanding the dynamics between indigenous notions of body and sexuality and intersections with modern sports.

In 2016 my fieldwork became transnational. A few of my friends from Buea Young Star FC and Unisport Limbe FC had managed to migrate to Europe despite the odds, and I visited them in June 2016 in Poland and Slovakia. I spent one month with them in their rented rooms and football clubs. The attitudes of my friends to migration and Europe had changed, and their new perspectives were crucial to the analysis that follows.

In addition to participant observation, I conducted approximately 110 semistructured interviews with young footballers, retired footballers, their partners, siblings, parents, grandparents, coaches, managers, and football officials, as well as men of God, wrestlers, wrestling elders, and sport journalists. I recorded 60 of those interviews. I also made many audio and video recordings of events that struck me as important, such as leisure time in the quarters, prayer sessions, club meetings, warm-up singing in dressing rooms, and training sessions. Research on men and masculinities would be incomplete without attention to the perspectives of women, and since football fields were predominantly masculine social spaces, I made conscious efforts to socialize with the footballers' sisters, mothers, and girlfriends, and to give their perspectives the attention they deserve.

Linguistic competence was a primary concern in a country known for linguistic diversity and inventiveness (Pool 1994: 44–48). Cameroon is officially a bilingual country, with English and French serving as administrative languages, the result of decades of colonial rule by France and the United Kingdom, which lasted until 1960. There are an additional 250 languages spoken in Cameroon. However, the vernacular in the Anglophone Southwest and Northwest Regions, especially in towns such as Buea and Limbe that are home to migrants from the country's other regions, is Cameroonian Pidgin English. I built on my knowledge of Krio, which I learned during my previous research project in Sierra Leone, and, while there are important differences between the Sierra Leonean and Cameroonian vernaculars, it provided me a base to quickly develop fluency in the early stages of fieldwork. Most of my interactions were in Pidgin English, except when my interlocutors insisted on speaking English, such as in churches and during prayers. Some interactions demanded a basic knowledge of Mboko Tok, a dynamic mixture of English, French, and Pidgin.

Originally a slang spoken by "common men" such as taxi drivers and construction workers, and which was popularized in the 1980s by the singer and protest artist Lapiro de Mbanga, Mboko Tok has been largely appropriated by young men and women in urban quarters who continue to add new words and expressions to its dynamic lexicon.[4]

As a White man in my late twenties, some of the first words I learned after arriving in Cameroon were terms that designate White people. *Waytman* was the most common one, followed by *sará* (used mainly by the Bakweri) and *oyibó* (a term borrowed from neighboring Nigeria).[5] When asked where I was from, I always (truthfully) answered "from Serbia" rather than "from Europe," in a conscious effort to distance myself from European nationalities with a history of colonialism, especially France, which many in Anglophone Cameroon consider the European country most responsible for the region's economic and political plights (Nyamnjoh and Page 2002). I was surprised that the young footballers would become keenly interested in the Serbian football scene and in opportunities to play in Serbia, demonstrating that their migration aspirations were not fixed to the global North.

Moreover, as a foreigner clearly interested in football, every time I initiated contact with young footballers or football club officials I had to insist that I was not a football manager interested in profit and that my goal was not to discover talented footballers and take them abroad to *waytman kontri*, i.e., Europe. The Southwest Region is not a regular destination for foreign talent hunters, but both of the football academies with which I closely worked at some point had partnerships with European managers or coaches who occasionally visited the area to scout for young footballers. Even after I had explained that my interest in sport was purely academic, entrepreneurial Cameroonians involved in football saw me as a resource for potential connections with European football clubs and managers. Even at the end of my twelve-month fieldwork, some encouraged me to enter the "business of football," which I never did.

Training with Buea Young Star FC in the first months of my fieldwork was a way to gain access to masculine spaces of Cameroonian football and to suspend, at least temporarily, the power inequalities and boundaries between Whiteness and Blackness that separated the footballers and me. Just like them, I had to submit to coaches' rigorous training regimes, at least for the first few months. On football fields, the difference in competence between myself and the footballers was obvious, as their football skills, tactical reasoning, and physical strength were far superior to mine. This led to many embarrassing jokes at my expense, but it also opened the door for friendships. In later months, my role became that of club assistant and photographer, which allowed me to focus more on asking questions and taking notes.

Some of my closest friends occasionally insisted that I was not a *waytman*, or at least not a stereotypical one. "Waytman? Usay yi dey?" (White man?

Where is he?), one of my friends would comment during social occasions, making a point to others present that I should not be viewed as a European. "You are not like other White men, you are simple. You are my brother." I was told this a few times by friends. After I asked them to clarify, they explained that I was different from most White people they knew who socialized with Cameroonians only when they had something to gain. I was of course very touched, as these acts appeared to go beyond simple hospitality and were genuine expressions of intimacy. At other times, however, I was crudely reminded that I was indeed a *waytman*, sometimes by those same friends, and that I was after all profiting from their friendships, in ways they could not profit from mine. This at times also signaled that I was becoming too inquisitive about sensitive details, such as witchcraft accusations or "fake" documents. My fieldwork was thus a constant negotiation between my role as a *waytman* researcher and an intimate "brother."

To my surprise, some of the more sensitive topics, such as the semilegal manipulation of travel documents, were public secrets. Even when the footballers were reluctant to discuss them directly, it was not very difficult to learn about them, but it made clear my responsibility to protect the anonymity of the people I worked with. Anonymizing was not always easy, since some of my key research participants were high-profile figures who could easily be identified by those familiar with football and politics in Southwest Cameroon. The names of key characters and football clubs in this book are pseudonyms, and some inconsequential details about them have been altered in an effort to protect their identities. The exception are well-known public figures, such as politicians and famous footballers, coaches, and club owners, whose identities could hardly be concealed.

Chapters and Arguments

In this book I argue that young men's aspirations to migrate to play football highlight issues that are central to the analysis of masculinities in post-structural-adjustment West Africa.[6] More generally, I argue that the athletic aspirations of young Cameroonians and their propensity to consult with Pentecostal men of God offer new insights about the nature of social mobility in the neoliberal age. To demonstrate this, throughout all the following chapters I seek answers to two simple questions: Why are so many young men in Cameroon attracted to mobility through football, despite being aware of the miniscule chances of success? And why do they gravitate toward Pentecostalism when there are ample other social and spiritual resources available to them?

In chapter 1 I outline the history of football in Cameroon and the Southwest Region from its introduction by European colonial administrators to the present-day commercialization of the sport. More importantly, the chapter details key structural conditions that fuel the precarity of life and livelihood of Cameroonian young men in general and aspiring footballers in particular. I demonstrate that young men's disposition to migrate through football is grounded in the prolonged economic stalemate and neoliberal austerity measures since the late 1980s, the proliferation of images of superstar athletes, and the expansion of the transnational market for football players since the 1990s.

Chapter 2 compares two of the region's most prominent but very different football academies, focusing particularly on how their "presidents" managed players. It shows how new football academies that consider aspiring footballers as commodities to be sold in transnational markets play a key role in molding young men to be willing to embrace new forms of precarity and to internalize neoliberal forms of agency as markers of adult masculinity.

Chapter 3 shows how morality is central to the ways young men attempt to face, on the one hand, diminishing livelihood possibilities at home and, on the other, the unpredictable transnational football industry. I focus on two key aspects that shape young men as moral and gendered subjects: their tenuous relationships with family members, reflected in young men's fears of being labeled "useless men," and the role of Pentecostal Christianity in shaping young footballers as "humble" men, focused on the sport, with faith in success despite unlikely odds. I show how the intersection between football aspirations and Pentecostalism shapes moral masculinities.

In chapter 4 I delve deeper into the spiritual aspects of football and demonstrate that magico-religious practices and Pentecostalism are deeply intertwined. The chapter scrutinizes the Pentecostal footballers' claims of rupture with "traditional" forms of spirituality and "demonic" forces, and reveals rupture as a key notion that allows the young men to fashion themselves as moral subjects, but one that reflects a desire for transformation rather than an accomplishment.

Chapter 5 focuses on young footballers' struggles to control and maintain their athletic bodies. I show how sexuality is a main source of embodied anxiety for the footballers and how Pentecostalism is a way of dealing with it. Beyond the material body, football and Pentecostalism emerge as moral and bodily regimes that shape young men as masculine subjects.

Finally, in the conclusion, I draw on ethnographic insights from the preceding chapters to return to the key topics raised in this introduction. As the chapters will show, the global market for football players relies on the willingness of young men to embrace new forms of precarity; however, crucially, this is a quality that is not simply "there" among young men but needs to be produced and cultivated. Part of this production is solving the "problems" of youthful masculinities, and Pentecostalism emerges for the footballers as a method to do exactly that. The intersection between football aspirations and Pentecostalism suggests that the ideology of neoliberal capitalism relies on the production of magical possibilities of extraordinary success but also on the faith that self-discipline, focus, and moral decency will bring social mobility, despite unlikely odds. Football dreams, Pentecostal faith, obligations to provide for the kin, and desires to migrate abroad fuel the precarity of masculinity in Cameroon, and beyond, in structurally adjusted West Africa.

Notes

1. I do occasionally refer to sorcery as "magico-religious practices" when I am looking to avoid morally charged terms like "witchcraft" or "black magic," even though my interlocutors regularly used them.
2. I borrow this term from the title of the European Research Council–funded research project "Globalization, Sport and the Precarity of Masculinity," directed by Niko Besnier, retrieved 7 September 2018 from https://global-sport.eu/project.
3. Throughout this book, I switch between the terms "club" and "academy." Technically, the two are not the same—"clubs" are teams that compete in national and regional leagues, and "academies" are football schools that train boys and young men under eighteen years old. In practice, however, the two overlap: some of the most successful clubs in national competitions call themselves "academies," and some football schools maintain teams with older players and compete in national and regional leagues.
4. The word "football" also has an equivalent in Mboko Tok—*ndamba*. However, the slang term is largely a part of a decades-old lexicon, out of fashion among young Cameroonians.
5. Another common term for White visitors is *mukala*, which otherwise refers to an albino. However, during my stay in Cameroon, the term was mostly reserved for Clinton N'Jie, a young Bakweri footballer with a light complexion who became a superstar during my stay in Cameroon, and who was nicknamed "Papi Mukala."
6. This book builds on a number of earlier studies of football in Cameroon. Arnold Pannenborg's doctoral thesis (2012) on "big men" who manage football clubs demonstrates how the sport is intertwined with Cameroon's politics and elite figures. This book goes a step further and situates Cameroonian football in a global political economy. Pannenborg's equally interesting MA thesis (2008) provides detailed descriptions of sorcery in football but very little reference to Pentecostal Christian spirituality. Jude Fokwang (2009) writes about marginalized Cameroonian men who promote self-discipline and imagine an alternative moral order through football, but he does so with no mention of Cameroonians' aspirations to migrate by playing the sport. Finally, Bea Vidacs in her *Visions of a Better World: Football in the Cameroonian Social Imagination* (2010) effectively applies Achille Mbembe's ideas (2001) to football. She writes: "As an ideal, at least on the level of desires and will, in Cameroon football represents an antithesis of the zombification, inertia, and impasse of the postcolonial condition, described so vividly by Mbembe and others. In practice, the general state of Cameroon constantly frustrates this desire, and one could subscribe to Mbembe's thesis and recognize in football the zombification he talks about, mirroring the general state of affairs of the country." Such discrepancy between desires and realities is also central to this book, which focuses more sharply on high aspirations and stifling realities of young footballers themselves.

CHAPTER 1

Dreams of Mobility
Football between Politics, Economy, Spirituality, and Transnational Markets

Football is ubiquitous in Cameroon. In Buea, the Southwest Region's capital, its presence in everyday social life is hard to escape. Every morning before 6:00 A.M., as the owners of grocery shops, boutiques, hair salons, restaurants, and bars are preparing for the working day, young men jog up and down the main road that connects the town's central places: the bus station, the university campus, the town stadium, the council building, the old Buea Town. Many are running for leisure, perhaps toward a small field where they will play *santé*, a casual game of football with friends before the working day begins. Others are headed toward the stadium, which will soon overflow with football clubs training for the next "interquarters," wildly popular local competitions.

Football images and words saturate everyday life. Taxi drivers adorn their vehicles with stickers that depict superstar players, with the English Premier League's Chelsea FC dominating drivers' dashboards. Their rear windshields bear the names of prominent football-related personalities: "Papi London" is the nickname of a prominent local businessman who funds football competitions; "Papi Mukala" is Clinton N'Jie, a young man from Buea who signed to play with the French elite club Lyon in 2011. Cameroonians gather in bars with TV sets to watch the latest matches of elite European leagues, to revel in performances of superstar Africans playing abroad, and to complain about the notorious volatility of the "Lions Indomptables," the "Indomitable Lions," the beloved national team that either fabulously shines or utterly disappoints in international competitions.

Besides this presence in everyday life, football is deeply embedded in Cameroon's politics and economy. Throughout the country's history, football has reflected changes in politics, the economy, and spirituality, but it has also driven them. In the Southwest Region, football reflects the country's specific colonial experience, the nature of the postcolonial state since its 1961 independence, the economic shifts that shaped the country's economy in the 1980s and the early 1990s, the ethno-regional cleavages, the spiritual life of the predominantly Christian regions, and the changes in the global football market in the 1990s and 2000s. The history of football clubs and, later, football academies in the Southwest Region parallels the history of this region's economic and political position in relation to Cameroon's other regions, to Cameroon as a whole, and to the expanding transnational markets.

The last point—interaction with transnational markets—is especially relevant for the arguments and chapters that follow. Since its introduction by the colonial powers, football in Cameroon has always been immersed in transnational circulation of people and ideas. However, transnationality gained importance with the expansion of the global market for football players and commercialization of global football in the 1990s. Since the late 1990s, young Cameroonian men have begun perceiving football as a new opportunity to migrate abroad and earn a living.

A story from the region serves as a case in point. In 2004, a newly formed Cameroonian football club assembled and trained a young team of under-21 players and, in conjunction with partners in Europe, arranged for the team to travel to Italy and take part in a youth competition. The team's performance at the tournament was mediocre at best, but they reportedly attracted the attention of football scouts. When the time came for the team to leave for the airport and return to Cameroon, half the team went missing. No fewer than ten players decided to flee the squad and try their luck individually in Europe. In the coming years, despite their uncertain status as undocumented migrants, two of the players who fled the squad made it all the way to clubs in the top tier of elite Italian football, and at least three more signed contracts in Finland, Switzerland, and Greece. Since this "incident," the club in Cameroon has been reluctant to send players for trials abroad. The story, similar to others of African footballers defecting abroad in order to pursue their fortune (Okeowo 2016), has become a cautionary tale for the region's football coaches and managers. For the young footballers with whom I trained in 2014 and 2015, the story was a confirmation of their belief that opportunities await in Europe and elsewhere abroad.

The history of the embeddedness of football in the region's social, political, economic, and spiritual life, and also in transnational processes embodied by global markets, is crucial to understanding young men's disposition to play football as a means to migrate and to the discussions and arguments I put forward in this book.

From Colonial Games to a Source of Regional Pride

Football arrived on the African continent by way of European imperial and colonial projects. The first recorded matches took place in South Africa in 1862, where teams played matches between "home-born" (British) and "colonial-born" (South African) White soldiers and civil servants. In the late nineteenth and early twentieth centuries, football matches were documented throughout the continent: in Oran (Algeria), Tunis, Cairo (Egypt), Dakar (French West Africa), Brazzaville (French Equatorial Africa), Léopoldville (Belgian Congo), and elsewhere. The first matches and tournaments were organized in coastal trading towns, such as Calabar and Lagos (Nigeria), Cape Coast (Gold Coast, today Ghana), and Zanzibar. Later on, the game spread to regions where railway systems were developed, such as Sudan, Cameroon, Southern and Northern Rhodesia, Congo, and Uganda (Alegi 2010: 2).

At first, football matches were reserved for European settlers, and these excluded indigenous populations. However, it was not long before Africans started participating. The British seem to have been more inclined to include indigenous populations from the very beginning of their colonial projects, while others (French, Belgians, Portuguese, and Italians) were somewhat slower. One possible reason for this is the combination of the ideology of "muscular Christianity" and the "civilizing mission" of British colonial projects. "Muscular Christianity" was an influential movement in nineteenth-century Britain that espoused physical exercise and maintenance of the athletic body as central to the development of moral personhood, based on values such as discipline, asceticism, and self-sacrifice. The movement's influence was such that sport became an important element of school curriculums throughout Great Britain and served as a method for producing disciplined and moral citizens. Thus, throughout their colonies where British colonial administrators sought to develop a public school system to "educate" and "civilize" indigenous populations into subservience to the empire, sports and physical education were included in school curriculums to help fulfill this role (Mangan 1998).[1] While the British imperialists were probably the first to include Africans in sports, other colonial countries soon followed, and by the 1930s and 1940s French and Belgian colonies also accepted that sports were an official part of their "colonizing mission." For instance, in Léopoldville (Belgian Congo), football was a way "to provide civilized black youth with healthy distractions and to complete their physical and moral education at the school of discipline and endurance that the practice of sport entails."[2] Football, as sports in general, played an important role in the making of moral subjects.

In Cameroon, football was part and parcel of the country's unique triple colonial heritage. The area was first colonized by Germany in 1884. In 1916, during World War I, the territory was divided between France and Britain, creating French (East) and British (West) Cameroon, with French Cameroon being much larger than the British territory. After French Cameroon's independence in 1960 as the independent République du Cameroun, the British-controlled territories voted in a controversial United Nations–organized referendum on their future administrative status. They were, however, not permitted to form an independent state. The northern parts of the British-controlled territories voted to join Nigeria, and the southern parts voted to join French Cameroon. In 1961 these southern parts became the Northwest and Southwest Regions of the new Federal Republic of Cameroon. This created an Anglophone minority in a predominantly Francophone country. Furthermore, in 1972 the federation was replaced by a unitary state and renamed the United Republic of Cameroon, and in 1983 it was renamed yet again as the Republic of Cameroon. This complex colonial history and postindependence centralization of power eventually exacerbated the "Anglophone problem," i.e., the Anglophone Cameroonians' sense of marginalization in a majority Francophone state, an issue that underpinned numerous protests, violent government reactions, separatist sentiments, and the currently ongoing armed conflict.[3]

In the 1920s, Europeans in the colony started forming football teams. Cameroonians were originally discouraged from participating in matches, which were reserved for Europeans and expats from other African countries already exposed to European norms (Senegal, Sierra Leone, and Gambia). The first teams with Cameroonian players started emerging in the 1930s in coastal towns such as Douala, a trend that then spread to Yaoundé and further inland. European colonial administrators allegedly included Cameroonians because they believed that allowing them to participate in depoliticized activities such as sports could have a "cooling down" effect: involvement would likely discourage political mobilization and deflate political frustrations. Still, since the French administrators considered all voluntary associations as ultimately political, all football clubs had to follow proper registration procedures conjured by the central French authorities (Clignet and Stark 1974). In the coming decades, Cameroonian teams developed in the economic hubs of Douala and Yaoundé. The national football association, Fédération Camerounaise de Football (FECAFOOT), was founded in 1959.

Football history in Cameroon's Anglophone Southwest and Northwest Regions is somewhat different from that of the Francophone regions, yet it is very much intertwined with the economic and political developments in the Francophone hubs of Yaoundé and Douala. The football history in Anglophone regions was closely intertwined with large-scale industrial enterprises—which would, after independence, be transformed into "parastatals"—and government departments that were tasked with infrastructural developments. Both of these—the large companies and the government departments—played an important role in the regions' economic and political life and were central in funding and supporting football.

The most prominent example of a large-scale company in the Southwest Region was the Cameroon Development Corporation (CDC). Its history begins with the first plantations on the fertile volcanic soil around Mount Cameroon, established by German planters, who expelled the Bakweri people, the original occupants of the land, to native reserves. After the British occupation in 1915, the plantations were expropriated from their German owners. By 1922 the British decided the plantations were too difficult to maintain. In a 1924 auction in London, instead of handing the land back to the Bakweri, they sold most of the plantations back to the previous German owners. After World War II, in 1945, the land was again expropriated from the German owners. Bakweri elites wrote petitions to the British Crown and the United Nations in a campaign to have the land returned to them as rightful owners. Despite their efforts, the British Trusteeship Authority largely ignored them and decided to lease the land to a newly established statutory corporation. In this way, in 1946, despite Bakweri elites' protests, the Cameroon Development Corporation was born. By decrees, the CDC was tasked with managing 104,000 hectares of fertile land, providing welfare and education for the employees, and operating to the benefit of all the inhabitants of the territory (Konings 2011: 136–38).

Throughout the rule of Cameroon's first president, Ahmadou Ahidjo, ownership and management of CDC lands continued to be a point of contention for Bakweri elites. The postcolonial state took over the management of the CDC, turned it into a parastatal, and used it as a state-regulated driver of modernization. This was a part of Ahidjo's "planned liberalism" development strategy throughout the 1960s and 1970s, which stimulated the growth of large parastatal enterprises and promoted extensive state intervention in the economy.

Despite tensions with ethno-regional elites, the CDC played a significant role in the Southwest Region's economic and social development. The agro-industrial enterprise produced bananas, semifinished rubber, palm oil, palm kernel oil, and tea (until the privatization of its tea plantations in 2002). In addition, the CDC, in conjunction with governmental agencies, played a significant role in regional socioeconomic development and modernization: building roads, providing employment, building water and electricity infrastructure, building schools, and providing medical care (Konings 2011: 59). The CDC was the second largest employer in Cameroon after the government. Moreover, many Anglophones throughout the decades continued to praise the CDC as their own enterprise. This became most clear when in 1994 the government attempted to put up the CDC for privatization. Bakweri elites, but also other Anglophone organizations, led the protests against privatization with signs such as "France: hands off Anglophones" and "Hands off or we will burn the plantations" (Konings 2011: 64). One Anglophone columnist commented passionately about what the CDC meant to the region: "The CDC is unlike any other corporation. It means native lands, especially those of the Bakweri. It means jobs for Cameroonians, especially the Anglophones. It is a symbol of Anglophone survival against all odds" (quoted in Konings 2011: 142).

In the Southwest and Northwest Regions, in the period of late colonial governance and in the first decades after independence, large-scale parastatals, together with government departments, were central actors in the organization and governance of football clubs. The CDC founded football clubs that would become some of the regions' most prominent. In the early 1960s, the CDC founded and ran the CDC Victoria Football Club in Limbe.[4] Limbe fans nicknamed the club "OPOPO," short for "One People One Power." It was still, in 2015, arguably the most popular club (now called Victoria United) in Limbe, despite its mediocre performances in regional competitions. Another prominent football club founded and run by the CDC was CDC Tiko in the town of Tiko, a thirty-minute car ride from Limbe.

Other notable football clubs in the first decade after independence were run by government departments. For example, Prisons Social Club of Buea, one of the oldest and most reputable football clubs in the Southwest Region, was formed in the regional capital in 1967 under the patronage of the director of the Central Prison. The Public Works Department (PWD), tasked with building roads and infrastructure in the region, organized football clubs in all the larger towns of Anglophone Cameroon, the most prominent being PWD Football Social Club of Bamenda in the Northwest Region's capital. Throughout the 1960s and 1970s these clubs—CDC Victoria, Prisons Buea, and PWD Bamenda—participated in national leagues and cups organized by the newly formed FECAFOOT. They had significant successes and held their ground against the more prominent Francophone clubs based in the political and economic capitals of Yaoundé and Douala. These clubs built their reputations as fan favorites, and to this day Cameroonians in the Southwest and Northwest have fond memories of the clubs' successes. The clubs acted as a source of pride and social glue in towns and regions. Significantly, they represented (and were financed by) parastatals and regional governmental departments, many of which were emblematic of the postindependence era's modernization and development through large-scale state-sponsored projects. At the same time, parastatals and governmental departments, and by extension their football clubs, were a source of regional and provincial pride.

Thus football, originally a foreign game, was intertwined in the early years of the Anglophone regions' independence from colonial rule with nationwide political processes, but even more so was an integral part of the socioeconomic development of the regions and the accumulation of Anglophone and regional symbolic capital. At the intersection of state-sponsored development and regional social life, football in the Southwest and Northwest Regions in this period of postindependence modernization is an example of the appropriation of a foreign game, one that was introduced as a colonial instrument to cool down political sentiments but was turned into a symbol of regional belonging.

Economic Crisis, Democratization, and Big Men in Football

In the late 1970s, economic conditions in Cameroon and on the world market affected the economic viability of parastatals and the government sector, and this was reflected in the changing patterns of funding football clubs. The development strategy of Ahidjo's postcolonial state had been successful in quickly transforming Cameroon into one of the most stable African economies. Yet, in some ways, Cameroon was not different from other African economies. It relied heavily on the export of a few agricultural products—cocoa, coffee, bananas, and palm oil. The sharp decline in commodity prices on world markets in the early 1980s strained the economy. The country maintained an impressive 7 percent growth rate until 1986, but this figure was largely the result of the discovery of crude oil in 1977.

In addition, the use of public enterprises and government agencies for gaining political capital led to an inflated public sector. State-owned enterprises grew from a handful in 1961 to no fewer than 219 in the mid-1980s. Importantly, state-owned enterprises became instruments for Ahidjo's regime to exert power by distributing state resources (jobs, rents, power, and prestige), rewarding political allies, and co-opting political opponents. Managers of large parastatals were reportedly often selected less for their competence than for their political ties. They had often previously served in top government positions before being appointed to manage parastatals. They constituted what some analysts have called the regime's "hegemonic alliance" (Bayart 1979), the bureaucratic-political elite developed around the president of the state and the ruling political party.[5] This patrimonial logic of governing was present in many postcolonial African states, but it was arguably particularly strong in Cameroon.[6]

In the late 1970s most parastatals and regional government departments began experiencing financial difficulties, and as a result their financial support of football clubs decreased. The Central Prison gradually phased out its financial support of Prisons Social Club of Buea. Despite performing fairly well compared to other parastatals, the CDC ceased its support of football clubs in the early 1980s, and CDC Victoria and CDC Tiko were separated from the large enterprise and renamed Victoria United and Tiko United. Clubs founded by the PWD suffered the same fate. Dwindling parastatal and government department support caused uncertainty for football clubs in the region and at the same time opened up space for influential individuals to fund and lead popular clubs.

Paul Biya took over Cameroon's presidency in 1982. Because of the drop in commodity prices on world markets, the government eventually had to borrow from the International Monetary Fund (IMF) and the World Bank, and in 1988–89 it reluctantly agreed to implement a structural adjustment program

(SAP). The neoliberal program resembled those applied to or imposed on many countries around the world, especially Latin America and Africa, aiming to dismantle the public sector, dissolve or privatize public enterprises, and liberalize trade and markets. As in many other countries in Africa (e.g., Ferguson 2006; Harrison 2010), the neoliberal reforms failed to deliver the promised prosperity. The country's GDP per capita continued to plummet throughout the adjustment program, dropping 42.4 percent between 1986 and 1994.[7]

The neoliberal SAP imposed on Cameroon by the IMF and the World Bank also involved significant political changes. The program insisted on the promotion of the model of "good governance," which was intended to democratize political life and limit the authoritarian regime. Many young people, especially disenfranchised youth in urban areas where resentment against the "hegemonic alliance" was particularly high, supported these changes. They hoped that the "changement" (change), a notion among disenfranchised youth that acquired the status of an ultimate solution to all social and economic issues, would lead to the dissolution of the political elite of the neopatrimonial state and finally bring the power of the "longs crayons" (educated elite) to the people (Ndjio 2008a: 130). Paul Biya was forced to introduce multiparty democracy in 1990, and new political parties emerged in the political arena.

However, the "democratization" agenda imposed by international financial institutions opened up space to express pent-up feelings of ethno-regional injustice and intensified the politics of ethnic citizenship (Geschiere and Nyamnjoh 2000). Most of the newly formed political parties had a clear ethno-regional base. Ethno-regional elites saw multipartyism as an opportunity to become more active and made attempts to take part in national politics by promoting ethno-regional interests (Konings and Nyamnjoh 2003). Since 1990, democratization in Cameroon has meant that political elites need to establish political bases and support in their own regions, i.e., to create political capital in their own "native" regions in order to partake in national politics.

Successfully running a football club became one way of gaining the support of the local population and advancing a political career. Throughout this period of economic and political turbulence, several "big men"—influential and powerful businessmen, entrepreneurs, and individuals with political ambitions—took control of football clubs. Some entered club management in order to gain political points, while others were ushered in almost against their will by football fans. The advantages of running football clubs that were already established as regional favorites became much clearer in the early 1990s, when political engagement became dependent on popular support in the region.

In the 1970s Ni John Fru Ndi, the owner of Ebibi Book Centre on Commercial Avenue in Bamenda (capital of the Northwest Region), emerged as a well-known businessman. By his own account, he was not interested in investing in football, which he considered a waste of money. However, PWD Bamenda supporters disagreed: in 1979, they pressured him, even tricked him, into running the popular but financially ailing PWD Bamenda. He lamented spending so much of his capital on a football club and claimed that his business ventures suffered (Pannenborg 2012: 73–74).

However, a decade later, with the introduction of multiparty politics, his leadership of the popular football club proved to be a good basis for his political ambitions. In 1990, Ni John Fru Ndi founded and became leader of the Social Democratic Front (SDF), the only party that represented a real challenge to the regime of Paul Biya in the country's first multiparty elections. Some have claimed that his road to success in the political arena started with his management of PWD Bamenda. In one interview, Ni John Fru Ndi confirmed that managing a football club had an impact on his political career:

> People came to know me and they saw my sacrificing spirit, and because of my ability to do certain things they came to respect me. When I formed the party, the spirit of what I had done in PWD [Bamenda football club] followed me into the party. People who had seen me on the field said: "If he's with the party we will support him because we saw how he handled his players on the field." (Pannenborg 2012: 123)

Thus, beginning in the 1990s, managing football clubs that enjoyed public support became closely intertwined with political ambitions. Financially ailing football clubs looked for prominent men, preferably native to the club's town or region, to finance and manage them. In turn, while managing a club was not necessarily financially profitable for these men, it often resulted in their increased visibility and recognition, which could lead to acquiring significant political capital.

For Ni John Fru Ndi, entering politics meant creating an opposition party to challenge the hegemonic alliance rallied around Paul Biya and his CPDM party and calling attention to the "Anglophone problem." For others, engagement with politics meant joining the ruling party. In 2000, Eteki Charles Dikongue, another prominent figure, was led almost against his will to run Tiko United. A pale remnant of the former CDC Tiko Football Club, Tiko United was financially ailing but locally very popular. In an interview, Eteki Charles Dikongue described how he was made a club president:

> A delegation of the club met me at my house in Limbe and pleaded with me to become the new president. At first I refused. I had too much work to do and becoming a president would take too much time. But then everybody pleaded and begged me. Eventually I had to agree. I'm originally from the Tiko area and I had to do something for my community. There was a Congress and they made me the new president. (Pannenborg 2012: 74)

Eteki Charles Dikongue was elected Tiko United president as a "son of the soil" (he was a Southwesterner born in Victoria and schooled in Tiko and Buea), an established civil servant (he was a Southwest Region delegate of the Public Works Department), an experienced football manager (he took part in managing another club in the 1990s), and a wealthy individual (a necessary requirement for a popular community club that lost most of its financial support). Notably, he was also in 2007 a Southwest Section president of the CPDM, the ruling party. The same year, Tiko United qualified for the first division national league after many years of playing in regional competitions, and in 2009, almost miraculously, it became the first Anglophone team in the history of Cameroon football to win the national championship. Winning the championship for the beloved town club cemented Eteki Charles Dikongue as one of the best-known and respected big men in Tiko and the Southwest Region. Thus managing a popular football club can bring substantial political and symbolic capital (Pannenborg 2012: 137–39).

In the 1990s, as democratization amplified the "politics of belonging" (Geschiere 2009) in Cameroon, belonging to an ethnic group acquired renewed importance and meaning. The Southwest Region is ethnically very diverse, but there are significant cleavages between "native" Southwesterners, such as the Bakweri and other ethnic groups near the coast who claim indigeneity to the land, and Northwesterners, or "Grassfielders," migrants from the many ethnic groups of the Northwest Region. This ethnic makeup and the attendant occasional tensions have roots in the colonial management of labor. In 1894 German colonizers finalized the colonization of the coastal region, alienated the land from its Bakweri owners, and established a plantation complex on the fertile volcanic soil near the coast. The Bakweri were neither numerous enough nor willing to work the plantations, so the Germans organized people from the Northwest to move to the Southwest to work. By the 1920s, most of the plantations' laborers were migrants from the Northwest. Many settled in the Southwest, renting the fertile land from its indigenous owners. Over time, in some parts of the Southwest, such as the coastal Victoria District, the migrant population almost outnumbered the "natives." The indigenous Bakweri began accusing the newcomers of disrespecting local authorities, seducing local women, and not investing in local development (Ardener 1996: 243–46). They began referring to the Northwestern migrants as *kam-no-go*, a derogatory Pidgin English term that encapsulated the perception that the newcomers were taking over and exploiting their land (Geschiere and Nyamnjoh 2000: 443). This issue became particularly relevant with the "ethnicization" of politics in the 1990s, when Bakweri elites appealed to the ruling CPDM party to protect them from the "strangers." The Biya government obliged by changing the constitution in 1996 and promising Southwesterners state protection from the supposedly dominant "Grassfielders."

In return, Bakweri elites largely supported the CPDM government (Konings and Nyamnjoh 2003: 17).

Football was not immune to the politics of belonging. In Limbe in the 1990s, running the aforementioned Victoria United, the widely popular successor of the defunct CDC Victoria Football Club, was a matter of ethno-regional belonging. When in 1994 Innocent Bonu, a barrister based in Limbe, became its president, his Northwestern origin and status as a "stranger" was problematic to some. For many, the helm of the most popular coastal football club should have been occupied by a "native." According to speculations, Henry Njalla Quan, an influential businessman born, schooled, and based in the Southwest, allegedly used his political leverage to oust Bonu (Jua 2004). Njalla Quan was a prominent member of the ruling CPDM party, a government delegate for the Southwest Region, and a native Southwesterner. He was born in Bimbia, a village close to Limbe, to a Bakweri mother and a foreign father (allegedly from Togo). He was also very close to the now late Paramount Chief of Limbe Manga Williams, who was his mother's younger brother.[8] In 1996, Njalla Quan took over the helm of the Victoria United Football Club. Two years later, the club qualified for the national first division. In 1998 Njalla Quan was appointed by President Biya as a general manager of the CDC, a financially ailing but still very relevant parastatal. Meanwhile, Innocent Bonu, soon after leaving Victoria United in 1996, formed his own club, Victoria Shooting Stars, which came to be regarded as a *kam-no-go* club. The two teams became fierce rivals. The rivalry between the two influential figures, a "son of the soil" and a "stranger," illustrates the extent to which managing football was an integral part of ethno-regional politics.

Christianity, Pentecostalism, and "Sorcery" in Football

Democratization in the early 1990s triggered another change in Cameroonians' lives: the proliferation of neo-charismatic Pentecostal churches. Before 1990, the government of Cameroon had imposed measures to restrict the registration of associations. These measures were based on a 1962 "anti-subversion" decree designed to discourage any organizations that opposed the government.[9] In December 1990 the decree was repealed through a series of laws, commonly known as the "liberty laws."[10] They guaranteed freedom of association, which resulted in the proliferation not only of new political parties but also of a large number of neo-charismatic Pentecostal churches independent from mainline and longer-established churches in Cameroon.

Christianity in Cameroon, as in most of Africa, had been introduced by foreign missionaries. The first to successfully establish a church in the Southwest Region was the Jamaican missionary Joseph Merrick, a member of the Baptist

Missionary Society in London, who founded the Jubilee Mission in the village of Bimbia, about eight kilometers from today's Limbe, in 1844. He paved the way for another Baptist missionary, the Briton Alfred Saker, who continued Merrick's work of spreading Christianity in the region. Saker is credited as the founder of the township of Victoria, today's town of Limbe, in 1858. After Germans colonized the territory, the Protestant Basel Mission established a church, which was eventually transformed into a Presbyterian Church (Akoko 2007b: 301). Roman Catholics and the American Presbyterian Mission soon followed (Ardener 1956: 107–8). This trio of mainline denominations—Baptist, Catholic, and Presbyterian—today still forms the basis of much of Christian life in Anglophone Cameroon.[11]

Pentecostal denominations began arriving in the Southwest Region in the 1940s. The Apostolic Church was founded by a Nigerian evangelist in 1949, and the Full Gospel Mission was founded by a German missionary in 1961. These were still, in 2014, two of the largest Pentecostal denominations in Anglophone Cameroon, but they were accompanied by an increasing number of smaller neo-charismatic Pentecostal churches.

In the 1990s, neo-charismatic denominations started to flourish and saturate the spiritual life of Southwesterners. Denominations differed in their doctrines, but most followed the common traits of neo-charismatic Pentecostalism that had become increasingly influential throughout West Africa (Daswani 2015; Marshall 2009; Meyer 1999), elsewhere on the continent (Engelke 2007; Haynes 2017), and throughout the world (Robbins 2004; Thornton 2016). They emphasized the gifts of the Holy Spirit, such as prophecy and healing; believers' individual experience of the Holy Spirit; vigorous dancing and loud prayers, including speaking in tongues; spectacular deliverances from evil spirits; the importance of becoming born again through baptism in the Holy Spirit; and a literal interpretation of the Bible. Many, but not all, churches in the 1990s adopted elements of the "prosperity gospel," a doctrine claiming that devotion to God and belief in the power of the Holy Spirit will lead to not only spiritual but also material prosperity.

The history of Pentecostal churches in neighboring Nigeria is relevant for understanding changes in the prosperity gospel in Cameroon. In Nigeria in the 1970s the doctrine of "holiness" and "righteousness" was dominant among Pentecostals. It emphasized eschewing material goods, retreating from the world, strictly controlling consumption, adhering to strict personal ethics, performing public confessions of past sins, exercising strict bodily discipline (exemplified by long periods of fasting and long night-time prayers), and condemning "toxic" behavior—lying, cheating, bribing, stealing, drinking, smoking, fornicating, and losing one's temper (Marshall 2009: 71). In the 1990s new Nigerian neo-charismatic pastors emphasized instead the miracles of material and spiritual prosperity in the here and now. The clearest expression of the prosperity gospel was the "name it and claim it" narrative, by which the believers were guaranteed material blessings from the outset: they needed only to name them and then claim them in the name of Jesus. Ethical conduct was still a part of the doctrine, but it took a back seat to the miracles of prosperity (Marshall 2009: 78–79).

Pentecostalism in the Southwest Region of Cameroon underwent a similar change. In the 1990s new Nigerian and Cameroonian neo-charismatic denominations began appearing. Many preached the prosperity gospel and appealed to many Cameroonians. Some older and more established Pentecostal churches, such as the Full Gospel Mission, followed their lead and joined them in preaching that faith would bring not only salvation in the afterlife but also material prosperity. What Robert Mbe Akoko (2007b) documented in the Southwest Region as the change in the gospel "from asceticism to accumulation" (2007a: 2) resembles the development of Pentecostalism in Nigeria from "holiness" to miracles and prosperity (Marshall 2009: 71–85).

But the lines between asceticism and accumulation doctrines most likely only appeared to be clear in the early 1990s because of the sudden proliferation of the prosperity gospel. During my fieldwork in 2014 they were not. Pentecostal denominations in the Southwest focused on miracles of prosperity but also insisted on strict personal ethics, such as complete abstention from alcohol and premarital sexual relations. This is comparable to developments in Nigeria, where most churches since the early 2000s could be situated somewhere on the "spectrum of 'holiness-prosperity' attitudes" (Marshall 2009: 85), with very few churches adopting versions at the extreme ends of that spectrum.

When one stepped away from the confines of churches and focused on the intimate lives of congregants, differences between denominations were even less clear. For instance, some Cameroonians were nominally members of "older" and more established Pentecostal churches, such as the Apostolic church, which emphasized strict ethical conduct; but they also sought counsel from individual prophets and evangelists from neo-charismatic denominations that focused on the prosperity gospel, such as the Nigerian church Winners Chapel. Some Cameroonians were members of mainline Christian denominations but also attended flamboyantly advertised "miracle conventions," "prophetic invasions," and festivals of "supernatural release," massive neo-charismatic events at which miracles and healings were performed. All kinds of Christians would watch DVDs or broadcasts of neo-charismatic televangelists, such as the enormously popular TB Joshua and his church service in Lagos. Thus Christians of all denominations were exposed to ideas of both strict asceticism and miraculous prosperity. It was also clear that neo-charismatic Pentecostalism was increasingly influential and appealing, especially to young people.

Football was also caught up in these changes. Almost all matches and trainings in which I participated began (and often ended) with a huddle in the center of the field and a prayer (see figure 1.1). For example:

> In the mighty name of Jesus, eternal rock of ages, mighty and everlasting father, we thank you for a day like this. Father, we thank you for our lives, we thank you because you are God. Father, we worship you, we bow before you, oh Lord . . .

The elaborate prayer, always different and improvised, would continue for about two minutes. Sometimes the person saying the prayer, perhaps a team captain or an exceptionally eloquent footballer, would address more concrete issues relating to football. Often the players would pray that they would not sustain an injury on the field. At other times, they would pray that, now that they had chosen football as their "career," they would be able to pursue their "dream" in good health. Some players would respond to these poignant moments by frowning with concentration and exhaling a long "yes," emphasizing the gravity of the spoken words. The speaker would finally conclude, "In Jesus's name, we pray." We all would respond with an "amen," the solemn moment would be over, and we would continue with the chitchat and warm-up for the training session.

This was a typical way of starting and ending a training session in all the football clubs I trained with or visited during my fieldwork. On a global scale, the image of a football team assembling in the middle of the field and celebrating a victory with a prayer was becoming more common since the 1990s,

Figure 1.1. Almost every training session starts and ends with a collective prayer. Buea, Cameroon, September 2014. Photo by the author.

mostly following the lead of members of the Brazilian national football team, who seized every opportunity to display their evangelical faith to football audiences worldwide (Rial 2012).

Prayers on the football field were not particularly new in Cameroonian football. But it was striking that an increasing number of young footballers were drawn to different iterations of the neo-charismatic Pentecostal movement and were eager to demonstrate their fervor. For instance, some of my football friends would attend "power house" events, small, improvised prayer cells in a person's living room attended by no more than fifteen people. Young pastors no older than twenty would lead the small congregations through passionate sessions filled with loud prayers and speaking in tongues. Young attendants would give testimonies of their sudden vision of the future, revelations from God, in which they were revealed a destiny of traversing the world and traveling through different countries. In addition, while many footballers rarely attended formal Sunday church services (despite nominally claiming that it was important to attend them), they regularly prayed in the privacy of their homes, sometimes in hour-long stretches several times a day, either by themselves or together with their friends or romantic partners.

Moreover, young footballers consulted with "men of God," whom they sometimes casually referred to by the acronym "MOG." These were individual preachers, prophets, pastors, or evangelists. The "title" of man of God could refer to a member of any denomination, but the footballers were most attracted to eloquent neo-charismatic preachers. Young men used the term more as a casual everyday nickname than as a formal or official label for a church leader. Everyone who was well versed in the Bible and vocal in preaching his (or, more rarely, her) faith could be nicknamed "MOG," regardless of church membership. For instance, Emil, the captain of Buea Young Star FC whom I mentioned in the first pages of this book, was frequently called MOG by his friends. Some men of God did not formally belong to any denomination but built their reputation on demonstrations of prophecies, insightful suggestions for solving everyday problems through prayers, or an exceptional zeal for "winning souls," i.e., evangelizing. Such was the case, for instance, with Saint Collins, a man of God in his early twenties, who was only marginally associated with Winners Chapel but built his reputation in Buea by working individually with people in need of spiritual counseling. Many of those seeking his help were young footballers. In chapters 4 and 5, I analyze these figures in more detail.

Christianity and Pentecostalism in Cameroonian football need to be considered in relation to a wide range of magico-religious practices that, according to Cameroonians, have always been part and parcel of the game. Cameroonians considered football in Cameroon (and Africa in general) as saturated with *jars*, a Pidgin English term that refers to a range of magico-religious practices in football (and other areas of social life).[12] The use of *jars* can include carrying pieces of tree bark or herbs with supernatural powers, bathing in specially prepared liquids, or marking the territory of the football field with special concoctions. *Jars* can be used to win matches, score goals, sabotage opponents, and obtain mystical powers from ancestors or occult organizations. *Jars* is not necessarily tied to specific ethnic groups or cultural traditions. Parallels to these practices in football are found throughout Africa, such as *umuthi* (Scotch 1961) or *muti* (Niehaus 2015) in South Africa, *juju* in Tanzania (Leseth 1997), or "sorcery" throughout the continent (Pannenborg 2012; Schatzberg 2006).

Uses of *jars* in football are secretive and notoriously difficult to pin down. Footballers and other Cameroonians use many terms to refer to magico-religious practices: *jars*, *medicine*, *juju*, "sorcellerie," black magic, and witchcraft. These terms are not absolute synonyms: while *jars*, *medicine*, and *juju* suggest a playful use of concoctions to score goals, "sorcellerie," black magic, and witchcraft suggest dangerous magic used to cause injuries to opponents, even to the point of spiritually sacrificing family members for a victory or lucrative career. However, the boundaries are far from clear. Like sorcery elsewhere in the world (e.g., Besnier 1996: 80), the borders between benign and harmful uses are blurred (see also Geschiere 1997). Moreover, footballers used all these terms interchangeably.

Despite Cameroonians' frequent talk about the prevalence of *jars* in football, not all were willing to openly discuss it in detail. One possible reason, besides secrecy and potential accusations of immoral behavior, was their awareness of Westerners' exoticization. In 1990 the famous Cameroonian national team made it clear that they did not enjoy the Europeans' fascination with the supposed Africans' obsession with witchcraft. François Omam-Biyik, who scored a goal in a legendary match against reigning world champions Argentina, said in an interview after the game, "We hate it when European reporters ask us if we eat monkeys and have a witch doctor. We are real football players and we proved this tonight."[13] During my fieldwork, while some footballers, especially those with whom I was close, would openly discuss this topic with me and occasionally bring it up themselves, others would indicate they were not happy with such questions.

The relationship between Pentecostal Christianity and *jars* in football is complex and important, and I discuss it in chapter 4. For now, suffice it to say that football in Cameroon is deeply embedded in, and constitutive of, spiritual life in the region, Christian and otherwise.

Commercialization of Global Football, Expanding Markets of Players, and Dreams of Mobility

In the late 1990s and early 2000s, changes in the global football industry and the expansion of the global market for football players added a new dimension to football all over Africa, including Cameroon. The number of transnational football transfers (i.e., movements of players between clubs) increased, and the trade of football players between clubs became more commonplace. Also in this period, football entrepreneurs throughout Africa began forming football clubs and academies with the mission to train young men for professional careers in sports and for migration abroad.

Transfers of African footballers from African to European countries started in the 1930s and gradually increased over the course of the twentieth century. During colonial times, France and Portugal recruited players from their African colonies, and by the early 1960s approximately one hundred players from the African continent played in French and Portuguese leagues (Poli 2006). One striking example of a pioneering football migrant from Cameroon was Eugène N'Jo Léa. Having migrated to France to complete his baccalaureate, he played in amateur leagues until he joined the professional club Saint-Etienne in 1954. With this team, he became a prolific goal scorer and went on to win a league title. An eclectic character, he was a fan of Dizzy Gillespie, played the trumpet, enjoyed reading Kafka, and received a doctoral degree in law. He took pride in his ascetic life of a sportsman: "I almost never go out in the evenings. Between my training, my reading and my music I have no time left to go to the movies or to a bar" (quoted in Lanfranchi and Taylor 2001: 175). He paved the way for many more Cameroonian footballers who plied their trade in French leagues between the 1960s and 1980s (Alegi 2010: 83), all of them from Francophone Cameroon.

In the 1980s a combination of new policies adopted by FIFA and African national football associations encouraged the global exchange of football players. The number of players from Africa started increasing, especially after Cameroon's national team, the Indomitable Lions, stunned the world with their performance in the 1990 FIFA World Cup. To the shock and surprise of international audiences, the Indomitable Lions reached the quarterfinals, the first African team to do so, and had even beaten reigning champions Argentina in the group stage. At that moment, the world once again "discovered Africa," this time as a new reservoir of talented athletes.

A crucial moment for intensification of global football migrations was the 1995 Bosman ruling, delivered by the European Court of Justice, which ensured that all football players from the EU were allowed to sign freely with any EU club after the contracts with their clubs had expired. This increased the mobility of footballers with EU nationalities within the EU. In 2000 this mobility effectively expanded (at least legally) to non-European players when the EU signed the Cotonou Agreement with African, Caribbean, and Pacific countries, which guaranteed the non-European worker's right of free movement within the EU. In the same period, financial inequality between clubs in Europe widened, and many European clubs began scouting West Africa (and

Latin America) for inexpensive young players (Alegi 2010: 98). These developments incentivized African footballers to sign contracts with European clubs that promised higher salaries than their clubs in Nigeria, Cameroon, Ivory Coast, Senegal, or Ghana.

Another central factor in the widening appeal of football was its commercialization through the influx of money from television rights and the spread of satellite television throughout the African continent (Lanfranchi and Taylor 2001: 236). Football is a prime example of how television rights in the beginning of 1990s played a crucial role in the globalization and commercialization of sports. In 1992, for example, Rupert Murdoch's BSkyB signed exclusive rights with the then newly formed English Premier League for £304 million; this was renewed for the 2016–17 season for £5.14 billion (Gibson 2015), cementing its control of the market and spearheading a new era in which the sport's governing bodies, teams, and clubs became subservient to the interests of television corporations. FIFA, the sport's world governing body, also greatly profited from television rights (Alegi 2010: 105). The corruption scandals that finally erupted in 2015–16 were precisely the outcome of the paradoxes inherent to a supranational entity with powers and budgets that rival those of a major state being run as a business by a tight-knit group of elderly men. The infusion of television into football also led to sponsorship deals, as multinational companies recognized the huge exposure available to them by sponsoring elite football (Law, Harvey, and Kemp 2002; Williams 1994).

Another key change took place throughout the 1990s: the advent of satellite broadcasting enabled TV coverage to reach the remotest corners of the world. Throughout Africa, the number of television sets grew exponentially, no longer the privilege of urban elites (Akyeampong and Ambler 2002: 15). Transnational television broadcasting blossomed, breaking down governmental monopolies and boosting the number of entertainment and sports programs at the expense of news and educational programs. Everywhere, satellite television broadcasts of sport events have seeped deeply into the everyday lives of ordinary people.

The spread of satellite TV in Africa enabled two crucial developments for football on the continent. First, the hours dedicated to live European football increased dramatically. The English Premier League, which was already popular on the continent, drew the attention of many football fans in Africa, who transferred en masse from football stadiums to bars with television sets. The European leagues were also attractive for many fans who wanted to see African elite players playing in Europe. For many spectators, European football became more attractive than local competitions (Akindes 2011). Second, satellite TV coverage of the African Nations Cup led to its exposure to an increasing number of foreign coaches, talent scouts, and football agents looking for the next prodigious player. Football clubs in Africa provided lower salaries compared to European clubs, and many footballers started recognizing the tournament as a platform to launch careers overseas (Alegi 2010: 111). Migration of footballers from Africa increased (Poli 2006; 2010), and the increasing real and perceived possibility of making a career abroad began occupying the imaginations of many young men on the continent. Thus the spread of satellite television played a crucial role in the commercialization of football in Africa and in the making of "imaginaries of exile" (Piot 2010: 4) through football for the continent's youth.

As Europeans discovered Africa as a pool of inexpensive talent, and as young people across Africa discovered the expanding market of football players, both European and African entrepreneurs and organizations started developing football academies in or near African capital cities mainly for the purpose of preparing players for the international football market (Darby, Akindes, and Kirwin 2007; Darby 2013). In European leagues, the number of players from African countries rose from approximately 350 in 1996 to 1,000 in 2000 (Alegi 2010: 98). In 2003, 1,156 players from Africa played in European professional and semiprofessional leagues (Poli 2006: 398). In 2015, the number of players from Africa playing in Europe rose to 3,036 (Poli, Ravenel, and Besson 2015). Since then, the transnational mobility of footballers has only increased (Poli, Ravenel, and Besson 2021).

These statistics indicate that the migration of footballers from Africa to Europe has increased since the mid-1990s. Yet the official numbers paint only a partial picture: they do not account for young men who reach Europe by means of "irregular" football-related migration. Much higher figures are provided by international not-for-profit organizations that seek to document and fight "human trafficking" in and through football. For example, the director of youth protection at the International Centre for Sport Security estimated in 2015 that at least two to three thousand young men are targeted by self-styled football agents to move out of Africa every year (Hawkins 2015a: 36). The unscrupulous agents promise the young men trials in clubs abroad, collect money from them and their families, and arrange for them short-term visas to travel for trials, but when the clubs do not show interest in the players (as is often the case) the agents abandon the young men, making them effectively broke and undocumented migrants.[14] The founder and director of another prominent organization, the Paris-based Foot Solidaire, estimated in 2015 that the number of young men victimized by deceitful agents each year is more than fifteen thousand (Guilbert 2015).

Yet even these figures are highly unreliable. Why do the numbers of these two organizations diverge so widely? For one, they are very rough estimations. Moreover, there is very little clarity whether the figures refer to football-related "human trafficking," as defined by, for instance, United Nations' conventions, or football-related migration in general. In fact, there is very little clarity whether these organizations make the distinction between the two. Conflation between exploitation and migration is common in media accounts and policy proposals that seek to curb football-related trafficking (Esson and Drywood 2018). The issue of exploitation in football-related migration is a complex one, and I will address it further in chapter 2. For now, suffice it to say that the numbers are impossible to verify and monitor because of the "irregular" nature of migratory trajectories of so many footballers. It is clear, however, that the scope of migration related to football is much larger than indicated by official statistics and that young men can become susceptible to trafficking and exploitation.

Moreover, the official numbers also do not account for many young men who migrate through various channels that have little connection with officially sanctioned football transfers and trials in order to make their way to lower-level European clubs. From the first migrations of African footballers to Europe, players' trajectories and experiences were heterogeneous: some advanced through universities, others were already economic migrants before taking up football (Lanfranchi and Taylor 2001: 168–69). One of my friends with whom I trained at the club in Buea pondered aloud about his possibilities to play abroad:

> I want to go and play in Europe. My age is twenty-one, which is not bad. I can go through my club president, but I don't have to go through him. I need some way, any way, just to get an invitation letter and go to Europe. And then I have people who will wait for me in Spain and Italy, I would go there. I have my cousins there. Then when I get there I can look for a club. I want to go out, I don't want to play in Cameroon. There is no money in football in Cameroon. There were first division teams asking for me to play with them, like Dragon [Club de Yaoundé], but I refused, I want to go out.

Young Cameroonian footballers attempt to leave the country by using kinship networks, acquaintances abroad, personal relationships with football agents, university scholarship programs, or employment opportunities abroad. Most of them reckon that once they leave Cameroon and reach their destination in Europe or elsewhere, they will be able to join club training sessions, showcase their skills to coaches and agents, and eventually sign a contract. Once abroad, the footballers sometimes join amateur clubs, clubs in low-level divisions, and youth academies that are not accounted for in official statistics on football migration. They prefer amateur clubs in Europe to professional clubs in Cameroon because they see them as springboards for their careers, places where they might be noticed by a coach or scout who could recruit them for a professional club. While in Cameroon, young men feel that their struggle and sweat on the football field is invisible to foreign agents and reckon that once they reach Europe or another destination, their efforts can bring positive results. Migration is for most young aspiring footballers a precondition to success.

By the turn of the century, even though Europe remained the most attractive destination for young footballers, African players could be found all over the world (Poli 2006: 404). For the now legendary 1990 Cameroonian national team, half of the players played in France, indicating a single migratory route from the postcolony to the former colonial metropole. By the 2010s the list of call-ups to the national team consisted entirely of footballers who played abroad, not only in France but in Spain, Turkey, Slovakia, Russia, China, the United States, and Qatar.[15] This illustrates a development in the transnational migration of football players, wherein the mobility of athletes is no longer confined to single routes between African capital cities and former European metropoles but instead encompasses the entire planet. In addition, the prime European leagues rarely buy players directly from African clubs; instead, most players move either through different countries, such as those of the Persian Gulf or Asia, or through lower-division clubs.[16]

In 2015 I identified twenty-seven football clubs in the Southwest Region. Some profiled themselves as academies aimed at nurturing young generations of footballers, while others were football clubs competing in divisional, regional, and national competitions. The region was also home to two international programs that can be termed "sports for development": the FIFA Grassroots project in Mamfe, and the Football Development Program (FDP) by streetfootballworld.org (part of the FIFA Football for Hope program) in Kumba. Almost every one of the hundreds of young men training seriously at one of the many official and unofficial football clubs dreamed of being spotted by a football manager and traveling for trials at clubs abroad. As an *oyibó*, *sará*, or *waytman* ("White European") interested in football, every time I initiated contact with a club or academy I would have to explain that I was not a football manager selecting promising players to take them abroad.

While on the face of it migration through football involves only a select few who train seriously and aspire to migrate by playing, the numbers and trends listed above do not capture the discrepancy between the number of young Cameroonians who hope to play football for a living and the number of those who migrate to play. For example, the largest football academy, Ecole de Football Brasseries du Cameroun (in Douala), which prides and markets itself as a producer of world-class footballers, in 2015 selected a new cohort of eighteen 13-year-olds from a total of 3,584 hopefuls who take part in trials organized throughout the country (see figure 1.2).[17] Considering that this is only one of many academies and that these are only 13-year-olds, it is clear that large numbers of boys and young men harbor dreams of a career in football even though only very few of them will "make it."

Footballers' desire to move abroad needs to be seen in the context of Cameroon's prolonged economic crisis and the general "migratory disposition" (Kalir 2005) of many young Cameroonians, namely their life orientation to

Figure 1.2. A billboard in downtown Buea announcing the beginning of the selection process for the most prominent football academy in Cameroon. June 2015. Photo by the author.

a migrating future. In the same period, the 1990s, when the transnational football market was expanding, young Cameroonians were suffering from the consequences of austerity measures imposed by the IMF and the World Bank and the disappointments of the "good governance" model of democratization. With austerity measures and the dismantling of the public sector, many civil servants were demoted or fired, and the number of available positions in the public sector decreased. The model of a "fonctionnaire," a person who pursued higher education and eventually used school certificates to reach enviable positions in the public sector, became less attainable and less attractive to young Cameroonians (Ndjio 2008b; Geschiere 2013: 56). At the same time, the neopatrimonial state elite rallied around Paul Biya's CPDM did not disappear with democratization, and state resources remained out of reach for the majority of young Cameroonians. Finally, the devaluation of the Cameroonian CFA franc by 50 percent in January 1994 was a severe blow to many Cameroonians' household budgets.

Young Cameroonians faced with decreased opportunities began developing alternative strategies for attaining a livelihood. Many young men looked to the informal economy and became street hawkers and petty traders. Some, mostly those in large cities such as Douala and Bamenda, began working as motorbike-taxi drivers, called *bendskin* in Pidgin English. This form of self-employment, developed independently from the state, provided many young men with employment and a reasonable income (Konings 2006). Another very different strategy was *feymania*, a form of swindling. The fraudsters were usually poor young men from urban neighborhoods, and few managed to become rich by swindling powerful Cameroonians (and later also international "victims"). Successful *feymen* who enriched themselves independently, and sometimes in spite, of the state, became new role models for many young men (Ndjio 2008b).

Perhaps the most striking strategy of young Cameroonians was their increasing orientation to a migrating future. Cameroonians' migratory disposition was evident in peoples' increasing reliance on migrants' remittances, which have strikingly increased in the 2000s. According to World Bank estimations, Cameroonian migrants remitted US$23 million in 1990 and US$22 million in 2000 (in current US dollars, adjusted for inflation). In 2017 however, remittances increased to US$316.6 million. In Anglophone Cameroon, the latest incarnation of a desire to be mobile is expressed through the notion of *bushfalling* (Alpes 2012; Atekmangoh 2017; Nyamnjoh 2011; Pelican 2013), a Pidgin English metaphor grounded in the image of a hunter stepping into the wilderness, i.e., the *bush*, away from home and bringing the game back home. But the wilderness that the term *bush* refers to is not in Cameroon but rather in *waytman kontri*, the "White" world, or "the West," a place where money can be earned and sent back home. Many young Cameroonians see migrating to the *waytman kontri* as the ultimate solution. *Bushfalling* as migration to the global North is the latest reaction of young people to the economic downturn and increasing unemployment since the early 1990s. Football is a novel and highly desirable way of imagining a future abroad and attempting to leave.

Thus, the young footballers' desire to migrate abroad is not too different from the desires of young Cameroonians in general. Both are grounded in the lack of imaginable stable future in Cameroon. And yet, for young footballers, being mobile through football has a much deeper meaning than a mere aspiration to earn a living. Rather than being referred to as *bushfallers*, mobile players prefer to be called "pro" or "professional." The term "pro" is an everyday nickname and a flattering title among peers that invokes tropes of high aspirations and a journey with a sense of purpose. Mobility through football is not only *bushfalling* but also pursuit of a childhood dream. It invokes images of struggle and sacrifice for personal fulfillment.

Moreover, playing football abroad for a living is a masculine aspiration. Young women faced with economic uncertainty in Cameroon also aspire to migrate but use different means, such as marriage with foreigners or *bushfallers*, university scholarships, and connections with informal migration brokers

(Alpes 2012). While women also watch and occasionally play football, it is predominantly young men who imagine themselves playing abroad for a living.

Football between Regional and Transnational Dynamics

Football in Cameroon is more than a game or leisure activity. The history of football in the Southwest Region reflects the changes in political, economic, and spiritual life. Football began as a "civilizing" mission implemented by colonial administrators, but the Southwesterners quickly appropriated it into an articulation of regional belonging. As the large-scale parastatal enterprises' financial support for football, as well as their economic impact in the region, withered away, prominent big men were ushered into the sport. With "democratization" in the early 1990s and the increasing importance of ethno-regional support for participation in national politics, involvement with the game proved useful to the big men's consolidation of popular support and political influence. Moreover, starting with the introduction of freedom of association in 1990 and through a slow but steady growth in number and influence, neo-charismatic Christian denominations have begun to make substantial changes to the social realm that Cameroonians always considered saturated with sorcery.

The history of the relationship of football with the region's politics, economy, and spiritual landscape also demonstrates that transnational processes are central to football. Football in Cameroon has always been embedded in global dynamics, ever since its introduction by colonial administrators. But transnational dynamics have become increasingly relevant with two more recent developments: one, the neoliberal structural adjustment programs that failed to recover the spiraling economy and left many young people struggling to come up with new livelihood strategies; and two, the commercialization of football on a global scale and the expansion of transnational market for players. These two large-scale developments grounded in a neoliberal ideology constitute central structural conditions that fuel the precarity of life and livelihood of young men who increasingly aspire to migrate and play football for a living. As many young men who are excluded from state resources see few opportunities for a decent livelihood in the country, enticing new opportunities, both real and perceived, to earn a living and reputation by playing the beautiful game have become increasingly attractive. These opportunities always involve migration, ideally to countries of the global North. There is, however, a flip side to these new opportunities for geographical and social mobility through sport: while many young men aspire to live the dream of playing to migrate and migrating to play, only very few succeed, and those who do are likely to end up in situations that render them susceptible to exploitation.

Notes

1. An interesting case in West Africa was that of Sir Frederick Lugard, a governor of the British Empire in Nigeria in the early twentieth century, who urged the creation of a public school system in the colony to "civilize" the indigenous population. He included "games"—i.e., sports—in school curriculums. However, his idea to use sport to "educate" the local population was based less on his zeal for muscular Christianity and more on his faith in the "civilizing" potential of the public school system, in which sport had already been embedded (Mangan 1998: 101–21).
2. *Le Courrier d'Afrique*, 22–23 November 1936, cited in Alegi (2010: 4–5).
3. For an extensive report on the conflict see Kewir et al. (2021), and for a thorough historical analysis of the "Anglophone problem" see Konings and Nyamnjoh (2003).
4. The coastal town of Victoria was founded in the mid-nineteenth century. The name was changed to Limbe in 1982 during the Ahmadou Ahidjo regime.
5. Since independence in 1960, Cameroon's political life has been dominated by one political party, the Cameroonian National Union, which was in 1985 renamed the Cameroon People's Democratic Movement (CPDM).
6. One cited reason was that the country had stark ethno-regional cleavages, and state resources were used to forge ethno-regional alliances among the various elite groups, which would lead to national unity and stability without serious coercion (Konings 2011).
7. From $1,726.84 to $994.64 (in constant 2000 US$). For a literature review of the economic and social impact of neoliberal reforms in Africa and Cameroon, see Konings (2011: 2–6).
8. Henry Njalla Quan's central role at the chief's funeral in 2005 even sparked rumors that he might be preparing to inherit the throne. He denied that he had such aspirations, but it was clear that he was close to the paramount chief. For an interview with Henry Njalla Quan, see "Mr. Henry Njalla Quan On STV Straight Talk with Jessie Bawak," YouTube, 18 May 2012, retrieved 18 December 2017 from https://www.youtube.com/watch?v=RC2VrBEhwNY.
9. In practice, all organizations not related to the ruling CPDM party, the only legal political party at the time, were labeled subversive.
10. See Republic of Cameroon, 1990, Law No. 90/053 of 19 December 1990 on the Freedom of Association; Republic of Cameroon, 1990, Law No. 90/056 of 19 December 1990 on Multipartyism.
11. Twenty-two percent of Cameroonians are Muslims. Most live in northern parts of the Adamawa Region, in the North Region, and in the Extreme North Region. It is difficult to assess how many Muslims live in Anglophone regions, where Christianity prevails. They are likely more numerous in the Northwest Region, home to around 350,000 Hausa Muslims. The capitals of the two Anglophone regions, Buea and Bamenda, each have two mosques.
12. Cameroonians pronounced this "/dʒɑː(r)s/" and suggested the spelling "jars." The word is an approximate synonym for *juju* or *medicine*, therefore used in the singular. The etymology of the word is not clear to me, but it does not directly refer to any kind of glass container. Arnold Pannenborg (2008: 133–34) did observe that some Cameroonian footballers in Buea kept their concoctions in plastic or glass jars. However, *jars* includes all kinds of objects, not only liquids or their containers. This is consistent with practices elsewhere, e.g., in Polynesia, where people use terms like "jars" and "bottles" to refer to sorcery even when no containers are involved (Besnier 1996).

13. Simon Burnton, "World Cup Stunning Moments: Cameroon Shock Argentina in 1990," *The Guardian*, 13 March 2018, retrieved 23 December 2018 from https://www.theguardian.com/football/blog/2014/feb/12/world-cup-25-stunning-moments-cameroon-argentina.
14. For a more detailed overview of how trafficking works in football, see Esson and Drywood (2018: 62–63).
15. Source: *Planet World Cup* website, retrieved 20 January 2017 from http://www.planetworldcup.com.
16. For a more thorough analysis of sport-related migration beyond the global South/global North binary, see Hossain (2021).
17. Frédéric Nonos, "Coupe Top 2015: 18 jeunes intègrent l'Efbc," *Camfoot.com*, 9 August 2015, retrieved 7 September 2017 from https://www.camfoot.com/actualites/coupe-top-2015-18-jeunes-integrent,21958.html .

CHAPTER 2

"This Is a Business, Not a Charity"
Political and Moral Economy of Football and the Production of the Suffering Subject

> According to the neoliberal perspective, to prosper, one must engage with risk. All neoliberal social strategies center on this. Managing risk frames how neoliberal agents are oriented toward the future. And it is implicit in this orientation that neoliberal agents are responsible for their own futures—they supposedly fashion their own futures through their decisions. By the same token, regardless of their disadvantages and the unequal playing field, actors are maximally responsible for their failures.
>
> —Ilana Gershon, "Neoliberal Agency," 2011

During my fieldwork in the Southwest Region of Cameroon, a reputable and successful football club and academy in Limbe was losing its most valuable players.[1] Unisport Limbe FC had an enviable infrastructure for training and lodging footballers, and the team participated in Elite One, Cameroon's top division. Yet young footballers were flocking to Buea Young Star FC, a small, ad hoc, and lower-level football academy in Buea. I was puzzled as to why footballers would leave the ranks of a well-established club that provided them with the experience of top-level football matches, high-level training, and a salary (albeit an unstable one) only to seek a position in a small club that barely had an organizational structure in place, was only competing in small regional competitions, and provided no income. They gave me a straightforward reason: Buea Young Star FC focused on selling players to clubs in Europe and offered them an opportunity to migrate. This opportunity, however elusive, attracted young footballers who dreamed of migrating and playing abroad for a living.

The contrast between the goals and leaderships of Unisport Limbe FC and Buea Young Star FC, which I will unpack in this chapter, illustrates the changing political and moral economy of football in the Southwest Region. While the previous chapter documented the globalization and commercialization of football, this chapter shows the consequences of these large-scale processes on entrepreneurship and management in football in Cameroon. In short, rather than developing competitive teams that represented towns and regions in national competitions, football clubs and academies in Limbe and Buea sought to partake in the transnational market for football players. To that end, successful clubs and academies, i.e., those that attracted young men who aspired to play for a living, were increasingly focused on commodifying young footballers by creating and estimating their market value and preparing them for export to clubs abroad. The consequence of this commodification, which was novel in Southwest Cameroonian football, was the production and cultivation of young men as subjects willing to forego their present obligations to make way for new modes of "suffering" oriented toward achieving future dreams and aspirations, however uncertain they were.

By taking political economy as a starting point, I seek to show how the changing constellations of global markets and the local sociopolitical context shape the economic and political activities in football in Cameroon. In a West African setting, economic and political activities are constitutive of a political economy that has been shaped by "negotiability, flexibility, resilience, innovation, and entrepreneurship . . . alongside the dangers of extraction and marginality in the global economy" (Guyer 2004: 6). By focusing on the political economy of football, I seek to capture how "global and local economic policies, institutions, activities, and processes of valuation produce cultural meanings with which people engage" (Adebanwi 2017: 4). Particularly for West Africa of the post-structural-adjustment period, the future, however uncertain, takes precedence over the present and the past (Johnson-Hanks 2005), and people are willing to submit to new forms of disciplinary power that promise inclusion in transnational circuits (Piot 2010). This development is especially pertinent in football, given the sport's global commercialization and the expansion of a transnational market for football players grounded in neoliberal ideas of free enterprise. In particular, football academies that focus on commodification and export of footballers act as mediators between the globalized football market and young Cameroonians' masculine aspirations and obligations.

Here I seek to document the exact role of new football academies in selecting and cultivating young men as subjects willing to embrace new forms of precarity.[2] In the academies, the value of "suffering" for the sake of an uncertain future emerges as central. My emphasis on suffering may be surprising in the context of a recent call in anthropology to move "beyond the suffering subject" (Robbins 2013) and consider subjects of anthropological inquiry as more than people who merely suffer. However, here I am concerned with how football academies produce and cultivate a suffering subject specific to the demands of the expanding global market. While young footballers in Cameroon routinely, as they say, "suffer" on the football fields, especially when they have to train and play without compensation, academy managers insist that they need to be taught a specific form of "suffering," one that asks them to disregard their immediate obligations and orient themselves to future success in a globalized market, however uncertain this success might be. As the Buea Young Star FC president would say: "[The players] need to suffer today so they will see the results tomorrow." The academies seek to teach the young men to take personal responsibility for their failures and successes and embrace the precarity that is inherent in the globalized market. In other words, the academies seek to inculcate young men with a neoliberal form of agency, as described by Gershon (2011) in the quote that opened this chapter, and to frame it as a marker of responsible adulthood.[3]

The moral economy of football in Cameroon needs to be understood as part of the moral economy of elites. Here by moral economy I mean economic practices that do not necessarily lead to maximizing financial profit but rather to establishing and maintaining social relations. The agents commonly considered to be part of moral economies are the disadvantaged, "the poor" (Thompson 1971) or "the peasants" (Scott 1976). However, the moral economy of football in Cameroon is inseparable from the moral economy of elites, i.e., the way that elites in Cameroon are created and legitimized through contributions to their ethnic or regional communities (Orock 2015). Cameroonians expect elite figures to contribute to the development of their regions of origin and then morally judge them and (at least in theory) hold them accountable to their communities, towns, and regions. In contrast to the agents of more common accounts of moral economy, the football presidents who are the focus of this chapter are anything but poor or disadvantaged. Rather, they are what Cameroonians call "big men," influential and wealthy individuals, either established or in the making. They manage or fail to convert their financial investment into other forms of capital, such as reputation and political capital, and this conversion depends on how Cameroonian football players, coaches, and football fans judge their investments and participation in football.

Death of a Big Man

The demise of one of the most prominent football academies in the Southwest Region illustrates the changes in the moral economy of football. Unisport Limbe FC was founded in 2000 in Limbe by a prominent highly ranked employee of a parastatal company. According to an account by a former coach, the founder had experience running and financing a small local football club in the 1990s, and in 2000 he assembled a formidable team of physical education teachers and football coaches. He established Unisport Limbe FC as an academy dedicated to boys aged twelve to eighteen, and in a few years added an adult football team with the goal of participating in Elite One.

In an interview in 2004, at a time when the transnational business of football was expanding (see chapter 1), the founder said that he was "determined to put top quality athletes into the market [and] shape the underprivileged children into people who can help their families tomorrow" (Pannenborg 2012: 163). In another interview in 2009, he identified his goals much more in line with ideals such as youth development, local sport development, and contribution to the national team:

> First, we want to give young people something to do in this part of the country where there are few leisure activities. Second, we are grooming young players so that they will be ready to play for the big clubs or even the national team. Third, we want to improve the level of our local football. (Pannenborg 2012: 163)

The founder was a member of the Southwestern elite. He was well known in the Southwest as an influential figure related to a parastatal that remained economically relevant despite the trend of privatization. He was a prominent member of the ruling CPDM party and a former highly positioned civil servant. Finally, he was a native Bakweri. He was respected in Limbe, and former Unisport Limbe FC footballers praised his management of the club:

> When the old man was there, everything was going well. If you play well and he likes you, you will never lack anything. When I played there he would not pay players too much, he would give salary of [CFA] 30,000, but if you came to him and told him that your mommy was sick, he would remove [CFA] 100,000 from his pocket and give you. A very good man.

Despite his originally stated goal of putting footballers in the market, the founder became known among the footballers as suspicious of foreign scouts and reluctant to sell footballers to clubs abroad. This mattered little, because he was known for taking "good care" of the academy staff and footballers, especially those from the Southwest Region, by providing financial assistance to them and their families. The club president participated in the moral economy of the elites through his investments in football and in some financially struggling footballers, investments that did not bring him financial profit but helped him establish a good reputation in the region.

In 2013 the general manager passed away. He was succeeded at the academy by one of his children, nicknamed "Junior," who was studying business administration at a university in South Africa. In 2014 Junior, who was in his thirties, told me that when his father was alive the aim of the academy was mostly "social development" and "helping disadvantaged children through sports." At the time, he continued, this was possible despite the fact that the club made no profit because his father had "good connections" with wealthy men who invested significant amounts of money in the club. Junior did not inherit those valuable contacts and lacked his own. He stated his mission to transform the academy into a self-sustaining business: he wanted to sell football players in order to make a profit and invest in the academy. He had ambitious plans for a sports center, tennis courts, and a swimming pool, which he planned to finance by grooming and then selling talented players to more prominent (and wealthier) football clubs.

In 2014 and 2015, Unisport Limbe FC had an enviable infrastructure, one of the most developed in the entire region. Four kilometers from Limbe, away from the bustling town and surrounded by farmland, the academy was on a campus that included two full-sized football fields, one grass and one sand; three dormitory blocks with bunk beds that could host approximately sixty children or adults; a large restaurant/dining room with a bar and television sets; a large conference room with tables, chairs, and a blackboard for meetings; a small leisure room with a television set and a ping-pong table; a large administration office decorated with trophies and photos of the late general manager; and a sumptuously furnished office for Junior. The dormitories had a regular supply of water in barrels, and the electricity worked most of the time. The academy owned two buses, one that could transport a football team of twenty-five and one to transport children between the campus and the schools they attended in Limbe. The academy employed a technical director, four coaches, an administrative assistant, a secretary, a doctor, two cooks, several drivers, and a groundskeeper. This infrastructure was developed in 2008 when the late founder decided to expand the academy premises that he first started developing in his native village three kilometers away. At the time, only a handful of football academies with a comparatively developed infrastructure existed in the region.

Unisport Limbe FC consisted of the abovementioned academy for boys aged twelve to eighteen as well as a men's team, which in 2015 competed in the Elite One first-division league. The academy resembled a boarding school. In July, boys were selected through football trials, and in September approximately thirty-five moved to the campus. The boys' parents paid yearly fees between CFA 800,000 (US$1,400) and CFA 1.3 million (US$2,275), which covered food, housing, football training, and tuition fees for schools in Limbe (which range between CFA 50,000 (US$87.5) for government schools and around CFA 150,000 (US$262.5) for some private schools). A few boys had partial scholarships and paid around CFA 300,000 (US$525). By way of comparison, the yearly tuition fees at a girls' boarding school in Buea amounted to CFA 300,000 (US$525). The academy also had about thirty day students who lived with their families in Limbe. These students only paid "symbolic" fees to the academy.

In the 2014–15 academic year, almost all the students housed at the campus were from Francophone families. Anglophone and Francophone Cameroonians arguably have different views of football as a career and future. Junior explained to me that Francophone Cameroonians were much more inclined to "invest in their kids' careers," since they believe that playing football can lead to a lucrative career. Indeed, most successful Cameroonian football teams, including the most prominent national football academy, the Ecole de Football Brasseries du Cameroun, were based in the large Francophone cities of Douala and Yaoundé.[4] One of the common refrains I heard from Anglophone footballers was that their parents insisted that education was the only way to progress in life and that football was a distraction. This complaint was especially common among footballers with families from the Grassfields (the Northwest Region) but was also present among young men from the Southwest. Footballers would contrast this with the more developed football infrastructure and "football culture" in Douala and Yaoundé, where pursuing a football career was an acceptable option for families. In Unisport Limbe FC, only well-off families could afford the academy's steep fees, and almost all were from Francophone regions. In contrast, academy day students who did not lodge at the campus and only paid symbolic fees were mostly Anglophone and more likely to be from poorer backgrounds.

Unisport Limbe FC was the only football academy in the region that strongly insisted on their students' school performance. All boarding students were registered in different schools in Limbe. The bus would deliver the boys to their schools every morning and collect them at the end of the day. They were ordered to keep their school uniforms neat and clean. Academy staff often complained that some boys were only interested in playing football and neglected their studies. Junior insisted that the boys needed to pass with acceptable grades and planned to develop a policy for the men's team to recruit only footballers with secondary school diplomas. The strong emphasis on education, unique among academies in the region, was grounded in Junior's understanding of the attractive but highly fickle nature of a career in sports. Consider this excerpt from the academy's website:

> While football has grown to become arguably the most popular and most played sport on the planet, with its top professionals being amongst the best paid athletes in the world, there is however no guarantee that being hyper-talented and undergoing a rigorous and efficient training program will lead to becoming a successful professional football player. . . . Ensuring the basic and secondary education of our trainees serves not only as a backup in case of a failed football career but also serves as a fundamental tool which will be beneficial to them during their football careers and even after their playing days.

Junior was also critical of changes in regional football under the influence of the expanding transnational market for football players. Despite the club's financial issues and Junior's proclaimed solution of selling footballers to wealthier clubs, he became reluctant in 2015 to enter the business of selling players. He was clearly shaken by the emergence of new small academies, clubs, and entrepreneurs in the region, which focused almost exclusively on selling players to clubs abroad, and by young footballers' attraction to them. In January 2015 he was visibly irritated when I asked him whether he had plans to sell players. The context of our informal conversation at the tribunes of a stadium in Buea was relevant: Unisport Limbe FC was playing a friendly match against Buea Young Star FC, a regional division team that was slowly becoming known for arranging trials for footballers in Europe and was becoming a magnet for young players. Junior used the opportunity to rail against the club:

> We are a professional team, not some amateur team that is only after selling players! If the players want to travel, they can go with their own traveling program, if their contract with us is over. We are here to build a team and play.... Also the kids at the academy, we have to first build up quality players, we cannot just sell them like that.

His reaction appeared to be a protest against the transnational football industry's "new scramble for Africa" (Darby 2000), in particular the football academies' search for talented young African footballers for the sole purpose of "exporting" them to wealthier countries. Sports scholars have identified a range of consequences that export-oriented academies can have for the development of African football and African economies more generally. While the clearest profit makers are the wealthy clubs in the global North that seek to extract Africa's talent and labor, often at the expense of the development of African football, some academies seem to have the potential of elevating the African game and in some ways even contributing to the social and economic development of the countries they are based in. Academies throughout West Africa come in many shapes and sizes, and their impacts cannot be easily generalized (Darby 2013; Darby, Akindes, and Kirwin 2007). What seemed to frustrate Junior, who was clearly interested in the development of local football and the more holistic development of local youth, was the increasing domination of small academies that were entirely business-oriented ventures, driven by the simple goal of making money from selling footballers to clubs abroad.

Despite the enviable infrastructure, the high profile of the founder, and the noble proclamations of goals of holistic development of young men, Unisport Limbe FC and Junior were losing their reputation in Limbe in 2014. Junior, whom people often referred to as a "small man" (in contrast to his father, who was a "big man"), developed the reputation of being unapproachable, arrogant, and brash, lacking a clear vision, and, most of all, being financially incompetent. These rumors concerned mostly the men's team, which was losing matches and was stuck at the bottom of the table, with relegation to the far less competitive second division looming.

Junior did not inherit his father's connections and influence. In 2015, he complained that the wealthy businessmen, influential political figures, and companies who had supported the club no longer did so. Financing the men's team became difficult. According to FECAFOOT officials, professional football clubs in Cameroon are obliged to pay their players at least CFA 100,000 (US$175) monthly. In the wealthiest Cameroonian clubs in 2015, such as Coton Sport FC de Garoua, footballers could receive up to CFA 400,000 (US$700) a month.[5] In addition, most Elite One clubs would pay their footballers occasional training bonuses for their meals and additional bonuses when they won. In 2015 almost all Unisport Limbe FC men's team players complained that they had not received their salaries for months. Normally, they received training bonuses of CFA 5,000 (US$8.75) a week and bonuses of CFA 25,000 (US$43.75) when they won, which in 2015 rarely happened. The club only occasionally fed players and paid for their trips to away matches. Players frequently complained that they were "hungry" and could not meet their families' financial demands, and that this affected their performance. Coaches complained that the club was in a horrendous financial state. They blamed Junior, accusing him of being deaf to the needs of his subordinates and disengaged from the Southwestern elite. Most importantly, the footballers were angry that the president was reluctant to sell them to overseas clubs. They saw him as hindering their ambition to "reach a higher level." They considered his reluctance to throw young men into the uncertain waters of the transnational circulation of footballers as close-minded and deaf to the rapid changes of the global football business.

The literal death of the big man and the subsequent demise of his powerless successor stood for another death: the breakdown of the moral economy on which the club had formerly relied. The moral economy of "development" (Orock 2015) grounded in large parastatals and regional elites, according to which elite figures create and maintain their positions by "developing" the town and the region, was failing in football. This breakdown was symptomatic of a wider transition in football management in the Southwest Region that was becoming increasingly disconnected from the established regional elites who dominated the game in previous decades. Instead, as will become clear below, successful football management in the Southwest Region increasingly relied on appealing to young footballers who were not interested in playing for Cameroonian teams but bent on migrating abroad.

Occult Interpretations

Cameroonians often assess, criticize, or praise figures in power by speculating that they are members of powerful secret societies (Geschiere 2017). The staff and players of the Unisport Limbe FC academy, as well as people in Limbe in general, speculated about the club's two presidents and their membership in secret societies. Rumors around different kinds of spiritual practices, either Christian or what Cameroonians called "occult," reflected people's perceptions of changes in the political and moral economy of football.

In 2014 and 2015, Junior hired on several occasions Mission for Christ Pentecostal pastors to perform what he called "psychological preparation" for the team before key matches. He occasionally hired pastors from the Presbyterian Church but believed that Pentecostal pastors engaged the players more effectively with their passionate exaltations and prayers. The pastors visited the team, preached from the Bible, and led footballers in long prayers. As Cameroonians often assume that football clubs and players are steeped in "sorcery," Pentecostal prayers were supposed to help distance the team from accusations of dabbling in such occult practices. In Junior's words:

> Psychological preparation is a part of the game. We are in Africa. Africans believe in black magic. There are probably other teams that instead of inviting a pastor, they . . . maybe . . . invite some traditional healer, or something, to perform some traditional rites. I am sure in Europe they have their own means of preparing games psychologically. I have not had the opportunity, I don't know what happens in Europe. Maybe there are some teams that invite pastors, maybe there are teams that invite Rosicrucians, or, what do they call them, people from Illuminati, I don't know. But we have our own way. We believe that Jesus is the ultimate, and we try to make all our players believe in the principles of Jesus Christ.

Junior's hiring of Pentecostal pastors was a significant departure from his father's rumored use of societies like Nganya, a prominent Bakweri secret society, to spiritually cleanse the football field on nights before crucial matches. One Pentecostal coach, who had worked in Unisport Limbe FC since the 2000s, described to me that the old general manager was particularly opposed to Pentecostal prayers in the club. In 2007, the coach said, the team lost an important match that could have qualified it for Elite One. The general manager blamed the coaches for the loss: he claimed that the night before they had led the players to "pray violently the whole night," and the players did not get enough sleep. He was clearly referring to Pentecostal prayers that encourage believers to dance vigorously and spend many hours on their feet. Fervent Pentecostal prayers occasionally continue deep into the night, and Pentecostals claim that long prayers, even when they invigorate their spiritual well-being, can be exhausting. The Pentecostal coach denied the charges: the prayers lasted no longer than twenty-five minutes, he claimed, after which all the players went to sleep. The coach believed that there were other reasons why the general manager disdained Pentecostal prayers, as he was allegedly a member of a secret occult society, most likely AMORC, a Rosicrucian order. All "big people," influential political figures in the country, were allegedly members, he said. "The people that hold the country are there, inside. . . . They have their own principles [of] how they pray." Hence the general manager's disdain for Pentecostalism, the coach insisted.[6]

However, the Pentecostal coach was reluctant to condemn the general manager's alleged membership in occult societies. This was striking, because Pentecostal Christians were usually quick to morally castigate such influential societies and their spiritual practices, real or imagined, and the Pentecostal coach considered occult societies antithetical to Christianity. He claimed that the general manager's membership was crucial to his procurement of funds, which he then cleverly used to run a successful club. The club therefore prospered thanks to the general manager's secretive membership. While the coach welcomed Junior's shift to Pentecostal prayers and frequently preached the Bible to the footballers, he also lamented the loss of the well-connected general manager (whom he characterized as a "good man") and his ungodly but beneficial networks. Several times I pressed him to give me his opinion on whether the club would do better if the young president was also a member of the Rosicrucian order. His replies remained ambiguous: "He would receive favors from them, because they would give money to their member. But it is his own choice. It depends on whether he wants to do like his father or he wants to live a different life."

This episode demonstrates Cameroonians' ambivalent attitude toward the demise of the moral economy on which football clubs relied. People were excited about the possibilities and opportunities that came with the new generation's governing of football, but they were also frustrated by the breakdown of the moral economy grounded in regional elites. Pentecostal Christians, as well as other Cameroonians, mobilized the imagery of occult spiritual practices and membership in secret societies to criticize the moral economy of the elites, but they also expressed anxiety about the changes and the inevitable uncertainties of new forms of governing in football. People did not draw direct links along the lines of "old/stable/demonic" and "new/uncertain/enlightened." Yet it was clear that they felt a broader transition was taking place as the transnational football market expanded and offered new possibilities and new uncertainties.

"This Is a Business, Not a Charity"

The promises of the transnational market for football players were central to the appeal of a newly founded academy in Buea. Buea Young Star FC was founded in 2010, and it quickly gained popularity among many aspiring footballers in the Southwest Region. Its founder and president was Kelvin, an aspiring entrepreneur in his late twenties, who, in contrast to Junior, did not belong to a well-known family. He was born in Buea to a father from the Grassfields and a mother from the West Region (most likely Bamileke). A former footballer and a football fan, he was keen to develop young talented footballers from poor backgrounds and help them sign contracts with clubs abroad, and to develop a profitable business based on selling football players. He founded the club with the help of two German partners, one a football agent in his late thirties and the other a football coach who specialized in developing young talented footballers. Kelvin also maintained a relationship with a Nigerian football agent who was based in Eastern Europe. In the club's 2011 promotional video, the German agent described the club's mission in a message aimed at young aspiring Cameroonian footballers:

> Always think of where you are coming from and where you want to go. You have to do all that you are able to do to realize your dream. With, probably, our support, we can realize for some of you the dream to go to Europe.

"Dream" and "Europe," terms that frequently go together in an industry that flourishes on hope despite miniscule chances of success, were in line with the aspirations of young footballers, many of whom had seen some of their friends travel abroad to play football and earn money, living out many young Cameroonian men's fantasy. Buea Young Star FC promised to cater to this aspiration, and many young men who played in several regional clubs joined it.

In 2015 Buea Young Star FC had none of the infrastructure of Unisport Limbe FC. Their first team had daily morning trainings at the Buea stadium, often sharing the field with another team, and the young team (boys aged roughly twelve to sixteen) trained a few times a week in the afternoon, after school. The academy had no academic program and did not require school attendance or membership fees.

The academy was officially registered but had no office. In contrast to the Unisport Limbe FC president, who ran club business either from his lavishly furnished office or from his luxurious house, Kelvin ran his business from his simple rental in Molyko, Buea's economic hub, only a few minutes' walk from the stadium, where the only sign of conspicuous consumption was an enormous plasma TV set. He was not poor, but his financial background and status were difficult to assess: much of his starting capital seemed to have come from his father, who used to work in a gas trading company. Kelvin seemed to have a substantial amount of capital at his disposal: in 2015 he married the daughter of a high-ranking civil servant and apparently spent CFA 3.5 million (US$6,125) for a lavish wedding reception at Buea's most expensive hotel. In contrast to the Unisport Limbe FC president, who was somewhat corpulent and well dressed in public (both signs of prosperity), Kelvin was slim, appeared young, and wore casual pants and a football t-shirt. His "office" in his living room was equipped with only one computer and an internet connection. Footballers would frequently visit him in his rental. He was often in the company of friends who assisted him in running the academy, some of whom had positions such as "team manager." These were not official positions but ad hoc titles that suggested an affinity to the club and a status of a friend. On one occasion, I was temporarily given a title of an "assistant coach" so I could sit on the bench during a tournament—a gesture of good will. I was never certain if or how much Kelvin's assistants were paid, but I assumed they received some financial compensation. The head coach received a fairly decent monthly salary of CFA 120,000 (US$210). In contrast to Unisport Limbe FC, Kelvin ran his club in a more informal manner.

Kelvin maintained good relationships with his foreign partners. Every year, the youth coach from Germany spent two weeks with the team, trained with them, selected twenty-five players who were to train with the team for the upcoming year, and, most important, selected the most talented candidates for trials abroad. The young president paid for his visits and his stay in an upscale hotel in Buea. A key purpose of this expensive exercise was a performance of meritocracy: a demonstration that an external "unbiased" person objectively observed the footballers and selected the most promising ones. In practice, this was not entirely the case, but to an extent the performance worked to circumvent the common Cameroonian accusation that club presidents chose footballers not based on merit but personal connections, kinship ties, and ethnic affiliations.[7]

For Kelvin, football was "a business, not a charity." Alongside his proclaimed desire to help young, poor Cameroonians reach their dreams of playing in Europe, profit (financial or otherwise) was his main goal. Selling footballers to international clubs was important. It was difficult to find exact information about sales and profits; however, a sketch of what went into selling a player, and some assessments of financial profits and the general economy of the process, can provide a rough picture.

After identifying a player with potential, Kelvin and the player would sign an official contract. If the player was under eighteen, Kelvin would consult the player's parents and ask for their permission. These were usually long-term contracts, from five to ten years, and could be extended. The contract stated that each time the player was sold to a club during this period, Kelvin would receive a percentage of the transfer fee, i.e., a fee paid by the receiving club to the source club, as well as a percentage of his salary. This was a common way of managing footballers. Occasionally, Kelvin would record a video of the player in action to present to clubs and managers abroad and write up a basic CV that listed the player's age, weight, height, position, and transfer history.[8]

He would then arrange and partially pay for the player's passports, visas, and airline tickets. Occasionally, he acted less as the head of a football club and more as a "doki-man," a migration broker (Alpes 2012; 2017). He would often arrange invitation letters from his European partners, a key requirement for visa applications; organize visa appointments at European embassies; and produce passports that falsified (reduced) the player's age. After having arranged the documents, Kelvin would send the player to his business partner, the Nigerian football manager based in Eastern Europe, who would find a club for him to train with, usually in a lower (third or fourth) division. In the first year, Kelvin would not expect the foreign club to pay the player. This would be a period for the player to develop his skills in a European setting and try to obtain a residence permit. The expectation was that the player would eventually be bought by another club and Kelvin would profit from the sale.

During my twelve-month fieldwork, Kelvin arranged trials and documents for ten players. For five of them, the document procedures failed or were deemed too expensive and protracted, while some left the club for an unrelated reason. The other five traveled to various destinations in Europe, including Portugal, Germany, Bosnia and Herzegovina, Poland, Latvia, Estonia, and Slovakia. Most visited at least two countries, following Kelvin's instructions. Some returned to Cameroon, either briefly or indefinitely. Three players found salaried positions on clubs in Eastern Europe.

Even when a player was sold, it was not clear whether the sale would be financially profitable for Kelvin. For instance, he sold one player to a small club in Eastern Europe where the player earned €350 a month. Kelvin took 20 percent (€70), which he then shared with the other participants in the "production chain": his two partners in Germany and his partner in Eastern Europe. Considering what he invested in the player, it is difficult to see how this sale could be financially profitable. However, Kelvin sold one player to a first-division club in Eastern Europe, and the player even went on to perform for the Cameroonian national team, which won the 2017 Africa Cup of Nations. In 2017, a widely used website that archives information about transfers in football estimated the player's market value at €250,000.[9] It is difficult to know what Kelvin collected (or is still collecting years after the sale), but the case shows that sending outstanding individual players abroad can be a lucrative business.

But profit alone does not sufficiently explain why entrepreneurs like Kelvin invest in football. While the reputation of Unisport Limbe FC was in a free fall, Kelvin increasingly enjoyed the respect of footballers, coaches, and football officials and administrators who lauded his efforts to support young Cameroonians in fulfilling their talents abroad. While some experienced football administrators and older coaches lamented the sorry state of the Cameroonian national league and the occasionally shady business practices that accompanied selling footballers to foreign clubs, they praised the Buea Young Star FC president for supporting young players' migration. In 2016 Kelvin capitalized on his growing reputation, ascending by appointment to a high position in a FECAFOOT regional bureau. Thus, investing in football in Cameroon remained a way of attaining social and symbolic capital, a continuation of practices of elite big men from previous decades (Pannenborg 2012). But while older big men, embedded in parastatal companies, political parties, and ethnic and regional elites, cemented their positions by investing in the local game, the new football entrepreneurs like Kelvin sought to build their reputations by selling players to clubs abroad.

Several issues need to be addressed at this point. One of them is age reduction, a public secret in international football. Finding ways to obtain passports that indicated a reduced age was common practice among Buea Young Star FC players and aspiring footballers in general. Even though international sporting bodies (such as FIFA) and national sporting bodies (such as FECAFOOT) consider this cheating, no footballers and very few football managers in Cameroon considered age reduction fraudulent or immoral. Footballers and managers such as Kelvin argued that while children in Europe trained at football from a very young age on good pitches and with expert coaches, Cameroonian kids had fewer training facilities available and needed more time to develop. According to this line of thought, Cameroonian footballers could not possibly compete with their European peers who had professional training facilities available to them and who had been training professionally for many years longer. The market for football players had become transnational, and in order to make the competition fairer, Cameroonian footballers had to resort to age reduction. Age reduction was thus for footballers far from a morally dubious practice but rather a necessary corrective, albeit a temporary one, to large-scale structural inequalities between the global North and the global South.

Furthermore, footballers carrying passports with a reduced age raises an issue that is a common focus of media and expert accounts of football-related migration, namely the trafficking of children. A number of high-profile clubs (such as FC Barcelona and Manchester City FC) have been recently found to have violated FIFA regulations that prohibit recruitment of minors (under eighteen years old), in particular Article 19, which prohibits clubs from transferring minors across borders. These regulations were put in place to curb child trafficking through football, a morally charged issue often raised by FIFA and other football governing bodies, human rights organizations, and journalists. Trafficking of minors is indeed a widespread problem in football-related migration (Darby, Akindes, and Kirwin 2007; Donnelly and Petherick 2004). However, the footballers' age reduction complicates the boundary between children and adults. Many aspiring football migrants in Southwest Cameroon were in their twenties and had their official ages reduced to sixteen or seventeen in anticipation of migration. The footballers were aware that clubs abroad wanted to sign young players (between eighteen and twenty-one) and that many clubs found ways to routinely circumvent Article 19 by placing minors in youth academies (Hawkins 2015a). The footballers' reasoning was that reducing age would give them another year or two to develop their skills, ideally in a youth club in Europe, unpaid by the club but sponsored by a trusted manager (such as Kelvin), until they could sign official contracts. Furthermore, the aspiring migrants, such as those whom Kelvin was trying to sell to clubs overseas, were not children, both in terms of age and social status. Rather, they were young men on the cusp of social adulthood, increasingly pressured by their families to begin earning a living and contributing to household budgets. Migration abroad was for them a way of dealing with rising obligations to provide as male adults, especially if their families invested money in their football training and migration. This point, not exclusive to Cameroon (Agergaard and Ungruhe 2016; Esson and Drywood 2018; Ungruhe and Esson 2017; van der Meij and Darby 2014), thoroughly complicates the morally charged accounts of child trafficking that have come to dominate public discourses about football-related mobility.

Secondly, selling football players (underage or not) in transnational markets evokes uneasy connotations in an African context. Estimating a market value and selling football players commodifies people. According to Appadurai (1986), the "commodity situation in the social life of any 'thing'" is a "situation in which exchangeability (past, present, or future) for some other thing is its socially relevant feature" (1986: 13). Commodification is then a process through which a thing (any "thing") becomes a commodity for exchange. Selling football players amounts to commodification of persons: football players emerge from a web of social relations that make them exchangeable commodities. This can be a particularly sensitive issue in the context of West Africa, where there are still ample memories of the slave trade, for example, expressed in masked dance performances in the Northwest Region of Cameroon (Argenti 2007), in ritual performances in Sierra Leone (Shaw 2002), and in long traditions of intellectual critique (Mbembe 2017). Cameroonians have a rich cultural and linguistic vocabulary to talk about the immorality of selling people. One example is *nyongo*, a form of witchcraft that emerged in colonial times and relates to greed, accumulation of wealth, and slave-like labor. In *nyongo*, or as it is known in different parts of the country, *ekong*, *famla*, or *kupe*, witches transform their victims into zombies and put them to work on invisible plantations. *Nyongo* can refer to people capable of using victims as slaves and getting rich from their labor, to a mysterious place where victims of greed are said to be slaving away, or to the greed itself. These discourses of *nyongo* are not simply remnants of tradition but instead are contemporary responses to modernity and globalization (Geschiere 1997: chapter 5; Nyamnjoh 2005).

However, the young footballers did not evoke this widespread imagery of the immorality of selling persons in the context of transnational football industry, nor did they see themselves as victims of a modern-day slave trade. From their point of view, as with young athletes from poor backgrounds elsewhere (Klein 2008), commodification offered an opportunity to migrate abroad and earn a living by playing the beautiful game. Migrating abroad, even for a short period of time, could bring much more financial and social capital to the young men than playing in Cameroonian clubs, most of which were dependent on the financial whims of Cameroonian investors and notorious for not paying regular salaries. Footballers were aware that opportunities for signing contracts with clubs abroad were also notoriously fickle, yet, for most of them, commodification that led to migration meant progress and a better chance for a livelihood.

Framing the issue of football-related mobility in terms of a modern-day slave trade, human trafficking, and exploitation of vulnerable persons appears rather in accounts of international organizations, journalists, policymakers, and football governing bodies. From high-ranking FIFA officers to investigative journalists, many have reported and raised alarms about the large numbers of young men who are exploited and trafficked through football-related migratory channels. This work is extremely valuable, as it meticulously documents the details of abuse and exploitation that are rife in the murky waters of transnational business of football transfers (Hawkins 2015a).

And yet, framing the entire migratory process in highly moralized terms of slave trade and human trafficking is not always helpful. It can be simultaneously too broad and too narrow. It is too broad when it tends to depict mobility as inherently exploitative. It is too narrow when it foregrounds shocking stories of outright abuse as archetypal accounts of human trafficking. One unfortunate result is that certain influential observers and decision-makers have come to disregard young football-related migrants' claims of being exploited as illegitimate. Paradoxically, conflating all mobility with exploitation and foregrounding the most horrific accounts of abuse fuels rulings of European courts that "the boys could not be victims if they had agreed to leave their home country" (Hawkins 2015b), arguments by owners of large football academies that the "wider business model" does not amount to "neo-colonial exploitation" (quoted in Hawkins 2015a: 127), and arguments by European immigration officers and antitrafficking organizations that young men's claims of exploitation are "bullshit" (quoted in Hawkins 2015b). The earlier-mentioned public secret that many aspiring footballers are not children further distances the young men from stereotypical images of victimhood and fuels arguments that the young men could not have been victims of trafficking or exploitation because they have "chosen" to migrate and stay in Europe. The false dichotomy of "agency vs victimhood" takes the center stage, and the young men's agency becomes a counterargument to their claims of victimhood.[10]

Moreover, as Esson (2020) has argued for the case of Ghanaian football migrants, conflating mobility with exploitation (i.e., the broad interpretation of trafficking) and foregrounding instances considered clearly morally reprehensible (i.e., the narrow interpretation of trafficking) are problematic, because both effectively conceal the underlying causes and structural conditions that make mobile Africans susceptible to exploitation.[11] The morally charged discourses of the modern-day slave trade and human trafficking on the surface reveal exploitation but can effectively obscure the structural conditions and inequalities that make the exploitation possible, and even likely, in transnational football migrations. These structural conditions in Cameroon and elsewhere in West Africa, detailed in chapter 1, are, one, the prolonged economic stalemate induced by neoliberal austerity measures that have left many young people with few options for a stable future in their own country, and, two, the commercialized global football industry that commodifies people, especially migrants. Furthermore, as it will become clear in chapter 3, young men on the cusp of adulthood, such as the young footballers from Buea Young Star FC sent to Europe by Kelvin, are also susceptible to exploitation, even if their stories do not fit stereotypical accounts of human trafficking.

Producing Suffering Subjects

Young men's aspirations to migrate were not enough to run a football academy. Kelvin needed to make sure that the footballers were disciplined, committed to training hard despite difficult conditions and uncertain outcomes, prepared to deal with the challenging (and sometimes exploitative) conditions they would encounter overseas, and ready to submit to his guidance and leadership. He played a crucial role in preparing young men for the precarity of a transnational athletic career.

As an entrepreneur and a gatekeeper of young footballers' access to the global market, Kelvin was less focused on managing Buea Young Star FC as a football team than on identifying talented individual players and managing their entry into transnational markets. Kelvin sought to develop close relationships and methods of supervision of individual promising players. He claimed that psychology classes he had attended at university allowed him to carefully assess not only football skills but more crucially the character of each individual player. On many occasions he discussed with me a player's individual characteristics: who was "stubborn" and who was "focused," who had a "zeal," and who was "disciplined." He was particularly critical of *strong-hed* (stubborn) footballers not willing to follow instructions, especially concerning migration. He complained about the two most common transgressions of footballers who manage to leave Cameroon. These were "running away"—i.e., hiding from the manager and the authorities, looking for other employment opportunities abroad, and staying in Europe illegally—and being defeated by the often-deplorable living conditions in the destination country and flying back to Cameroon of their own accord.

The consequences of Kelvin's priority to train individual footballers rather than the team as a whole became clear to me during a meeting between the coach, the team captain, and the club president. In 2015 Buea Young Star FC competed in the regional (third) division against teams of the Southwest Region. The players sometimes referred to it as the "devil league" because club presidents were not obliged by FECAFOOT to pay their players or provide them with daily or weekly training bonuses. At the time of the meeting, the club was not performing well. We all sat around the table, opposite the television set that was broadcasting a rerun of an English Premier League match between Arsenal FC and West Bromwich Albion FC. The coach argued that the main reason for the club's low performance was that the footballers had not received any kind of compensation for more than three months:

> Most of these players that are in the club now, they are not small children. They are big people, and all of them have some [financial] responsibilities. Now, players did not receive training bonuses for two or three months, and this affects the results. That is the main problem. . . . For this [low] level of football, or let me say for these players in Buea, if you want to see the results you must give them training bonuses.

Kelvin disagreed, arguing that most players were not eligible for training bonuses and that giving bonuses to everyone was not an effective business model. Moreover, it clashed with his key objectives for the academy:

> The objective for the club is not to win the league. The objective is to train people who have potential and then select the best and send them out of the country. For this season, for me, I only don't want the team to be last. So this does not bother me too much. I only worry about the performance of individual people that we need to select and prepare to travel abroad.

The focus on preparing individual players for the transnational market is clear. Note that not winning a league competition did not indicate a lack of ambition. An important incentive for Kelvin to remain in the regional "devil league" was the fact that the administrative rules were much looser. While Unisport Limbe FC had to carefully follow the administrative instructions of FECAFOOT in order to play in Elite One, in the "devil league" there was more space to manipulate players' documents and tamper with their reported age. Engagement with global markets seemed to work better from the gray areas of unregulated spaces in Cameroonian football.

Furthermore, Kelvin's focus on developing individual players led him to a model of allocating club finances that was strikingly different to clubs such as Unisport Limbe FC. Kelvin continued:

> I will not invest in every man equally. I can only put down money for something that is marketable, for something that has a prospect for future. I will put down money for something that will give me profit later. So I must concentrate on people that have some prospect.

Again, the commodification of players is clear and grounded in assessment of future value: which players are likely to bring profit in the future. Moreover, in Buea Young Star FC, commodification led to the nurturing of footballers who were equally oriented to the future and focused on success in football. Kelvin continued:

> [The players] need to suffer today so they will see the results tomorrow. Not ask [for money] now, but understand that you need to put your best into your training, so you can have the results later. . . . Also, there are match bonuses, if you win the match, you get [CFA] 3,000. In my own ideology, that is better. If I come to the training and do not receive a training bonus, but I know that I will get 3,000 if I win a match, I will do what? I will fight to win, I will give my best!

Finally, Kelvin framed suffering for the sake of the future as a sign of maturity and adulthood:

> Not every man in Buea can play this professional football! [*points to the Premier League match on the television set*] Only *one-one* [i.e., "very few"]. . . . And they are not children, they are growing a beard! They know what they want to do in life, so they need to do it.

Note that Kelvin's way of addressing the uncertainty of success in professional football was strikingly different to that of Unisport Limbe FC's president. While Junior in Limbe emphasized education as an alternative and addition to a future in football, Kelvin argued for single-minded determination and focus on the sport as a solution to the vagaries of an athletic career.

Importantly, Kelvin framed focus and determination as signs of adulthood. His allusions to adulthood are strikingly different from those brought up by the coach whom Kelvin was arguing with. Knowledgeable of local football and of the needs of young men, the coach worried about the footballers' obligations to provide for their families. Meanwhile, for Kelvin—the gatekeeper to transnational markets (and the one who had the last word)—the markers of adulthood were grounded in qualities that allowed young men (who were "growing a beard") to compete in transnational markets, namely the capacity to suffer for the sake of future success. Here we see how a football academy operates on the fact that young men are on the brink of becoming adult male providers and how an individual who runs an academy as a business seeks to shape them to comply with the demands of the market and his own business interests. In this way, the young men are taught to take personal responsibility for both their failures and successes and effectively internalize embracing the precarity of the globalized market as a marker of adult masculinity.

Finally, Kelvin's evocation of suffering demands more attention. "We are suffering" is a common refrain among Anglophone Cameroonians. Just like Nigerians (Larkin 2017: 48–49), Cameroonians speak of "suffering" during times of economic hardship and when their hard work fails to deliver. Cameroonian footballers in the "devil league" often "suffer"—when they are forced to train on badly maintained pitches that are conducive to injuries, when they are asked to play demanding matches on empty stomachs, and when their efforts result in meager (if any) financial returns. And yet the president of a prominent football academy insisted that young men needed to be taught the value of "suffering," a value they appeared to be lacking.

It is clear that Kelvin sought from footballers a specific kind of suffering, one that was oriented toward success that was elsewhere and in the future. While previously the footballers would suffer on bad training pitches for the sake of representing a club, achieving local glory, and earning a small income, club presidents like Kelvin trained young men to suffer in order to qualify for moving abroad and competing in transnational markets. As will become clearer in the next chapter, the capacity for this kind of suffering would become important once footballers migrated abroad and were confronted with the arduous and sometimes exploitative conditions in foreign clubs.

It turns out, then, that the subject with the capacity to suffer for the sake of an uncertain future—a prerequisite for an opportunity to succeed in a competitive and unpredictable football industry—is not a given among young African men who aspire to migrate. Instead, it is produced in academies such as Buea Young Star FC that are grounded in ideas of business and commodification. In other words, the suffering subject, the subject in economic distress prepared to suffer for a better future, is not simply "there" for the global markets to use but needs to be produced and nurtured, and it emerges from spaces and relations that rely on ideas of free global enterprise.

Political and Moral Economy of Football: Embracing Precarity

Focusing on entrepreneurship and management in football reveals that the political and moral economy in twenty-first-century Cameroon increasingly relies on engagement with transnational markets. While in postcolonial Cameroon managing football used to be grounded in influential regional organizations, such as parastatal companies, ethno-regional elite networks, or political parties, nowadays successful football management depends more on creating and maintaining transnational networks. Moreover, when the analysis of moral economy is expanded beyond the exclusive focus on the disadvantaged and considers the making of elite figures, it is revealed that the elites' legitimacy is increasingly intertwined with transnational markets.

This is not necessarily new: politics and economy in Africa have a long history of "extraversion," i.e., "mobilizing resources derived from their (possibly unequal) relationship with the external environment" (Bayart 2000: 218). But the establishment of football academies such as Buea Young Star FC is quite new in the Southwest Region of Cameroon, a trend that began in the 2000s. Recent changes in the Southwest Region's political economy of football, which transitioned from social and political entrepreneurship to economic entrepreneurship, led to the creation of football academies that focus on commodifying young men. The increased prominence of such academies is clearly a response to the expansion of the transnational market for football players, but it is also driven "from below," as young men faced with diminished opportunities in the local economy flock to the academies that promise them a possibility to migrate overseas.

Crucially, young men are taught in such academies to prioritize suffering for the sake of the future, however uncertain, over present needs and obligations and to take personal responsibility for failures. Academies formulate this value as a sign of adulthood and maturity that needs to be inculcated. In this way, young men are taught to embrace a new form of precarity, one that comes with the expansion of the global market for football players, and to internalize neoliberal forms of agency as markers of adult masculinity. Global markets thus rely on the willingness of young men to suffer for the sake of an uncertain future, but, crucially, this is a quality that is not simply "there" among young men but needs to be produced.

This begs the question: How are young men dealing with the opportunities and demands of the transnational football industry and of growing pressures from their kin to begin providing? In the following chapters I explore their perspectives and practices in more detail.

Notes

1. Elements of this chapter have been previously published in "'This Is a Business, Not a Charity': Football Academies, Political Economy, and Masculinity in Cameroon," in *Sport, Migration, and Gender in the Neoliberal Age*, ed. N. Besnier, D. G. Calabrò, and D. Guinness (London: Routledge, 2021), 213–30.
2. For a similar perspective on the social production of migrants who endure despite the hardships, see Gaibazzi's (2012, 2015) accounts of "cultivating hustlers" in West Africa.

3. For an analysis of neoliberal governmentality and agency in the globalized football industry, see also Esson (2013, 2020); Hann (2018, 2021). For an important nuanced perspective that argues that athletes who participate in sport industries are more than individualized entrepreneurs of the self, see Hopkinson (2019, 2021) and Crawley (2019, 2021), on Ghanaian boxers and Ethiopian long-distance runners, respectively.
4. One exception was Coton Sport FC de Garoua, the most successful Cameroonian football club in the past decade, that was based in the North Region though is in Francophone Cameroon.
5. For the sake of comparison, schoolteachers in government schools earn around CFA 100,000 (US$175); however, in some private schools, teachers' wages could be as low as CFA 25,000 (US$43.75). A secretary at Unisport Limbe FC earned CFA 60,000 (US$105). Some civil servants, e.g., programmers employed by the General Certificate of Education (GCE) board, would earn up to CFA 500,000 (US$875). The official national minimum wage in 2014 was CFA 36,270 (US$63.5), well below the workers union representatives' demands of a CFA 62,000 (US$108.5) minimum wage. See "Cameroon to Increase Minimum Wage from 28,000 to 36,270 FCFA," Business in Cameroon, 22 July 2014, retrieved 6 December 2017 from http://www.businessincameroon.com/public-management/2207-4959-cameroon-to-increase-minimum-wage-from-de-28-000-to-36-270-fcfa.
6. For a related discussion of convergences and tensions between Christian prayers and athletic training, see Guinness (2018). Note that the coach did not directly refer to a Bakweri secret society, such as Nganya, but to one that he perceived as European, originating from the Vatican and the Catholic Church. Many Pentecostals see their faith as a moral challenge not only to traditional African ancestor cults but also to longstanding Christian institutions, such as the Catholic Church.
7. During football matches on all levels (from small regional leagues to national team matches), when a certain footballer clearly underperformed, Cameroonian spectators often labeled him a "coach's player" or "president's player," indicating that his position on the team was not a result of merit but of a close personal relationship with team decision-makers. There was much talk of club presidents and coaches taking bribes for fielding certain footballers.
8. Footballers would often make these videos themselves, as something to show to potential managers.
9. http://www.transfermarkt.de.
10. It needs to be mentioned that this is not a criticism of the nuanced investigative journalism of Ed Hawkins's best-selling book *The Lost Boys: Inside Football's Slave Trade* (2015a) but rather of policymakers and antitrafficking organizations that see young men's agency as a counterargument to their claims of exploitation.
11. Esson (2020) has also astutely observed that the young footballers, as Black African men, do not fit the archetype of human trafficking victims, which in the eyes of White European service staff further undermines their claims to being exploited.

CHAPTER 3

Becoming Useful and Humble
Moral Masculinities in Uncertain Times

One morning in October 2014 I was late for training with Buea Young Star FC.[1] My teammates were already walking away from the dilapidated football field where they trained daily. One of them, Nelson, a tall defender in his early twenties, approached me, visibly excited. He had just received a phone call from Kelvin, the club president who was also his personal agent and had promised to place him with a club in Europe. "He said I will travel very soon. Maybe tomorrow." This was very good news: his main goal was to migrate and to begin playing for a living on a European club. Nelson had very little idea of where he would travel: some of the rumored options were Croatia, Latvia, Germany, and Poland. He had no more than a day or two to prepare for the trip. He was nervous but excited to leave.

But there were at least two more footballers on the club who, according to other players, coaches, and managers, played better and had more potential. Why did Nelson get a chance to leave instead? To me, this was a demonstration of the unpredictability of transnational football, a fickle industry in demand of young athletic bodies. For example, at the time of selection, one of the club's outstanding footballers had an injury, which led to him not being selected. Another one, Akwe, in his late twenties, was considered too old to perform, even though he exhibited superior skills. In addition, Kelvin frequently changed his mind about which player to send abroad and when, responding to fleeting opportunities to place players with one or another European club. The event also pointed to the unpredictability of migration from Cameroon in general. For example, a few of my teammates at the time had applied for visas in European embassies, and while some were successful, others were rejected on the suspicion that they had falsified their age. The staff at European (and other) embassies frequently rejected some visa applications while accepting others, and applying for visas for many Cameroonians, including young footballers, was like playing the lottery (see also Piot 2019).

My teammates were acutely aware of the uncertainties of visa applications and the transnational football market, but they had other explanations for why the other two footballers were not selected. They represented the epitome of a stereotype of disobedient footballers in Cameroon: irresponsible, alcohol drinkers, gamblers, and womanizers. By contrast, Nelson, who was incidentally a dedicated Pentecostal Christian, was well behaved, responsible, focused on training, and monogamous, and thus in the eyes of my teammates he deserved the opportunity to migrate. My teammates were much more concerned with issues of moral standing and problematic masculinity, and they turned to these issues when seeking explanations for successes and failures.

In Buea and Limbe, young aspiring footballers' transnational aspirations and the demands of the competitive football industry intersected with notions of morality and masculinity. The footballers, like young men in general, struggled to avoid being judged as what was locally known as "useless men," a morally charged haunting trope defined as the failure to achieve social adulthood by providing for one's family, or failing to be seen as making a serious attempt to do so. Many were also joining increasingly influential neo-charismatic Pentecostal Christian denominations that preached that dedication to the Holy Spirit brings success and material wealth, and these players were fashioning themselves as "humble," "focused," monogamous, and "God-fearing," distancing themselves from the masculine tropes of both conspicuous "urban" manhood and "traditional" village manhood. These young men fashioned themselves as moral subjects, at once seeking to fulfill the obligations of provider masculinity as well as the demands of the transnational market of football players that sought not only athletic and talented young men but also those disciplined and focused on the sport.

In this chapter I follow Nelson, Akwe, and their teammates to unpack the making of moral masculinities between new and old aspirations, demands, and evaluations. The goal is to understand the role of gendered morality when people deal with uncertainty. As I have outlined in more detail in the introduction of this book, moral masculinities are ways of being a man that emerge from men's struggles to do and be good, to deal with others' moral judgments and evaluations, and to orient themselves to moral values. They are constructed at intersections between different domains of social life, such as kinship, ethnicity, religion, and transnational markets. Three domains emerge as central in Cameroon: how young men negotiate notions of masculinity on football fields and how novel forms of masculinity emerge with (real and perceived) novel opportunities to migrate abroad to play; how relations with kin figure as central to the young footballers' migration projects and articulations of adult masculinity through obligations of financial care; and how Pentecostal Christianity plays an increasingly important role in shaping young men's participation in transnational markets.

As the young men deal with the demands of provider masculinity and the unpredictable market of football players, masculinity emerges as a product of navigating moral judgments and self-fashioning as moral subjects. The self-fashioning is driven by aspirations of seizing new real or imagined opportunities granted by globalized markets and fulfilling long-standing demands of economic redistribution. At the same time, however, as the above vignette illustrates, moralized discourses about problematic masculinity can effectively obscure the fickleness of globalized markets and the difficulties of reaching adulthood in the era of economic uncertainty. To account for this, there is a need to move beyond representations of young men as victims of large-scale economic processes and to consider ways they fashion themselves as moral subjects; but there is also a need to critically assess how moralized discourses about masculinity can obscure large-scale economic and political conditions that shape young men throughout the countries of the structurally adjusted global South.

Negotiating Masculinities on Football Fields

The following story of Akwe's rise and subsequent downfall demonstrates how notions of masculinity take shape on and around football fields in Cameroon. When I met him in August 2014, Akwe had already acquired somewhat of a legendary status in Buea. His beginnings in football were familiar: he started playing as a child on school fields with overgrown grass, until as a thirteen-year-old he took part in the Ecole de Football Brasseries du Cameroun's annual tournament. The coaches spotted him, and he started regular training. He quickly advanced through several teams in the Southwest Region, competing at the regional and national levels, and eventually started intermittently earning wages for playing. He was a redoubtable attacker and frequently scored goals. He was most fond of reminiscing about how football fans would occasionally *dash* him (i.e., give him an informal gift) small amounts of money to show appreciation for his performance. He would use these small gifts to buy items like soap, body oil, mobile phone top-ups, fruit, soft drinks, or roasted corn; when he would receive larger donations, i.e., those of more than CFA 10,000 (US$17.5), he would invest in football boots or training shirts.

Many experienced footballers around Buea remembered fondly the informal gifts of money from football fans around town. In 2014 this practice was more infrequent, but it could still be witnessed during "interquarter" tournaments, widely attended competitions between villages and town neighborhoods that take place during the rainy season (between July and September) throughout the country. I witnessed it only once, in all its glorious theatricality. In one interquarter match in September 2014, a footballer scored, and a fan ran into the field to join the players in celebration. The man ran straight toward the goal scorer and forcefully slammed a wad of bills onto the ecstatic player's sweaty forehead. Some bills stuck to his head, while others flew around him, forcing him to frantically collect them from the ground before the referee finally ushered him back to his position so that the match could continue.

The fact that Akwe collected so many of these gifts bore witness to his emerging status as a *Buea pikin* (child of Buea), an urban popularity particularly associated with football. The local popularity he gradually garnered through his football performance was also made possible by his ethnicity. He was a Bakossi, a native of the Southwest Region. Had he been a "Grassfielder," an immigrant from the Northwest, it would have been significantly more difficult for him to achieve the status of local favorite.[2] The image of the *Buea pikin* refers to a form of personhood that is inextricably tied to a locality and, in the case of footballers, a form of youthful masculinity that is built on positive relationships in one's immediate social surroundings, including with neighborhood and town peers, extended family members, and elders.

It did not take long for Akwe to be spotted by Kelvin, who at the time was in the process of founding Buea Young Star FC, the football academy whose single goal was spotting and training young talented footballers and sending them to Europe for trial matches (see chapter 2). Despite his lack of experience in the football industry, Kelvin offered to use his contacts in Europe and send Akwe for trial matches with European clubs. What followed was a long process of dealing with all the barriers to West Africans' mobility to Europe: obtaining travel documents, arranging invitation letters from football clubs, dealing with visa rejections, and collecting money for costly airfare. After two years of struggle, Akwe finally managed to leave the country. He traveled to Europe twice, spending a few months training with decent football clubs in Germany and Eastern Europe before returning to Buea, where he claimed that one of the clubs abroad was offering him a professional contract.

During his intermittent returns to Cameroon, Akwe was able to capitalize on his experience of mobility. He strategically returned just in time for interquarter tournaments and lavishly displayed the skills he had perfected abroad. The crowd and his teammates were in awe. Consider how Akwe's friend and teammate Emil (introduced in the introduction), while "hanging out," responded to my request to *langua mi stori* (tell me a story) of an interquarter match he had played with Akwe:

> There are some men, like Akwe, right? You need to buy Akwe at least one crate of Booster [whiskey cola] if you want him to play. When you tell him that you will give him *mimbo* [alcohol], anything in the shape of a bottle, you will see good football! . . . That time when he just came back from *waytman kontri* [Europe], they asked him to go play at the Limbe City Cup. . . . That boy played some football, he made

my heart skip. . . . See! As the goal post is here, he takes the ball along the left line, attacks the post, dribbles, passes the goalkeeper, leaves everyone behind along the sideline. He scores! Limbe goes crazy. . . . And me? I just stand at the field, my head starts to ache, I don't understand what happened. I just stand, and say, "Ebangwese Akwe, you have come back!" [*We all laugh*]

Emil's narrative was inspired and full of awe, but it also indicated a problematic aspect of Akwe's reputation: his overindulgence in alcohol. After his first return from *waytman kontri*, Akwe established himself as a *don man*, a term that loosely referred to being a connoisseur of urban style characteristic of young men in Cameroonian town neighborhoods. The style included fluency in Mboko Pidgin (a distinctive version of Pidgin English associated with the street scene), a hip style reminiscent of hip-hop stars, and a propensity for *mimbo* (alcoholic drinks) and an occasional *mbanga* (joint). For some time Akwe also sported the ubiquitous *cock*, a Mohawk-like haircut popularized by football superstars like the Italian-Ghanaian international Mario Balotelli and for many Cameroonians a visual marker of playful youthful masculinity associated with football stardom. But by the time he was back in Cameroon for the second time, Akwe had acquired a reputation for enjoying *njoka* (nightlife), which involved the consumption of beer and whiskey, late-nights in numerous nightclubs, and a string of sexual partners. Cameroonians closely scrutinize young footballers' behavior: men drink and party, especially popular footballers, but serious aspiring athletes must abstain. They are subject to criteria that do not clearly emerge from specific past events, such as rituals (cf. Lambek 2012), but rather from their life orientation and future expectations. In this context, Emil's spirited story was morally ambiguous: he expressed excitement and admiration but also, and more subtly, a critical commentary on Akwe's practices.

Local football matches and competitions, such as the one in Limbe in which Akwe and Emil participated, were important social events for young Cameroonians. The smallest and most informal events were matches of *santé*, where between six and fourteen young men split into two teams, occupied a free piece of a grassy field, put up makeshift goalposts, and simply played football. Occasionally, there was money involved: each player would chip in CFA 500 or 1,000, and the winning team collected the bounty. One could run into these impromptu matches early in the morning, before the working day began, or in the late afternoon, before darkness would fall at 7:00 P.M. In towns such as Buea and Limbe, they usually took place in and around stadiums or on the football fields of primary schools and high schools. In the villages throughout the Southwest Region the most convenient spots were *ewoka wesua*, the "wrestling fields" in Mokpe (the language of the Bakweri). Each Bakweri village had a grassy field that served as a central location for important village social events. This is where young Bakweri men throughout the dry season took part in Sunday wrestling bouts (*wesua* or *pala-pala*); where secret societies of the Bakweri such as Maale and Nganya performed public dances; where people organized feasts and funerals after deaths of traditional chiefs or otherwise notable persons; and where Pentecostal churches organized their "outreach" activities in which charismatic prophets attempted to win the souls of their fellow Cameroonians. These fields were ideal spaces for young men to organize informal *santé* matches and socialize.

Interquarter competitions involved more elaborate organizing. They were played on various levels. Some were small-scale tournaments between villages or town quarters played on *ewoka wesua* or on school football fields, organized and funded by village chiefs, quarter chiefs, local entrepreneurs, and church communities. Others were large tournaments played in towns' central stadiums, such as Buea Omnisport Stadium and Limbe Centenary Stadium. These were well-funded tournaments organized by the municipalities, large telecommunications companies such as Orange and MTN, or prominent and wealthy entrepreneurs and companies. All the tournaments, from the smallest ones in the villages to those in the stadiums, involved a considerable amount of organization: teams applied with their own "presidents" and "coaches" who provided players with football jerseys and half-time pep talks; remunerated referees and linesmen officiated the matches; match commentators expressed words of thanks and praise for the guests of honor, such as prominent coaches and entrepreneurs; organizers of well-funded competitions hired medical workers and security personnel; and organizers provided trophies and financial rewards for the winning teams. These competitions, organized throughout the country, were very popular. For example, in July 2015 a quarterfinal match between Middle Farm and Cassava Farm, two Limbe quarters, attracted more spectators to Limbe Centenary Stadium than an elite division football match between Unisport Limbe FC and a visiting team from Douala.

Interquarter football competitions were important social spaces in which young Cameroonians formulated and performed masculinities. These tournaments, especially the smaller ones that took place in villages and on school football fields, were often rough competitions between competitive young men who did not hesitate to engage their opponents in physical altercations and perform strong tackles that targeted their opponents' shins. In addition, interquarter competitions always took place during the rainy season, between June and September. The grass fields turned into slippery bogs of mud and stone, and the persistent fog characteristic of the rainy season at the foot of Mount Cameroon could be so dense that one could not see the goal while standing at midfield (figure 3.1). Thus, the weather exacerbated the rough conditions in which the young men competed. Cameroonians, especially managers and coaches of higher-level football teams but also young footballers, repeatedly

Figure 3.1. Interquarter match on a muddy field in Buea Town. Buea, Cameroon, July 2015. Photo by the author.

warned me that I should be extremely careful if I took part in these competitions, as I would be tackled and run over by rough boys from town quarters and villages. As a *waytman* who clearly did not grow up on interquarter football, I was perceived by Cameroonians as not sufficiently tough to take part in these fun, but demanding, competitions.

Unsurprisingly, experienced footballers contended that taking part in such rough competitions was central to the formation of good players. One could not be a competitive footballer unless one had taken part in interquarter competitions and proved one's physical strength, stamina, technical skill, and competitive spirit on the muddy fields against the tough guys from quarters and villages. This was most clearly articulated to me by Valentine Atem, a footballer who retired in 2014 after playing professionally in Cameroon, Ghana, Azerbaijan, and Germany, a venerable football legend in Buea and Akwe's idol: "I believe strongly that every player in Cameroon must first play interquarter. . . . When you are small, when you play in interquarter, in my time, you would learn so many things. It gave me spirit, hardness, and culture of the game." In this context, Akwe, who over the years honed his skills by participating in these competitions, was a dominant figure who frequently awed spectators and peers.

However, with the increasing professionalization of football in Cameroon, and with the expansion of the transnational football market and perceived opportunities for young Cameroonian footballers to travel and play abroad, participation in interquarter competitions acquired new meanings and became a more ambiguous context for the negotiation of masculinities. One of my friends from Buea Young Star FC, nicknamed Lahm (after Bayern Munich defender Philipp Lahm), a dedicated member of the Apostolic Church and a close friend to several charismatic Pentecostal prophets in Buea, showed up to an interquarter match in June 2015 and loudly bragged in front of other young men that he did not intend to play:

> I will not play anywhere! Every day I go to training, after that I go home, I eat, I pray, I sleep, that is all. A coach of the veterans called me to play a match for them, only for my enjoyment, and they would give me 30,000. I refused! He was looking at me like I was crazy. But you can get the highest injury in this small football! And my president does not want me to play interquarter football.

Lahm's last point referred to the recent practice of higher-level football teams and academies forbidding their players from taking part in interquarter competitions. For instance, Unisport Limbe FC threatened their players with monetary fines if they "caught" them playing. They argued that players frequently suffered injuries in these rough tournaments and then were not fit to perform in official matches. Similarly, Kelvin, Buea Young Star FC president, discouraged the individual players he was preparing for trials abroad from participating in the tournaments, albeit using another method: he would pay them to not participate. The logic: good footballers were drawn to interquarter tournaments because they wanted to awe spectators and peers but also because they could earn significant amounts of money. Even though interquarter teams were nominally composed of young men from given quarters, the "presidents" and "coaches" of these teams would regularly hire good footballers, such as Akwe and Lahm, to play and boost their teams' chances of winning. The practice of hiring players who were referred to as "pro" most likely started in the 1990s, just as in local competitions in Senegal (Baller 2014), at a time when on a global scale football was increasingly being entangled with money. In some cases, in addition to the possibility of free alcohol and socializing, the "pro" players would be offered anywhere between CFA 5,000 (US$8.75) for playing a regular match and up to CFA 50,000 (US$87.5) for playing in tournament finals. These were significant amounts for the young footballers, whose income (if any) was often sporadic but who experienced increasing pressures from their kin to contribute to household budgets. The manager of Buea Young Star FC thus decided to demotivate his most precious players by paying them in advance. Lahm's emphasis that he had denied the lofty offers from interquarter coaches was a performance of more "serious" long-term plans that included moving abroad.

The young footballers would also avoid interquarter tournaments because of rumors of missed opportunities to sign contracts abroad because of interquarter matches. One such story was told to me by a Unisport Limbe FC goalkeeper, who was looking for opportunities to migrate abroad to play:

> I had a friend in Mount Cameroon FC [a well-known football club], he and some other players were supposed to go to Italy to play a tournament. Everything was already arranged, he just had to wait. Instead, he went to play interquarter in Muea [a small town close to Buea]. That field in Muea is so bad, there is so much mud in the rainy season. He played a match there, fell, broke his foot. So he never went to Italy to play. Many times it happens, that a player is just about to go abroad, plays interquarters, and something happens.

The implication was that his friend was drawn to play the match because of a handsome fee or a casual opportunity to have fun, enjoy beer, and good food, common staples of interquarter competitions. An increasing number of young footballers with ambitions to migrate framed interquarter competitions as spaces of temptation—where one could enjoy local popularity, alcohol, and money—as well as danger in the form of an injury that could destroy an opportunity to migrate.

Footballers occasionally needed to negotiate and give convincing reasons to their peers for not taking part in the ubiquitous character-building and name-making competitions. Some would simply not show up at the football field, while others would give various excuses for not playing, most commonly that their football boots were too damaged from repeated use on rough pitches or that they were injured. Otherwise, like Lahm, they would brag about their "presidents" having higher plans for them, including playing abroad.

In addition, Lahm's claim that he was keeping himself to the house and away from the streets referred to his regime of self-discipline, or at least the performance of the cultivation of a disciplined personhood that stayed away from vices associated with interquarter football. His boastful performance emphasized the supposed immorality of those who engaged in masculine vices of alcohol and nightlife, a reputation that followed footballers like Akwe, and the need to distance oneself from the kind of masculinity based on these vices. It is also significant that both Lahm and Emil were dedicated Pentecostal Christians. Pentecostal young men were most outspoken against the supposedly abhorrent vices of young footballers and the supposed immorality that lurked around Buea quarters.

At times, young footballers would distance themselves from these masculinities by ridiculing the physicality of amateur football, which they characterized as "typically African." For example, Lahm's elder brother, who was also present at the June 2015 interquarter match, rarely missed a chance to ridicule a tough defensive tackle: "African man likes physical football, you see?! In Europe instead they like technical." He characterized his own style of playing as "technical," developed through formal training in professional football clubs and training camps and aimed toward the "European" ideal of football.

Related to the characterization of African football as "physical" was the trope of *kontri-nayn*, a common term used by players and coaches to mark a man who played football roughly and mindlessly. *Nayn* stood for "number nine," an attacking position in football, supposedly the only position such a person could play, as he had no knowledge of football tactics and positions and could only elbow his way toward the goal. *Kontri* referred to the village, the countryside, marking that the player was from a place where he had little access to structured training. While many accepted that the physicality of the *kontri-nayn* could be an asset for a footballer if a coach could effectively harness his physical potential through structured technical and tactical training (supposedly, the famous Didier Drogba of Ivory Coast started as a *kontri-nayn*), the footballers used it as a put-down, one that pointed to the supposed brainless physicality of men from villages who attempted to play football. This contrasts with the ideals of rough and physical interquarter football as a crucial training ground for young athletes and a character-building exercise for young men. Even though masculinities related to *kontri* were different from those related to a "quarter"—when used as negative markers in football, one pointed to the village and brutish physicality, and the other to masculine urban "vices"—some footballers marked both as local expressions of masculinity inappropriate to their aspirations of transnational mobility, orientation toward imagined Europe, and structured nurturing of athletic bodies.

Interquarter competitions and football fields were thus social spaces where young men formulated, performed, and negotiated forms of masculinity. On the one hand, they were proving grounds where young footballers and men in general were being made. On the other hand, an increasing number of young men saw them as places of danger and temptation. On the slippery football fields, masculinity was never complete but always a negotiation and an ongoing project, and even the seemingly sovereign, or "hegemonic" (Connell 1987), expressions of masculinity were unstable and prone to contestation. These negotiations were taking place in local settings but were profoundly influenced by global dynamics, particularly the global football market's expansion and the new (real and perceived) possibilities of becoming transnationally mobile by playing football.

The Danger of Becoming Useless: Family Obligations

For many young Cameroonians, aspiring to become mobile is also an attempt to demonstrate to their elders that they are on their way to becoming responsible men. A key project in the young men's struggle for respectable personhood is being able to live up to the moral demand of providing for the family.

The fame that Akwe had acquired through playing in interquarter matches and having short stints of playing abroad was short-lived. His last stay in Cameroon in 2014 extended many months after the local competitions were over, and his teammates started asking, "Why is he still in Cameroon?" There were many explanations for Akwe's extended stay, all related to the uncertainties of transnational mobility. His old passport had expired, and a new one was expensive. The Southeast European country where he was supposed to migrate had no embassy in Cameroon, and the visa application process was unclear. A football agent in Europe on whom he relied for help with documents reportedly had problems with alcohol abuse and neglected his responsibilities. Finally, the manager of Buea Young Star FC decided that Akwe was becoming too old to play and refused to invest in his career, despite his talent and skills. Akwe's teammates, however, were not convinced, and for them the issue was clear: Akwe had irresponsibly returned to Cameroon only to drink with his friends, play local football, and bask in his fame, wasting his manager's and his parents' time and money instead of remaining in Europe, where he should have worked hard to find a club to play for and repay the money he had raised among his relatives. Avoiding problematic masculinity did not necessarily lead to success: there were a number of footballers, old and young alike, who managed to migrate abroad despite their reputations as *strong-hed* (stubborn) men who failed to follow managers' and coaches' orders. Yet for Akwe's teammates, masculine vices remained central explanations for failures to capitalize on talent.

Akwe discarded these accusations as unfounded gossip and was reluctant to discuss them at length. To me, having spent many days with him during the course of my fieldwork, the rumors and accusations seemed vastly overblown: it was clear that he struggled to acquire papers to migrate, meanwhile earning small amounts of money through local football and investing most of it into his two small children's daily meals and medical bills. However, even Akwe's father, a retired civil servant, who invested a considerable amount of money (CFA 650,000, around US$1,150) to finance his son's promising career abroad, was disappointed that Akwe was supposedly turning into a "useless man," one seemingly uninterested in taking up his growing responsibilities and providing for others. During our long conversations, the father expressed deep discontent with the fact that Akwe still lived with him at the family house in Buea and would repeatedly avoid facing other members of the household.

From *Buea pikin* to *don man* to "useless man": Akwe's story is that of a rise and fall in status and respectability. A performance of football skills attained in *waytman kontri* is a bodily performance of lavish possibilities and a bright future, but it is only temporary. Such moments of failure demonstrate that masculinity is subject to evaluation and contestation, and that people evaluate masculinity differently in different settings. They also demonstrate that performance of masculinity relies on potentials for economic reproduction and engagement with precarious new economic opportunities.

The image of the "useless man" is particularly relevant to moral and relational aspects of becoming a man in Cameroon. As in other parts of West Africa, it is especially men who seem to be subject to labels of "worthlessness" by their kin and elders (Masquelier 2013: 480; van Stapele 2015; Vigh 2016: 243) and who attempt to achieve substantive personhood by becoming a "big somebody" (Kleinman 2016: 260) or achieving a status of a "grand" or a "big man" (Melly 2011: 368). For young footballers, and men in general, in the Southwest Region, the fear of becoming "useless" related most strongly to the failure of proving one's worth to one's kin. This usually took the form of fulfilling obligations to provide financially for junior brothers, sisters, and cousins, as well as elder family members, such as parents, grandparents, uncles, and aunts.

Since the mid-1990s, as opportunities for a stable income in Cameroon diminished, migrating abroad has increasingly emerged as the most viable option for young men to avoid becoming labeled "useless" by their kin. Football had a peculiar place in these moral evaluations, and with the increasing presence of an image of a lucrative football career, the perceptions of kin toward the sport have been changing. Kelvin, the Buea Young Star FC president, explained:

> You should understand, when I was small, between 1990 and 1995 . . . you go to the field to play ball, and when you come back, your mommy and your papa will beat you! They will say, "Where did you go? You cannot go to the farm? What is this football?" Because they did not see the importance of football. But in 1998, 1999, 2000, when [Samuel] Eto'o Fils started to play, you could see mommy and papa would even buy you boots and a ball, so you can take them to the field and play! [*Laughs*] . . . Parents encourage it now because they know that there is money in football. Before they used to believe that footballers are useless people, that they have nothing.

These claims are difficult to verify, but there is truth to them. Stories about parents beating their boys if they deemed that football was distracting them from work or school abounded but were mostly retold by men in their late twenties or older. As images of superstar athletes proliferated and football was emerging as a novel way to make a living, especially abroad, these stories were being slowly replaced by those of parents investing in young footballers' travel arrangements. Still, there were considerable variations. For instance, as indicated in chapter 2, parents from the Grassfields were particularly known to insist on formal education for their children as central to avoid becoming "useless," and they were particularly suspicious about football as a source of a stable future. Parents in the Southwest Region seemed more inclined to consider football as a possible lucrative investment in the future. One reason given to me was the proximity of Douala, the country's largest economic hub, where the presence of large football academies and a fairly developed football infrastructure, such as stadiums, training fields, and a history of successful football clubs, made a career in football seem more attainable.

The accusations of becoming useless also referred to an unwillingness to "struggle," to show effort to live up to one's potential. This is how Akwe's father expressed his disillusionment with his son's still living in his family house:

> He is not supposed to be here. I am sick, and it affects me, not only financially but also spiritually. When you talk to your mother, is she not glad that you are making your own life to get independence? That is how it is supposed to be. . . . God gave him a different level, but he does not use it.

The term "spiritual" did not explicitly refer to a religious sentiment but to the father's unease with the fact that Akwe, in his father's eyes, continued relying on others for support and made little effort to reach adulthood. Adulthood was marked by two different but related notions: one was financial, whereby others would depend on him instead of him being dependent on others; the other was self-realization and fulfillment of exceptional talent.

The term "useless men" also pointed to a moral obligation. Beyond Akwe's case, it was common to hear men of older generations—parents, uncles, grandparents—chastising young men who failed to show initiative for progress. They would refer to the young men as "idle," i.e., as those squandering their potential by spending time with friends in quarters. For example, I was told that Middle Farm, a quarter in Limbe, was an "idle park," a place filled with young men only interested in sitting around and wasting their time gossiping, drinking beer, and playing *jambo* (a gambling card game). This was also reflected in football. I was told that Middle Farm was full of very talented young footballers—their team always performed well in interquarter competitions. Why, then, people wondered, did so many fail to capitalize on their talents, especially at a time when Cameroonian individuals were successfully turning football skills into careers abroad? At times, people blamed the state for not providing infrastructure and support for developing young players, thus their occasional comment: "Cameroon wastes talent!" However, evoking tropes of young men's "idleness" and "uselessness" suggests that the blame more often fell on the young men themselves, who failed to demonstrate the initiative to work and develop themselves—in this case to train seriously, to struggle to migrate abroad, and, once they migrated, to remain abroad. Thus the label "useless" referred to the failure not only to earn and redistribute money but also to demonstrate the effort to become "somebody." Elsewhere in West Africa, men and women pursue entrepreneurial and migratory projects despite small financial returns because they seek to achieve a respectable personhood by demonstrating struggle and avoiding being labeled as "useless" (Fioratta 2015). Thus money is important, but so is the demonstration of a substantial initiative for movement toward progress. The notions of "idleness" and "uselessness" in Cameroon were similar, but they also seemed to be gendered: the morally charged labels usually referred to young men who were supposedly squandering their future and talents by wasting their time gossiping in their quarters, drinking beer, and being content with playing interquarter football competitions. Those labeling young footballers who enjoyed playing local football as "useless" and "idle" seemed, however, to ignore that there were in fact very few opportunities to migrate abroad and turn football into a lucrative career. Moral judgments and evocations of problematic masculinity can therefore conceal the fact that opportunities for transnational mobility and careers in professional sport are rare and precarious.

Pentecostal Christianity played an important role in young men's fear of becoming useless. Pentecostal preachers, often young people in their early twenties, promoted what could be called a "proactive" approach to life: a vision that one's faith in God, dedication to God and the Bible, and a positive disposition toward problems in life are crucial to overcoming what they called a "spirit of laziness" and eventually poverty and stagnation. Consider this brief exchange between Tabe, my friend from Buea Young Star FC who had recently started attending the services of Christ Embassy Church, and Pastor Sally, a female preacher, during a casual visit to her house:

Pastor Sally: How are you?

Tabe: *A jos dé.* ["I am just there" in Pidgin English, a common casual greeting.]

Pastor Sally: You are just there!? What kind of an answer is that!?

Tabe: I am so excellent and full of glory!

Thus Pentecostal preachers urged their followers to cultivate the disposition of "positive thinking" not only in church services, comparable to what has been widely documented throughout Africa and worldwide (e.g., Gilbert 2015; Soothill 2007; de Witte 2012), but also in everyday interactions. The subtle everyday injunctions, extensions of the "name-it-and-claim-it" neo-charismatic ideology, by which one's fortunes begin with a proclamation of the glory of God and one's belief in miraculous possibilities, were designed to encourage young people to snap out of their supposed lethargy, inculcate them with a positive disposition toward movement and progress, and counter the supposed prevalence of stagnation and idleness.[3]

For the most part, Cameroonian parents welcomed the Pentecostal methods of cultivating a "can-do" disposition among young people. While elsewhere in Africa the Pentecostal injunction to "break with the past" in practice came down to breaking bonds with family members (Engelke 2010; Meyer 1998), Cameroonian Pentecostal preachers rarely preached to their young followers that they should forego their relationships with and obligations to their kin. Tensions between young Pentecostals and their non-Pentecostal family members usually revolved around attitudes toward ancestral worship, when young Pentecostals accused their elders of being too steeped in "traditional" practices, or issues of Christian worship, as Pentecostals considered the mainline Christian denominations old-fashioned in their worship. However, obligations to provide for kin remained central for young men.[4]

Yet Pentecostalism, in conjunction with the pursuit of a football career, could create tensions between young footballers and their kin. Consider what a young Pentecostal pastor in Limbe regarded as major problems and solutions for young Cameroonians:

> The biggest problem with young people is they don't have a dream. Here in Africa, people don't think from early on what they want to be in life, what they want to do, and people also don't support young people and give them counseling. . . . They need to find a dream and focus to achieve it.

Young aspiring footballers, especially those influenced by Pentecostalism, certainly had a "dream," i.e., a clear vision of the future and a coherent idea of what they wanted to become. As I have shown in the previous chapters, the notion of a "dream" permeated the world of football, as academies advertised to young people by encouraging them to realize their "dreams" of playing their favorite sport and making a living with foreign clubs.[5] The notion of a dream was prominent in young footballers' prayers. Footballers were also keen to emphasize the importance of "focus" as central to success in the highly competitive sport, which in practice meant attempting to direct all their energy to training and finding ways to cross Cameroon's borders. Moreover, as I showed in more detail in chapter 2, young men in academies such as Buea Young Star FC were actively taught to "suffer" for the sake of an imagined future and to prioritize future goals over present obligations and needs. Thus notions of a "dream" and a "focus" that Pentecostal preachers emphasized found fertile ground among young aspiring athletes.

However, migrating through football was an exceptionally elusive goal. An exclusive focus on succeeding in football risked foreclosing other possibilities, however volatile, of attaining financial independence, such as education, farming, small business, trade, or work in an informal economy. Young footballers' parents and elder siblings demanded that young men begin earning a livelihood, and they could lose patience for the footballers' infatuation with the sport and dreams of distant success. Thus footballers who chased fickle opportunities to "make it" in football were particularly at risk of becoming labeled useless by their parents and elder siblings.

Some football managers were aware of young men's fears of being labeled as useless and used their obligations toward kin as a tool to secure their investment in players. For example, Kelvin made sure that Buea Young Star FC footballers leaving Cameroon would not attempt to return to the country on their own initiative, by amplifying the players' fears of returning to Cameroon empty-handed. He offered to pay for only half the expenses of the player's trip (passport, visa application, airfare, accommodation) and asked him to provide the other half, knowing that the young man would need to borrow the money from parents and relatives. This way, the manager ensured that the indebted player would be obliged to pay off the loans and that, once in Europe, he would train hard to land a contract. The president thus insisted that the gendered expectations of the family were central to the young footballers' athletic performance and ultimately their economic value in the transnational football market. Aware of the manager's strategy, family members saw it as a mechanism that forced the young men to transform themselves from *strong-hed* (stubborn) boys into "serious" men.

Kelvin's effort was effective. Consider how he managed Ayuk, another strikingly fast right-winger for whom Kelvin in February 2015 arranged a trial with a club in Eastern Europe (see also the opening vignette in the introduction). The president asked Ayuk's elder sister Malaika to contribute to paying for a passport, visa, and a plane ticket. A few weeks after Ayuk departed, I visited Malaika to ask for details about her investment and her relationship with Kelvin. She explained, "He always does it like that, tells the family to give half of the money for traveling, so that they [the footballers] take traveling seriously." She had taken a bank loan and invested CFA 450,000 (US$790) in Ayuk's trip. I commented that this was a lot of money—Malaika was a part-time seamstress, and her husband traded in clothes and clothing materials, and thus money was hard to come by. "It is a lot? It is not a lot! That plane ticket costs how much? If Kelvin was not there to help him . . . God really blessed Ayuk, and Kelvin, he helped him a lot!" She was grateful to Kelvin for providing an opportunity for Ayuk to try his luck abroad and did not regret the money invested; her attitude resembled those of the many Cameroonians who repeatedly gave money to migration brokers who promised to take their juniors abroad (Alpes 2017).[6] The implication was that Malaika expected Ayuk to find a club in Europe and pay back her investment.

In May 2016, I visited Ayuk in Slovakia, where he played for a third-division club (figure 3.2). We sat in a single-room apartment that he shared with a teammate from Nigeria. We talked about his experiences in Europe. "Uroš, I am suffering. Life is not easy. While in Cameroon, I thought in Europe I will find money just waiting for me around the corner to pick it up! [*He laughs*] But since I came here I never found good money. This Europe is hard!" Ayuk was earning €400 per month with his club, enough to pay for rent and food but not much more. "Sometimes I cannot sleep at night because I think of people in Cameroon, how they suffer, I want to help them, but there is no way. Everyone asks for money, they believe I reached Europe and that everything is great now. When my phone rings and I see a number from Cameroon, I'm afraid, I start

Figure 3.2. A Nigerian footballer and his Cameroonian teammate (in the background), recent arrivals on a third-division club in a village in Slovakia. June 2016. Photo by the author.

trembling!" Throughout our conversation, Ayuk's mobile phone kept buzzing: his younger brother was asking for CFA 65,000 (US$115) to transfer to their grandmother who had retired to her village in the Manyu Division.

Returning to Cameroon was not an option for Ayuk. "I even wanted to go back, but Nelson [his former teammate] convinced me not to. He told me that now I needed to struggle since I had the opportunity to leave Cameroon, maybe there will be no more opportunities like this." Ayuk had thought about returning because of the horrible conditions he encountered the first time he arrived in Eastern Europe: appalling accommodation, being physically attacked by racist football fans of the opposing teams, and an exploitative wealthy Polish businessman who sought to profit from cheap African football labor. But the uncertainty of mobility between Cameroon and Europe led him to stay and suffer. "And I can go back only if I have money to *dash* [give as a gift to] people, because if you go back empty-handed everyone will curse at you. Like they cursed at Akwe. You know what happened to Akwe, right? They will say you are a useless man."

Ayuk's experience in Slovakia, especially the strained relationship with his demanding family, which is common among migrants (e.g., Lindley 2009; Sabar 2010), was ample demonstration of how material goods, primarily money, become enmeshed with emotions, such as love, obligation, and fear, constituting transnational "affective circuits" (Cole and Groes 2016) between migrants and their kin back home. The circuits metaphor is appropriate, as it highlights both the effort to remain connected and the potential for conflict and disconnect. Different institutional and individual actors—state institutions that limit young men's border crossings but also demanding kin who deter young men's return—work to curtail the mobility of young migrating Cameroonians.

More generally, the trope of the "useless man" demonstrates how modes of masculinity are built on relationships of dependence and care. Many young Cameroonian men express both an obligation and a desire to repay their elders and to provide for their juniors. With that in mind, having dependents emerges as a cornerstone of moral masculinity. One feminist version of ethics, the ethics of care, challenged the myopic views of ethics located only in abstract principles, or human action in relation to these principles, and put forward a gendered and relational idea of ethics (Noddings 1984). While the feminist perspective predominantly attributed the ethics of care to women, the demands and desires of young Cameroonian men to provide financial care suggest its relevance to men. The term "useless man" that refers to a lack of financial care and the demise in reputation that comes with it points to financial care as a moral value shared by many Cameroonians, one that is profoundly relational and gendered (see also Vigh 2017).

As the allure of building a future by playing football abroad becomes increasingly visible in the Southwest Region, the evaluation of young men as moral subjects is increasingly taking place in the context of global processes. While the presence of the transnational market in places such as the Southwest Region provides novel opportunities for young men, it also brings novel ways of failing to those young men who focus all their attention on entering the market.

The Importance of Being Humble: Pentecostalism, Gendered Morality, and Dealing with an Uncertain Future

In many ways, Nelson was the opposite of Akwe. His teammates had nicknamed him "Jesus," a reflection, in his own words, of his calm demeanor, which contrasted with many other footballers who were "hot." His teammates described him as "humble," meaning that he followed the instructions of club managers and coaches, both on and off the field, where they closely monitored young players' actions and dispositions. Being "humble" contrasted with being *strong-hed*, which meant missing training sessions, frequenting night clubs, and succumbing to the allures of urban life.

Nelson was born and bred in Buea but was not a native of the Southwest Region: his parents were originally from a village near Nkambe, a town in the northernmost subdivision of the Northwest Region. When I met him, he was renting a room in a small wooden shack, cluttered with a bed, cupboard, small table, stove, and television set, without a toilet or much room to move. Nelson continually expressed his dedication to "move up in life" away from poverty and stagnation.

Nelson's parents lived far away, in their home village near Nkambe. Despite being fluent in his *kontri tok* (native language) Yamba, which he used on the rare occasions when he spoke with his parents, Nelson was somewhat of an exception among the young Grassfielders in Buea who were forced to stay in close contact with their family elders in villages in the Northwest Region. He felt abandoned by his parents and was critical of his father, a retired army officer and village chief who had fathered nine children with two wives. Nelson was particularly disapproving of his father's polygynous marriage, and role as a "cultural man" who "never entered a church" or provided him with education and financial backing:

> He is a village chief and a big man. He never paid for my school fees; instead, he would go to the village, *dash* [give] to people 500,000 francs, buy *mimbo* [alcohol] for people, they would drink until they were drunk. Meanwhile his child was not going to school.

Here Nelson criticizes "traditional" masculinity, especially that of dignitaries, which relied on attaining "big man" status in regulatory societies, engaging in polygamy, fathering many children, and ostentatiously spending in village settings. The Grassfields region is also known for its hierarchical and gerontocratic political structures that have long subjugated young men (Argenti 2007: 28–29; Warnier 2007: 36). Far from being privileged as the son of a chief, Nelson felt he was denied basic assistance and left to fend for himself. He attributed these characteristics to a "village mentality." Like many of his peers in Cameroon, he castigated the "cultural man" who disregarded the struggles of youth. But he was even more disparaging of youth's ostentatious behavior in Cameroonian towns. He struggled to keep himself isolated from "bad friends" and "distractions," which at times presented a challenge in his neighborhood known for *jambo* (small-time gambling) and drinking joints. He spent most of his time in or around the house rather than on the street. Moreover, Nelson emphasized his dedication to being a God-fearing Christian. He was a member of one of the many Pentecostal denominations that had proliferated in the Southwest Region and closely followed the advice of "men of God," the Pentecostal Christian pastors who encouraged young Cameroonians to dream big and remain devout to experience God's miracle of success.

For some, notably the migrant Grassfielders who settled temporarily or permanently in the Southwest Region, the contrast between Akwe and Nelson confirmed the stereotypes that contrasted the masculinity of coastal men from that of northwest migrants. As the stereotype goes, the men native to the coastal regions are lazy and only interested in "enjoying life." In contrast, the Grassfielders are more "serious," future oriented, focused on upward mobility, and renowned (as well as criticized) for their "spirit of entrepreneurship" (Warnier 1993). This stereotyping harks back to colonial times, when coastal people were reluctant to work on plantations established by German colonizers and were labeled "unprogressive" and unwilling to work (Ardener 1996: 245–46). On the surface, the contrasting cases of Akwe and Nelson conform to these stereotypes. Yet young men regardless of geographical or ethnic origin espoused values of "discipline" and "hard work" and were drawn to Pentecostal Christianity. Footballers in particular, both Grassfielders and Southwesterners, looked up to a new masculine idol: Eyong Enoh, a soft-spoken Pentecostal Christian, born in the Southwest Region, who played with some of the most prestigious football clubs in Europe and on the Cameroonian national team. Notably, the footballers did not so much admire his football skills as his humble predisposition and propensity for hard work. The values of "discipline" and "hard work," seen as central to success in football, together with Pentecostal morality, transcended stereotyping based on ethnicity.

Kelvin was adamant that Nelson's humility would ensure him success in the transnational sports industry. He selected Nelson for trials abroad, investing money in his costly trip to Europe and expecting a significant return. Nelson took over the spot of several of his teammates, Akwe included, even though the latter arguably displayed superior football skills. In his decision-making, Kelvin was considerably influenced by his main partner abroad, a football coach from a small town in Western Europe with experience in coaching young footballers. When I met the coach on one of his annual visits to Buea, he repeatedly emphasized that Cameroonian footballers were talented but lacked focus and discipline, a common stereotype that sport officials in the global North express about athletes from the global South (Besnier 2015: 857; Guinness 2014; see also Ralph 2007). On several occasions, he also directly compared Nelson with Akwe, praising the former as an exemplary figure for all other young footballers at the academy and lamenting the latter's "unprofessional" disposition. For the coach, Nelson was fit to enter the transnational circuits of footballers, while Akwe was not.

Many West African footballers struggle once they reach Europe (Banaś 2016), and Nelson was no exception. His destination was a far cry from his dreams of making it in *waytman kontri*. He landed on a fourth-division club in a village in Poland, where, like Ayuk in Slovakia, he struggled in new structural conditions to establish himself as a legal resident while at the same time attempting to train and perform in terrible conditions. While Nelson was not duped by profit-seeking managers, like so many young West African footballers (Esson 2015b: 47; Hawkins 2015), he ended up on a club that specialized in bringing in cheap West African players hungry for success and keeping them in substandard living conditions with no basic amenities or salary. Struggling to fight his way through the racist verbal incidents and physical attacks by violent fans, Nelson endured nine months before finally acquiring legal resident status and signing a contract with another club, which provided him a starting salary and a decent apartment. However, he never considered returning to Cameroon. He insisted that, now that he had finally emigrated, it was time to "struggle" abroad despite the hardships. At least staying abroad would bring opportunities for social mobility, while returning to Cameroon would never bring a better future. Recall also from Ayuk's story that it was Nelson, an exemplary "humble" footballer, who convinced him to continue struggling despite the exploitative conditions and uncertainty. Here it becomes clear how values that academies seek to inculcate in young men—those of suffering and perseverance despite limited opportunities (see chapter 2)—become central once the young men encounter difficult conditions abroad. Nelson's and Ayuk's stories also demonstrate how this suffering through the difficulties of transnational migration and the competitive football industry becomes a moral and gendered imperative grounded in young men's desires to provide for their families, meet the demands of adult masculinity, avoid becoming "useless," and demonstrate dedication to movement toward progress.

The Pentecostal gendered morality that Nelson subscribed to—avoiding alcohol, nightlife, and women—proved beneficial to him in Poland. When I met him there in May 2016, he was praised by the Polish club manager, who emphasized the benefits of Nelson's way of life for performance in football. The club manager was impressed with footballers from Africa he had encountered until that moment, whom he perceived as more disciplined and driven in their pursuit of a football career than their Polish teammates. Soon after, the club manager hired Nelson to play for his club on a long-term basis.

In addition, Nelson continued to follow the church services of the hugely popular Nigerian neo-charismatic prophet and televangelist TB Joshua. One Sunday morning we watched together an internet livestream of the service. Nelson was visibly moved. "It gives me hope, and also faith. This is how I get my inspiration, by watching this church." He recounted to me an episode from the church service he had seen the week before my arrival in Poland, a testimony of a Nigerian football player.[7] The testimony began with failures in trial matches with three different clubs in Italy. The footballer eventually returned to Nigeria to attend the service in the megachurch in Lagos and receive blessings from the prophet. Soon after, the footballer was given another opportunity for a trial, this time in Slovenia, where he performed extraordinarily well. He signed a long-term professional contract with one of the most prominent Slovenian football clubs, which went on to win the national league title. This was a story of struggle, God's miraculous intervention, and finally success, which clearly made a strong impact on Nelson, who prayed to be spotted and signed by a higher-level club. Thus Pentecostalism was useful for Nelson in two separate but related ways: it provided him with gendered morality that converged with the demands of football coaches and managers, but it also allowed him to deal with uncertainty and the possibility of success, however elusive.

In the Southwest Region, football coaches and managers, especially those who rewarded humility with mobility, often attempted to mold youth into good men, calculating that they would have a better chance at making a profit from them. Although some coaches and managers were Pentecostal Christians, many were not, and the managers did not specifically look for devout Pentecostal footballers. Rather, they looked for "humble" and "disciplined" young men. Many young footballers found the Pentecostal gendered morality, combined with the promise of prosperity despite the unfavorable odds and their disadvantaged economic background, attractive and useful for fulfilling the demands of managers and coaches. They presented themselves as humble, monogamous, and orientated to mobility and a cosmopolitan future, and they were prepared to struggle abroad despite the unfavorable circumstances, all the while criticizing the hypermasculine tropes of both conspicuous urban manhood and "traditional" village manhood.

Nelson's example is representative of the way that contemporary religious morality emerges for many young Cameroonians as a way to address poverty and stagnation. Pentecostalism is thriving in many places where neoliberal economic adjustments have eroded old forms of sociality (Haynes 2013) and becomes central in dealing with social and economic insecurity. Elsewhere in Africa, other contemporary religious movements with a global reach, like reformist Islam, have also allowed people to deal with the growing uncertainty (Larkin and Meyer 2006). For many Cameroonians, the prolonged economic crisis that has plagued the country since the 1980s is also a moral crisis that involves sexual infidelity, corruption, and witchcraft (Fokwang 2008; Johnson-Hanks 2005: 366). For young Cameroonian men who attend Pentecostal churches and avoid urban vices, Pentecostal Christianity provides spiritual and ideological resources for self-fashioning as moral subjects in the context of economic downturn and difficulties of reaching social adulthood.

For footballers in particular, Pentecostal morality has become a way to both deal with and engage the uncertainties of transnational mobility and football career. Nelson's relationship with his manager and the European coach's comparison demonstrate that the economic evaluation of football players in the transnational market is not only an evaluation of athletic ability but also a moral evaluation of gendered acts. Pentecostalism provides young footballers with gendered morality that converges with the demands of football coaches and managers.

But religious morality does not ensure success in football. While Nelson succeeded, many Pentecostal footballers I met remained without passports and contracts. For instance, Emil, whom I have quoted earlier, never left Cameroon, despite his zeal for football, numerous attempts to migrate, and dedication to Christianity. Pentecostalism in football emerges as a site of production of an alternative form of masculinity that should have a better chance of overcoming local challenges and becoming transnationally mobile, and is attractive for the young men because it provides them with ideological tools for self-fashioning as moral and gendered subjects. Yet Pentecostal morality cannot guarantee success in the fickle industry and in reaching meaningful adulthood by providing for the family. Pentecostalism provides young men with resources to improve on their chances in precarious conditions, but these resources are ideological.

Like other global sports, such as rugby (Guinness 2014) and baseball (Klein 1991), the transnational football industry favors disciplined athletes. The morality inscribed by Pentecostal churches resembles the demands of sports managers and coaches. Elsewhere in Africa and in Latin America, Pentecostal movements promote similar masculine values, such as monogamy, distancing from "traditional" masculinity, abstention from alcohol and promiscuity, and self-control (Lima 2012; Pearce 2012; van Klinken 2012). It is not surprising that these values match those promoted by coaches and managers. But crucially, contemporary religious movements over the world emphasize a moral dimension to people's actions. In early 2000s Nigeria, Pentecostal denominations played a key role in shaping the view that the HIV/AIDS pandemic, poverty, and inequality were the consequences of Nigerians' immoral behavior (Smith 2004). In Tanzania, while Pentecostal women consider their pre-conversion sins as the consequence of difficult socioeconomic circumstances, men more often speak in moral terms about their unchecked desires and individual sinful inclinations and emphasize the importance of self-control and responsibility (Lindhardt 2015: 260–62). In Cameroon, Pentecostal denominations are not the only institutions through which people formulate and transform moral masculinities. But the surge in their popularity among young footballers points to how expectations of transnational industries, of which professional sports is one of the more demanding and unpredictable, become translated into moral imperatives and demands of transformation of masculinity. It is in this context that footballers, as indicated in this chapter's opening vignette, view each other's failures not so much as a result of structural inequalities and uncertainties inherent to the industry but in terms of gendered moral shortcomings.

Masculinities, Morality, and Uncertainty in Sport

Cameroonian footballers are not simply stuck between high aspirations and limiting economic realities, they also actively struggle to make themselves into moral subjects. Some of them seek to reconfigure masculinity to contrast tropes of manhood that many Cameroonians associate with football players. They challenge tropes of "urban" and "traditional" masculinity and imagine a mobile future. Moreover, football clubs and academies headed by managers who promise the possibility of mobility are not only spaces where athletic bodies are trained but also those where moral and gendered subjects are made between new and old expectations, demands, and aspirations. The gatekeepers of young men's mobility select certain men as eligible for participation in the transnational market while excluding others. Those who fail or decline to conform to the regimes of production of "humble men from the global South" become labeled as unprofessional and unmanageable by the gatekeepers of mobility in international sports, as well as "useless" by their families and peers. Moral evaluations are thus central to the ways young men seek to overcome diminishing livelihood possibilities at home and engage real or imagined opportunities promised by globalized markets.

The notion of moral masculinities enables us to understand moral judgments and orientations toward moral values as central to the construction of gendered subjects. People construct moralities and masculinities at the intersection of different domains of social life. For many young Cameroonians, football has emerged as one of these domains, but it is inextricable from other contexts, such as their relations with kin, their religious practices, their economic circumstances, and their ethnicity. Formulations of moral masculinities rarely take place in bounded cultural settings. Instead, men formulate modes of masculinity by engaging with large-scale global forces (the transnational market of football players), their home environments (their kin), and their generational peers (friends and fellow footballers in the neighborhoods). On these different scales, men are subject to moral evaluations that are central to how they construct themselves as men.

Crucially, however, moralized discourses about masculinity can effectively conceal large-scale structural conditions that shape and limit young men. The footballers' struggles and aspirations reveal how dealing with different forms of precarity becomes translated into issues of morality and masculinity. Like many young people elsewhere, young Cameroonian footballers are acutely aware of their position on the margins of global circuits and the uncertainties inherent to transnational markets. At the same time, many interpret their failures and successes in terms of moral shortcomings, moral decency, and masculinity. Evocations of masculinity and morality reveal why young men strive for the unlikely and suffer through hardships, but these can also obscure the precarious realities of transnational migration and globalized markets and the elusiveness of social adulthood in structurally adjusted West Africa.

Notes

1. Elements of this chapter have been previously published in "Becoming Useful and Humble: Masculinity, Morality, and Association Football in Cameroon," *Anthropological Quarterly* 94(3): 411–42 (2021).
2. As I have shown in chapter 1, throughout the twentieth century many "Grassfielders" settled in the Southwest Region. At times their children and grandchildren in the coastal areas are labeled as unwelcome immigrants by the "autochthonous" populations who claim that the self-interest-seeking "allochthones" from the north exploit them (Geschiere 2009: 42; Konings and Nyamnjoh 2003: 14–15). In 2015 the coastal town of Buea in the Southwest Region was home to a mix of Bakweri, an ethnic group who claims indigeneity to the land; migrants from other divisions of the region, such as the Bakossi or Banyangi, whom the Bakweri refer to as "Southwest brothers"; and the "Grassfielders," migrants from ethnic groups of the Northwest Region, the so-called "allochthones" from the north.
3. Christ Embassy Church, also known as Believers' LoveWorld Incorporated, a widely popular church based in Nigeria, is a typical example of the cultivation of "positive thinking." In 2016 its founder and leader, Pastor Chris Oyakhilome, published the book *The Power of Your Mind*. The book jacket read: "Put your mind-power to work and be all God wants you to be! There are no limits to what you can achieve, and absolutely no restrictions to how high you can propel yourself, when you put your mind-power to work."
4. Perhaps the original Pentecostal injunction to break bonds with family members has been overstated, both by Pentecostal Christians and by anthropologists writing about them. This might be because of excessive focus on striking discourses about "demonic" traditions and ancestral worship rather than on subtle everyday practices and interpersonal relationships. Close readings of some ethnographies of the Pentecostal "break with the past" reveal that this break is at the very least a constant struggle and never a finished process (Meyer 1998: 329) and that Pentecostals can feel obliged to financially support their elderly kin even when they believe they are steeped in "demonic" practices (Engelke 2010: 195).
5. The prevalence of the notion of a "dream" is not exclusive to Cameroon but a staple of football academies throughout West Africa. For example, one of the largest football academies in Ghana is called "Right to Dream."
6. Maybritt Jill Alpes documented that parents in Buea would give between CFA 1.8 and 2.5 million to migration brokers for "travel programs" (Alpes 2017: 307). Thus investments like those of Malaika (CFA 450,000) and Akwe's father (CFA 650,000) were significant considering their economic situations, but these investments were still significantly lower considering the fees of migration brokers.
7. The church in Lagos records and diligently archives all its services, and I was able to watch the recording of the particular service on YouTube.

CHAPTER 4

"Tapping the Power"
Ruptures and Continuities in the Spiritual World of Football

As glimpsed in previous chapters, Pentecostal Christianity, an increasingly influential spiritual movement in Cameroon, has found its way into football. During my fieldwork in 2014 and 2015, football players were increasingly attracted to Pentecostal denominations. Many read the Bible and prayed on a regular basis, attended Pentecostal services, consulted with the charismatic "men of God" (pastors and prophets), and presented themselves as dedicated Christians.

The presence of Pentecostalism in football is intriguing, because Cameroonian footballers and fans of the game have long considered the sport to be saturated with "sorcery." As I indicated in previous chapters, many Cameroonians insist that the occult-like practices they call *jars, medicine, juju*, "witchcraft," "sorcellerie," and "black magic" permeate the sport. With the growing importance of Pentecostal Christianity among footballers, the question of the use of *jars* in football has acquired new meanings. Pentecostal footballers were particularly diligent and worried about the prevalence of what they saw as a demonic presence in football and were committed to offering alternatives. Football in Cameroon became a rich field to explore tensions and convergences between magico-religious and neo-charismatic practices.

Pentecostal Christians in Africa and the world over often claim that their faith in the Holy Spirit represents a point of rupture with the past (e.g., Engelke 2004; Marshall 2009; Meyer 1998; Robbins 2007; van Dijk 1998). The act of conversion, when the person becomes a born-again Christian, is a central moment that signifies rupture with a previous way of life. In practice, the rupture is often enacted as a radical break from relations with family members, "traditional" social structures, ancestral spirits, and "demonic" forces that tempt people to sin.

This break with the past, however, is a perpetually unfinished process. Pentecostals' claims of breaking away from "traditional" forms of spirituality often appear as "discursive and strategic" (Engelke 2010: 184), which suggests that their talk of discontinuity and rupture reflects a desire rather than an accomplishment. As Engelke (2010) has argued, "[t]he discourse of discontinuity is a powerful and often arresting form of talk within Pentecostal and charismatic Christianities. But our attention to language has to be complemented by an attention to lived experiences. . . . it is in what people do and with whom they relate that rupture gains much of its force and meaning" (Engelke 2010: 196). Indeed, in practice, Pentecostals rarely agree among themselves about how one should make a break with other forms of spirituality, and they frequently debate which practices are acceptable and which are not when making the break (Daswani 2013). The logic of Pentecostal Christian conversion is often embedded in other social forms, either other forms of Christianity or forms of "traditional" spirituality that preceded Pentecostalism and continue to exist (Gifford 2004; Peel 2000; 2016). In some cases, in their efforts to engage in "spiritual warfare" (Rio, MacCarthy, and Blanes 2017; van de Kamp 2011) against forces they label as demonic, Pentecostals can become entangled in the discourses and practices of witchcraft and continue reinforcing them with newfound force (Newell 2007). Thus, there are also elements of continuity, either with older magico-religious practices or with other Christian denominations.

The problem of spiritual ruptures and continuities is an important one for young Cameroonian men. As outlined in previous chapters, Pentecostal Christians fashion themselves in opposition to other forms of masculinity, such as urban youthful masculinity and "traditional" village masculinity. Young Pentecostal men see themselves as moral subjects and formulate alternative forms of masculinity in contrast to other forms. This self-fashioning is, I suggest, grounded in Pentecostal logic of rupture with other forms of spirituality and with modes of action deemed immoral. And yet, the rupture is difficult to enact and maintain in everyday practice, and even though Pentecostal rupture promises a solution to uncertainty and moral ambiguity, it cannot fully avoid them.

The challenge is then to overcome the opposition between rupture and continuity and the impetus to advocate for one over the other and see how rupture and continuity coexist and produce new social forms (see J. D. Y. Peel comment in Robbins 2007: 26–27). As will become clear in the following sections, Pentecostal footballers in Cameroon also insisted on a radical break with *jars* (magico-religious practices) in football. Simultaneously, for many footballers, Pentecostalism was attractive because the Christian Holy Spirit seemed to operate in the same "spiritual world" as *jars* and provided them with an effective source of power that followed a logic similar to that of the magico-religious practices.

In football, spiritual practices are striking, because footballers' debates over them focus on how they affect material reality (see Meyer and Houtman 2012;

Vásquez 2011). The potent but vulnerable bodies of young athletes are central, as the footballers depend on their physical strength and stamina, and grave and unexpected injuries can end their careers before they even take off. Uncertainty is unavoidable in competitive football: who will suffer from injuries, what will be the outcomes of important matches, and who will be selected from among the many to show his skills in front of coaches and managers? The footballers' debates over how spiritual practices affect material reality revolve around three key questions: whether they "work," i.e., bring victories and success on the field; how they affect their athletic bodies—their main instruments of action and the key source of their efforts; and what is the role of material objects and the rituals that surround them. In particular, I focus in this chapter on the use of material objects, such as *medicine* and *jars*, as well as Pentecostal Christian objects, such as anointed stickers and anointed oil; on the notions and practices of prophesy and "spiritual eyes"; and on issues of power and effectiveness of engagement with the "spiritual world."

The notion of the "truth" or "reality" of spiritual powers has been a recurrent theme for anthropologists writing about non-Abrahamic magico-religious practices and beliefs, who have long wavered between the positions that they could not possibly be real (Evans-Pritchard 1976), that the discourses made them have real consequences (Geschiere 1997), that they were indeed real and that anthropologists needed to accept them as such (Viveiros de Castro 2015), and that the possibility was open for some of them to be real but that their reality was uncertain and a frequent point of disagreement among people (Graeber 2015). In particular, some of the proponents of the recent "ontological turn" in anthropology have argued that anthropologists need to humble themselves and accept their participants' claims of the reality of spiritual forces at face value (Holbraad 2010), consider their claims literally rather than figuratively (de la Cadena 2010), and see them as constitutive of a reality that is alternate to the reality of the ethnographer (Martin Holbraad in Alberti et al. 2011). I agree that claims about spiritual forces need to be taken "seriously" (Viveiros de Castro 2011). However, what I mean by this is accounting for the lively debates about these claims and the pragmatics and politics of their everyday use (see Cepek 2016; Meyer 2016; Vigh and Saus 2014). Cameroonians' debates about the truth and reality of spiritual forces are nuanced and far from settled and claims about them are diverse, filled with skepticism and doubt, and inseparable from their practical use and from the moral judgments about using them. These debates become even more complex as magico-religious practices become entangled with Pentecostal Christian practices, and both of these with "Western" science, suggesting epistemological uncertainty and hybridization (Tonda 2002) as more appropriate analytics than ontological alterity (Holbraad and Pedersen 2017).

Rupture as a Moral Statement: *Jars* and Pentecostalism in Football

Discussing *jars* and how it relates to Christianity leads to a conceptual trap: it runs the risk of unifying practices of *jars* into a coherent religious system, which it is not, and opposing it to Christianity as a coherent belief system (see Asad 1993; Ruel 1982). Rather than taking them for granted as separate and complete structured systems of beliefs, it is more useful to see how young men, especially footballers who engage with Pentecostal denominations, separate the two in everyday discourses. This allows for an approach that takes their discourses seriously while at the same time allowing space for critical examination. Moreover, *jars* is almost always performed in secret, so to discuss what it constitutes, one needs to rely on rumors, accusations, interpretations, and highly moralized recollections.

In what follows, I outline the way Pentecostals talk about the "spiritual world" in football by following Emil, the argumentative and extroverted captain of Buea Young Star FC, one of the central figures throughout this book whom I have already introduced in previous chapters. Emil was born and grew up in Fundong, the largest town of the *fondom* (chiefdom) of Kom in the northwestern Grassfields. As a boy, he considered joining a *medicine man* (traditional healer) as an apprentice to learn about the trade but instead converted from his parents' Catholic faith to Pentecostal Christianity and became born again while at school. After moving to the Southwest Region to study at the University of Buea and play football, he became a member of the Apostolic Church, one of the largest Pentecostal churches in Anglophone Cameroon. Even though Emil encouraged me and his teammates to join the congregations, he did not attend church regularly. Rather, like many other Pentecostals, he spent many hours in his home in deep solitary prayer. In Buea Young Star FC, his teammates nicknamed him the team's "man of God" because of his elaborate prayers before and after trainings and his avid interest in what he called the footballers' "spiritual life." Emil and I established an everyday routine: almost every morning after training sessions at the Molyko Omnisport Stadium in Buea, we walked together to our respective homes, which were only a few minutes apart, and discussed matters of the state of the club, some individual players' trajectories, and issues of "spirituality" in football in general.

For many Cameroonians in the Southwest Region, especially those involved in Pentecostal Christian denominations, people live two separate but interrelated lives: a "spiritual" one and a "physical" one. The spiritual life precedes the physical life. As Emil explained, "Before anything happens to you in the physical life, it has already happened in the spiritual." The two are separated but interrelated: actions in the spiritual have profound effects on the physical. Cameroonian Pentecostals therefore reproduce the dualism between the spiritual and the physical and establish the hierarchy between the two, only to immediately collapse the distinction. This can be seen as a common Protestant tension between, on the one hand, the separation between the spiritual and the material and, on the other, the need for the immanence of God in the material world (Lambek 2014: 15–17), or it can also be seen as a recognition that this dualism is present everywhere in thought yet transcended in practice (Lambek 2006).

Importantly, the spiritual realm is also occupied by "the devil": the malevolent spirits that Christians usually link to ancestral traditions. Pentecostal Christians attempt to engage with the spiritual realm by evoking the Holy Spirit through deep prayers, meditation sessions, and Bible reading. As Pentecostal Christians would have it, others prefer to visit traditional healers who dabble in witchcraft and occultism, using *juju*, *medicine*, or *jars* in order to exert effect in the spiritual world and reap its fruits in the physical. The key point is that when Cameroonians speak of the "spiritual," it involves both the powers of the Holy Spirit and the powers of *jars*. It will become clear in the following that Christians make clear moral evaluations to separate the two, but for now, we can observe that both are marked as "spiritual."

Many Cameroonians see a football match as a battle, not only of the physical prowess of football players, their athletic skills, or their coaches' tactics but also of the two sides' spiritual forces (Pannenborg 2008). Cameroonians occasionally talk about the *jars man*, otherwise called *medicine man*, traditional healer, or *nganga*, "controlling" the game with his spiritual powers. The spiritual battle is usually prepared by traditional healers before a match and away from the field. The battle itself takes place in the spiritual world, above and beyond the immediate match, and has profound influence on the outcome.

For example, in one story that Emil told me, Buea Young Star FC was playing a high-stakes match at the Molyko Omnisport Stadium against a strong opponent. The father of Akwe, the team's striker whom I wrote about in previous chapters, was there to watch the match. Concealed in his fist was a *medicine* prepared by a traditional healer, which he used to control the outcome of the match. At one moment, while the team was losing, he lifted his hand and pointed toward the goal of the opposing team. Less than a minute passed, and Akwe scored a goal, equalizing the score. The match became difficult, and it was time for the opposing team's spiritual powers to respond. As it turned out, the opposition's *jars man* (who was presumably among the match spectators) was also powerful. He concealed his own *medicine* in his fist and directed an attack on the striker's father. The father's *jars*, previously so effective, started burning in his hand and finally caught fire, forcing him to drop it on the ground and effectively neutralizing his powers. Both teams had powerful *jars*, and the match ended in a draw.

Jars could be almost any kind of object: a blade of grass, a thread, a piece of tree bark. It could be a ring or stone that a player wraps in a thread and sprays with perfume. There are many ways of using *jars*. If they are small objects, players can conceal them in their waistbands, boots, or socks. The players or the *jars men* might bury the objects in the football field, near the goalposts, for example. Other forms of *jars* came in the shape of a potion prepared by a *jars man* that the footballers applied to the surface of their bodies: prior to the match, they would wash their faces with the potion, rub it on their hands and feet, or cover their entire bodies by bathing in it. Footballers claimed that they could smell the *jars* on their opponents' bodies during football matches. In other examples, footballers "applied" *jars* to the inside of their bodies: *jars* could be drunk or eaten.

Jars practitioners often needed to follow strict instructions from the *jars man*. For example, Emil witnessed while with one of his previous clubs in his hometown of Fundong that the *jars man* instructed players to ingest an edible or drinkable substance, such as animal fat or a mixture of herbs, on match day at exactly 4:00 A.M. The expected result of this particular *jars* was to allow the footballers to run faster and have more stamina. From Emil's story, the outcome was unclear, but the key point was that *jars* often came with highly specific instructions and prohibitions that needed to be carefully followed if one was to experience its benefits.

Jars was often used far away from football fields. Players used it in secret locations, in the privacy of their homes, or in their family compounds. Emil recollected how a former striker of Buea Young Star FC traveled to his family's village in the Manyu Division to visit a powerful *jars man* whenever he had difficulties scoring goals. After his return to Buea, he again began scoring regularly. A visit to the village was crucial: Cameroonian footballers insisted that the most powerful *jars* was in the countryside, where people, especially elders, were well-versed in "traditional" practices. This was especially true of the Manyu Division, which many young men in Buea believed was a remote area brimming with powerful and mysterious *jars*. Two reasons could account for this. First, the Manyu Division, which borders Nigeria, was the birthplace of Obasinjom, an important cult agency (*njom* in the Ejagham language) with a set of masked dancers who performed magico-religious and cleansing practices (Röschenthaler 2004). The power of the association was well known in Buea, since the Bakweri purchased it from the Banyangi people of the Manyu Division in the 1950s in an effort to combat different forms of witchcraft (Ardener 1996).[1] Second, roads between Buea and the villages in the Manyu Division were in a particularly bad state, making the trip difficult. Young Bakweri footballers who played in regional division clubs dreaded traveling to Manyu division for matches precisely because of the excruciating trip. This contributed to the perception of the area as remote.

At other times, the use of *jars* might take place on and around the football field but away from inquisitive eyes. In one example already mentioned in chapter 2, the former president of Unisport Limbe FC reportedly hired Nganya, a Bakweri secret society with access to ancestral spiritual powers, to perform rituals at the Limbe Centenary Stadium the night before an important match in order to cleanse and "prepare" the field for a victory. Because the Nganya society is secretive, it was unclear (to me and to most Cameroonians) what these rituals entailed, but most likely they involved food offerings, pouring libations, and consulting the ancestors in an attempt to win matches (see Pannenborg 2012: 94–95). Cameroonians, and especially Pentecostal Christians, cited this as an example of the use of *jars* in football, i.e., the use of spiritual powers of the occult.

Another striking example was the ability of some *jars men* to forecast the outcome of the match. A person with such "vision," Emil insisted, could predict the final score, identify players who were about to score, or predict who would suffer injuries. *Jars men* were credited with having an exclusive insight into spiritual world activities that determined what was about to transpire on the field. This was in line with the well-documented instance that traditional healers all over Cameroon, but also elsewhere in Africa (e.g., in Mozambique; see West [2005]), put a substantial amount of effort into developing a "second pair of eyes" that allowed them to see beyond the boundaries of the physical world (Geschiere 2013: 72).

What results did footballers expect from practicing *jars*? First, to enhance their physical performances: run faster, have better stamina, or jump higher to win more headers (or, for the goalkeepers, save more shots on goal). Second, to improve their skills: take more precise shots or dribble past their opponents more successfully. For example, consider how Emil described the exploits of Akwe, who, according to him, used to use *jars* in order to perform better:

> The *medicine* that Akwe was using, but now he stopped, was the one where he would use the potion [*wata*] that his parents would prepare for him. He would wash his face, his hands, and his feet with it. When he would enter the match, oh God . . . he would play well! He would play that ball so you would not believe it was him. Him alone would dribble the entire team and score!

At other times, footballers used *jars* to cause their rivals to lose focus or stamina. Footballers referred to these as "spiritual attacks," i.e., attacks aimed at other footballers performed in the spiritual world. The most striking "spiritual attacks" that footballers talked about were not those aimed at the opposing team's footballers but rather those performed by individual players to their teammates with whom they were competing for a position on the team. A common example was a substitute footballer who used *jars* in order to cause an injury to his teammate and take over his position on the team (see also

Pannenborg 2008: 111–13). In one of the more amusing stories I was told by Emil, the goalkeeper of Unisport Limbe FC was suspected of using *jars*, since he was strikingly short for a goalkeeper and yet regularly outperformed all other goalkeepers on the team and was almost always selected in the starting eleven. On one occasion, before a friendly match, he was removed from the starting lineup. Jealous of his teammate, he contacted his *jars man* and paid him to use *jars* on the goal posts in order to sabotage his rival. However, he was not careful: one of his teammates overheard his phone conversation with the *jars man* and informed the team coach. As the match was about to start, the coach, determined to teach his goalkeeper a lesson, made a last-minute tactical change: he put the unsuspecting goalkeeper back in the game. The deed had already been done, and it was too late to reverse the spiritual attack: the envious goalkeeper had a taste of his own *medicine* and embarrassed himself by conceding no fewer than five goals. Emil told this story with a particular gusto, laughing at the fate of the envious goalkeeper.

This story demonstrates several points related to the use and discourse of *jars* in football. First, *jars* can be used to overcome physical limitations, such as height for a goalkeeper. In this instance, *jars* resembles performance-enhancing doping practices that amplify the body's potential in order to perform better, something that athletes everywhere are driven or tempted to use in competitive settings (see Kovač 2016). Second, *jars* can be used to hurt others out of envy. This suggests instances of witchcraft as "harm to persons or their belongings inflicted by human and spiritual beings" (Rio, MacCarthy, and Blanes 2017: 4), which are observed throughout the world. The variety of practices that Cameroonians attribute to *jars*, and the fact that footballers regularly use this term as a synonym for witchcraft, suggests that this definition is too narrow and fails to capture the term's variety and ambiguity (see Geschiere 1997; 2013). Third, *jars* can turn against its practitioners, who will eventually need to pay the price for dabbling in the fickle world of mystical powers and attempting to hurt others. This was a common refrain among Cameroonians, especially Pentecostal Christians, who emphasized the immorality of the use of *jars*. Finally, Emil's retelling illustrates that *jars* is the object not only of moral condemnation but also of fascination, humor, and playfulness.

Despite playful attitudes toward *jars*, sentiments of horror and fear abounded. Players and their friends and families attributed serious career-ending injuries to "spiritual attacks" and "spiritual poison." In one of the more disturbing interviews I conducted, a former aspiring footballer explained how his athletic ambitions ended abruptly at the age of sixteen. He was already recognized as a promising goalkeeper at a football academy in Tiko when he mysteriously broke his leg during a friendly match: nobody was around him, there was no physical contact, and the ball was not even in his vicinity. He was taken home and treated by medical doctors, but the recovery was excruciating, and the wound would not heal. Suspecting a spiritual attack, his family hired a traditional healer who shed some light on what had happened. On a particular day before the incident, the boy had washed his football boots and left them out to dry outside his family compound. Somebody, perhaps a jealous neighbor, used this opportunity to apply spiritual poison to the boots. The boy wore the boots to the friendly match, and the tragedy ensued. His recovery was painful and long, and only after several months and with a combination of herbs prescribed by the traditional healer was he able to walk again. He was eager to return to football, but his mother would not have it: she would not allow her son to be involved in an activity so saturated with dangerous spiritual activities, and his dream of a professional career was over.

Emil's and others' stories show that *jars* could come in many guises and serve many purposes.[2] At one end of the spectrum, it was seemingly innocuous and playful, albeit contested, and had performance-enhancing goals. At the other end were much more sinister spiritual "attacks" and "poisons" that were, according to Emil and others, a result of the fierce competitive nature of the sport and feelings of envy of another's success. *Jars* was linked to both the longstanding cleansing practices of secret societies and the witchcraft attacks on powerful individuals. Thus the lines between practicing witchcraft and protecting oneself from it were blurred in footballers' accounts. Emil recognized the gradation of seriousness and malevolent intentions of different kinds of *jars*. Yet at the same time, being a member of Pentecostal Christian denomination that advocated a "break with the past," he characterized all instances of *jars* as "the devil," "evil," and "darkness." This is how he responded to my question of whether one could combine *jars* and Christianity:

> You cannot combine [God] with *jars*, because God says that you should not worship any other God, and *medicine man* worships some other God.... No *medicine* is a good *medicine*, no *jars* is good *jars*, because nothing good comes out of evil.... To become the best in life, there are only two things you can do: either you dine with the devil or you dine with God. You cannot be in the middle.

This shows how Pentecostal Christians took part in the "construction of heathendom" (Meyer 1998: 322) by categorizing all indications of "traditional practices" as "evil" and "darkness" and aligning themselves with what they called the forces of "good" and "light." As elsewhere in the world, Pentecostals rejected any form of syncretism.[3] Pentecostals like Emil seemed to be aware of the wide range of practices of *jars* but subsumed them all under a single category, structured the imagined area of *jars* as clearly bounded, and positioned themselves against it.

Moreover, this discourse of rupture was framed in moral terms (see also Daswani 2013), i.e., the supposed break from the past was a moral statement, a form of "moral absolutism" (Eriksen, Blanes, and MacCarthy 2019: 158) that sought to offer a singular morally charged solution to an otherwise plural and uncertain world. Cameroonian footballers like Emil, but also others, spoke about the "spiritual" battle in football in clearly moralizing terms: Christian practices in terms of "spiritual life" and "spiritual health" and *jars* as "spiritual poison" and "spiritual attacks." This was not particularly new or surprising. What was important, however, was that Pentecostal footballers took the powers of *jars* more seriously than did mainline Christian denominations, were determined to battle it, and, crucially, as I will demonstrate in the following sections, sought to provide strong alternatives to its powers. As will become clearer, despite the discursive and moral rupture (or perhaps precisely because of it), the practices of Pentecostal footballers resembled those of *jars* and had similar goals.

"Tapping the Power" of God

Not everyone in Cameroon agreed that the uncertainties of football—goals, results, injuries—were so profoundly dependent on activities in the spiritual world. Many footballers, especially those with experience of playing outside of Cameroon, laughed off *jars* as either a silly superstition not worthy of attention or a remnant of tradition confined to the countryside. Valentine Atem, the Buea football legend I mentioned in chapter 3, recalled some of his early matches in interquarter tournaments in the mid-1990s. After scoring a series of miraculous goals in a village tournament, the opposing team accused him of using and concealing *jars*. They forced him to strip down to his underpants to reveal the hidden token he must have been hiding somewhere on his body. Valentine happily obliged: he stripped naked in the middle of the field and allowed himself to be inspected for *jars* by the opposing players, who quickly realized they could not find anything. Valentine put his clothes back on, the match was restarted, and he continued to plow through the opposing side's defense and score many goals. "It was a lot of fun," he reminisced with a grin, and insisted that *jars* constituted harmless fun and silly superstition.

Some experienced Cameroonian football coaches I interviewed, and Cameroonians in general, repeated the often-heard mantra meant to demystify spiritual powers: "*Jars* does not play football." One regional league team coach argued that *jars*, and especially traditional healers (whom he called "native doctors"), is ineffective:

> If the native doctor has that power, well, he has children, why can't he give it to his children to go and play football and score goals and have money? Let us be practical. . . . Why can't they raise their children and give them those powers so they can

be professionals, so that they can play in Paris, Zagreb, Chelsea? They would earn a lot of money and build their father a house, a mansion. But if you see where those native doctors are living, you can't even sit there. They are living in poverty.

This kind of skepticism about the effectiveness and genuineness of traditional healers was common. Notably, such claims were often accompanied by statements that if *jars* was indeed effective, footballers would not have to train at all—it would have been enough to simply seek the assistance of traditional healers.

Those with a more "modern" approach to football, inspired by Western coaching techniques, also relegated the role of spiritual powers in football to a less than central aspect of the game. John Mayebi was one of the region's most successful coaches: in 2009, with Tiko United FC, he won the Elite One championship; it was the first time in the national league's history that an Anglophone region club won the title. For him, *jars* had no inherent powers that players or coaches and managers could harness and use. He argued that no amount of *jars* could replace hard work and training:

> We used to believe in those things, but with advancement, some of us have gone deep into football and realized that the only *juju* is training. So, we give a different name to those things. . . . The name we give it here, in football, as coaches, we call it, in French, *préparation psychologique*, psychological preparation. They have virtually no powers, the only thing they do is psychological.

This discourse of "advancement" was reminiscent (although not exclusive) to that of the coaching camps, one- or two-week-long courses for football coaches, sometimes organized and led by European coaches, designed to provide Cameroonian coaches with "expert knowledge." Elite One team coaches were usually expected to attend them—indeed, coach Mayebi showed me his diploma that qualified him to coach high-level teams. It was notable that he referred to a term in French: most coaching camps took place in the Francophone capitals of Yaoundé and Douala. This "expert knowledge" relied on four pillars of coaching:

1. Physical preparation—improving players' strength and stamina;
2. Technical preparation—improving players' skills with the ball;
3. Tactical preparation—teaching players to apply tactical principles;
4. Psychological preparation—preparing players to endure under competitive conditions.

Coach Mayebi placed *jars* in the last category. Although he preferred players to not use *jars*, he occasionally allowed it when he assessed that it was beneficial to player performance. But for him *jars* had no direct connection to material reality: the physical actions of running, ball contact, and tactical principles. He argued that the use of *jars* in Cameroonian football has decreased significantly, by "60 percent." Notably, he also argued that much of it was replaced by Christian prayers.

It was, of course, impossible to verify whether the use of *jars* among footballers decreased in the 2010s. Perhaps it was marginalized by the combination of the onslaught of Pentecostal churches with an agenda to eradicate it and the implementation of international coaching strategies that supposedly demystified its power. But often practices akin to witchcraft do not disappear with modernity but instead are transformed by it, and new instances emerge (Geschiere 1997). In particular, Pentecostalism does not eradicate witchcraft but can instead amplify it (Newell 2007). Another possibility is that the use of *jars* in football did not decrease but only became more secretive and continued away from the fanfare of public sporting events and the eyes of an inquisitive *waytman* researcher.

There is, however, yet another possibility: that some footballers discovered Pentecostal Christianity as a novel source of power that allowed them to engage in the spiritual battle of football and harness spiritual powers with physical consequences similar to those of *jars*.[4] Returning briefly to Emil, he hinted at the way that an individual engagement with the Holy Spirit, one of the main goals of Pentecostal Christians' intense prayers, could have physical consequences that were invaluable for footballers:

> When I am about to play a match, I sit in my room, for one or two hours, and I worship in His presence. When I want to play, I meditate with God. The way that I play on that day is different. When I go to the field, I am unstoppable. . . . That is the power of God working in me.

Unlike for Coach Mayebi or older players like Valentine Atem, who relegated the spiritual aspect of football to categories of "psychological preparation" or "fun," for Emil engagement with the spiritual world had profound physical consequences. Even though Emil made a sharp discursive rupture and breakaway from *jars*, as all Pentecostal Christians do, the physical consequences that he experienced resembled the performance-enhancing consequences of *jars*.

Emil was not the only one who, as many Cameroonian footballers say, "tapped the power" of God, hoping for physical consequences observable on the field. The first time I met Njoh, a footballer in his early twenties, in the Unisport Limbe FC team dormitory, I was struck by his eagerness to speak about how his faith affected his football performance. He was a Bakweri, a native of the region. It was his second season on the team in Limbe, where he moved after spending two years with Buea Young Star FC. He was a member of the Apostolic Church—Emil's denomination—where he followed his parents and his long-time girlfriend who were also members. Given that most of the matches in the Cameroonian first division took place on Sundays, he was rarely able to attend church services. This did not bother him much: just like Emil, he worshiped in the privacy of his own room, either by himself or with his partner. Njoh's telling of one of his experiences of the power of God on the football field shows how the physical consequences can be central for footballers:

> One time we were playing a match against New Stars, at the Centenary Stadium [in Limbe]. The first half was very difficult for us, they were controlling the game. I discovered that during the course of the game I lost a lot of strength. I was very, very weak, I was very, very tired! That was just before the end of the first half. But, then we went to the dressing room, and we went out again for the second half. I entered the field. I spoke the word of God, I spoke it inside me. I said "God, renew my strength!" Believe me, automatically I felt some sensation! Inside me . . . And I was strengthened to play that match exceptionally. I mean, I played the match, and I discovered I wasn't even tired! When the match finished, I wanted to continue playing! I discovered then it was God who renewed my strength. And since that time, I continued to speak that word. Any time I play a match I can never get tired! It is not by my own might and my own power! It is by the spirit of the Lord.

Physical consequences of spirituality were central for Njoh: not too surprising for a competitive athlete. The material body is central for understanding the appeal of Pentecostal Christianity, and the body becomes the "harbinger of ultimate truth and authenticity" (Meyer 2010: 756). Njoh reiterated that he was able to harness and use the power of God ("I use God's power, the power of the Holy Ghost"), that he was able to do so by speaking the word of God ("there is power in your tongue"), and, crucially, that this brought him tangible results ("anything you want to do in the field, it works"). He also argued that there were "demonic powers" that "worked" on the field for those who "believed" in them. The source of his own power, however, was "superior" to theirs. In his own eloquent words, typical of Pentecostal Christians:

> The power of God is the highest power, it is supreme, superior to any other. . . . God gives me dominion to trample upon snakes and upon scorpions. So when you come with your demonic power, I have no fear, because I know where I am standing. I know where my power comes from. . . . And right inside the field of play I can declare those words while I am marking you, those words that I have been saying in my closet: "I have dominion over you, you cannot stop me." So I cannot lack strength when I am playing, I always have supernatural abilities, because I know that my abilities are from God. When you come with your ability from any other power that is not of the same Holy Ghost, you can never prevail over me.

The Pentecostal break from the past is not only a renouncement of "tradition," one that Pentecostals casually characterize as "demonic," but also an alignment with Christian tradition (see Engelke 2010). Crucially, "strength" and "ability," central for footballers as competitive athletes, become entangled with "power."

Aligning with the Holy Ghost allowed Njoh and other Pentecostal footballers to access an alternative source of power that promised physical benefits. His statements about the "power of God" that "always works" are not necessarily literal: Pentecostal Christians use words to imagine and construct a better reality rather than to simply describe it. But it is clear that the Holy Ghost was a novel source of power with stakes in the "spiritual battle" of football, a power with profound influence on the physical world and the athletes' bodies.

Pentecostal Objects

We have seen that *jars* often involved the use of objects, such as thread, stones, rings, or tree bark, imbued with magical properties. Some Pentecostal Christian pastors also provided objects, such as anointed stickers, anointed olive oil, holy water, or salt. As the following case will show, a focus on Pentecostal objects and how people use them and with what purpose can complicate the views of rupture as central to the appeal of Pentecostal Christianity.

As stated previously, Buea Young Star FC footballers often characterized Emil as the team's man of God, emphasizing his in-depth knowledge of the Bible, eloquent prayers on and around the field, and constant concern for the players' spiritual life. Yet Emil insisted that he had his own man of God, a person that surpassed him in knowledge and power. He often recommended that his teammates pay him visits when he assessed they needed assistance or protection.

In December 2014, I accompanied Emil and Akwe on one such visit to Saint Collins Aliche, Emil's friend and self-styled man of God. Saint Collins was around twenty-two years old, a recent graduate of the University of Buea. He was born near the southwestern town of Kumba to a Nigerian father and a Cameroonian mother. After being involved in starting a Christian ministry in Kumba as a very young man, he moved to Buea to pursue his studies. He worshipped on Sundays in Winners Chapel, a Nigerian neo-charismatic denomination founded in 1983 that has since become a transnational megachurch. On the spectrum of Pentecostal churches that ranges from emphasizing holiness to emphasizing miracles (see chapter 2), Winners Chapel represented the latter (Gifford 2004: 173).

Winners Chapel was the subject of substantial controversy in Cameroon. In August 2013, a nine-year-old girl reportedly collapsed and died in the denomination's branch in Bamenda (the Northwest Region's capital) where a pastor was casting out demons that had supposedly possessed her. This led President Paul Biya to close approximately one hundred Pentecostal denominations, mostly in Yaoundé and Bamenda. This was the second wave of Pentecostal church closings in Cameroon, the first one having occurred in 2011 when the president cast the churches as a threat to national security. CNN quoted the deceased girl's mother: "I want the government to stop these pastors who use mysterious powers to pull Christians and kill them for more powers. All my children have run away from the Catholic Church in search for miracles, signs and wonders." The mother's invocation of the "power" that neo-charismatic pastors supposedly harness and its "mysterious" origins is indicative of how some Cameroonians, especially dedicated members of mainline denominations, see Pentecostal churches as entangled with witchcraft. Pentecostal pastors protested that the president ordered the closings because the churches criticized the government. By 2015, most Pentecostal churches had reopened.[5]

Saint Collins was not a pastor from Winners Chapel but an independent man of God: he provided individual counseling to those seeking his advice. He insisted that he was not a formal pastor ordained by church authorities but a "committed Christian . . . loving to do the work of God." Like many other extroverted men of God in the Southwest Region and their counterparts in the Nigerian neo-charismatic churches, Saint Collins exuded confidence. He often wore smart clothes, such as his favorite gold-colored shirt, clearly resembling those worn by flamboyant Pentecostal pastors in Nigerian and Cameroonian megachurches.

It was not entirely clear how Saint Collins made a living, but as a recent university graduate he was most likely financially dependent on his parents. Importantly, Saint Collins gladly accepted small gifts of money and food from people who came to him for advice and prayers, but he did not charge for his services. Christian men of God never do, or at least are not expected to. This is a way for them not only to demonstrate their dedication to "the work of God" but also to differentiate themselves from traditional healers who do charge their clients, sometimes demanding very high fees.

When Emil, Akwe, and I visited him in December 2014 in his family house, we had no particular agenda. After a while, he presented us with a wad of his "anointed stickers." The size of roughly two bars of soap, printed on glossy paper, the stickers showed an image of a well-dressed Saint Collins, holding a Bible and pointing at it, as if he was preaching. His name and phone number were on the sticker, and a quotation: "You are disconnected from whatsoever Satan is using to connect you to himself. Mathew 10:1." This was not a direct quotation from the Bible, even though it was presented as such. More likely, it was a quotation Saint Collins attributed to himself, with an added reference to a Bible verse that refers to powers of healing and casting out evil spirits.[6]

The stickers were more than just the marketing tools of a young entrepreneurial man of God: they were anointed by his prayers. Saint Collins instructed me on how to use them: "You can put them on top of your entrance door if you want your house to be covered in the power of God. The power of God is coming from that sticker and is reflecting like a ray, like a star that shines." Otherwise, "You can also put it on your skin"—meaning one can either press it against one's body during prayers to induce healing or simply carry it around in a pocket or a bag for general protection against evil spirits.[7]

Saint Collins hastened to add important instructions: "The sticker does not contain any power itself. It is only a medium for God's power, a medium that God can pass through and manifest himself. In order for it to work you have to believe in God." This is one of the most common instructions provided by Pentecostal men of God regarding anointed tools, such as stickers, olive oil, holy water, or salt: the material objects contained no power in them but were only mediums for God's power, and their effectiveness depended on the user's belief. This was a crucial way in which Pentecostal men of God differentiated the objects they were using from the "fetishes" of *jars*.

After some more casual conversation, it was time for me to be delivered from evil spirits. Saint Collins instructed me to stand in front of him, close my eyes, and raise my hands slightly. I had previously gone through a few deliverances, so the situation was not particularly new to me. He placed his palm on my forehead, tilting my head slightly backward and upward. I immediately heard a commotion behind me and soon realized that Akwe and Emil had stood up and were standing behind me, one of them carrying a chair, anticipating that I might fall to the ground, and preparing to catch me. The man of God started spinning me slowly in circles. He kept repeating in an increasingly impassioned voice, "Thank you Jesus, thank you Jesus. Free him in the name of Jesus." Between the repetitions, he forcefully blew air around my face and neck.

After a few minutes, he took a sticker in his hand and pressed it on my forehead, returning me to a previous position. "This sticker is highly anointed," he uttered. After some more moving around, he exclaimed, "Something is leaving you now." His repetitions became louder, and he started moving and spinning me faster, making it difficult for me to avoid falling. Finally, he stopped, I opened my eyes, and we briefly discussed some of his prophecies and suggestions.

On that particular evening, neither Akwe nor Emil went through deliverance or prophecy, but they were not particularly concerned. Instead, as we were leaving, Akwe showed me a bundle of anointed stickers he had collected from Saint Collins's stack. "This is the most important thing. This is like the oil I told you about," he said, referring to anointed oil, another common object that Pentecostals use in their prayers.

What is striking in this vignette is the central place of material objects that stand for mediums of the power of God, in this case anointed stickers. Pentecostal stickers were ubiquitous in Buea—on people's entrance doors, walls, or inside cars, promoting any of the number of Pentecostal denominations or men of God (figure 4.1).

Figure 4.1. Pentecostal stickers, ubiquitous in cars and homes. Buea, Cameroon, May 2015. Photos by the author.

Stickers were not the only material objects that Pentecostals used to "tap the power" of God. Saint Collins claimed that almost any object could be anointed with prayers. Some material substances were used more frequently and seemed to be more conducive to the power of God, such as anointed oil. On one occasion, while I was visiting Saint Collins at his family compound, he was visited by one of my teammates from Buea Young Star FC who had issues with his passport and visa application. Saint Collins sent him out to buy a small bottle of Goya brand olive oil, which is commonly available in grocery shops. After he returned, Saint Collins rubbed the oil on his hands and pointed toward my teammate's feet. "I want to pray for this place," he said. My teammate put his feet on the table, and Saint Collins applied oil to his feet and calves. They both closed their eyes, and Saint Collins prayed ferociously, with an intense frown and beads of sweat emerging on his forehead. "Let these legs serve you in your career, in your future! In the name of Jesus!" After the prayer session was over, my teammate left, taking the bottle of (now anointed) oil with him.

Several of my other teammates and other footballers had their own bottles of anointed oil. Some applied them to their feet and calves before important matches. Others, for the sake of rationing, would add a few drops of the oil to the body lotions they used daily. My teammates in Buea Young Star FC who managed to arrange trials in Europe carried their bottles with them abroad.

The use of physical objects in prayers contradicts Pentecostals' claims that each person can individually establish a direct link with the Holy Spirit through dedicated prayer. Many Pentecostals claimed that they had no need for material objects and that they engaged the Holy Spirit solely through prayers. Emil, for example, almost never used any objects in his everyday prayers. Yet Pentecostals rarely condemned the use of oil or stickers. Among footballers, use of Pentecostal objects such as anointed stickers, oil, water, or salt was rarely contested. Football players used Pentecostal objects in public, as opposed to *jars*, which was confined to secretive private spaces.

The use of objects as mediums is not unusual among Pentecostal Christians throughout the world, but it is sometimes controversial. Pentecostals in Ghana use many different mediums to engage with the Holy Spirit: cameras, objects, and their own bodies (Meyer 2014). There is a significant amount of debate among Ghanaian Pentecostals on whether the use of certain materials, such as sand that represents ancestors, is appropriate for use in prayers: some pastors fear that they might lead to the proliferation of ancestral spirits from which Pentecostals are attempting to break away (Daswani 2013). In some cases, some objects are deemed appropriate, while others are not. Friday Apostolics in Zimbabwe are particularly committed to what they see as immaterial faith, and they even consider the Bible an inappropriate medium. However, other material substances, such as sticky honey, are deemed appropriate. This reveals the work of attributing prohibitive materiality to certain objects and permissible materiality to others (Engelke 2012). In Nigeria, the setting most similar to that of Anglophone Cameroon, there is considerable diversity in how Pentecostals deal with materiality: pastors generally discourage believers from using objects in their prayers (Marshall 2009), but the hugely popular megachurch Synagogue, the Church of All Nations (SCOAN) distributes small bottles of "Morning Water" as mediums for God's power. These are indications that what outside observers qualify as material, the believers might consider spiritual instead (Meyer 2014: 316).

Does the use of Pentecostal material objects in football in Cameroon point to continuity with the use of *jars*? Dedicated Pentecostals who emphasized radical rupture would disagree. But everyday spiritual practices suggest complicated dynamics between rupture and continuity. After hearing rumors about Akwe's alleged implication in *jars*, I attempted on several occasions to gently confront him with these accusations and get his take on the relationship between *jars* and Pentecostal practices. As expected, he denied the accusations and emphasized his Christian upbringing—his family attended a Baptist church. Yet the way he experienced the use of Pentecostal tools and the power of the Holy Spirit in the field of play was instructive:

> Most of the times when you use anointed oil or holy water, after you rub it, inside you feel light, you feel lively. Even in the field you can do some things you could

never ever do. It is just like magic. Because when you do it, the Holy Spirit is in you, you can do all kinds of things. Also, you have a lot of luck. I can just kick the ball anyhow and it will just enter the goal.

Here Akwe explicitly equated Pentecostal Christian practices with "magic"—surely he would have been corrected by his Pentecostal friends if they had been around. The benefit of Pentecostal tools was that they could bring miraculous results on the field of play, not unlike those that footballers sought from *jars*. The last sentence of the quotation illustrates a common gripe among football coaches who complain about footballers' overreliance on *jars*. They think footballers who use *jars* selfishly strive to score goals, believing that objects imbued with spiritual powers will enable them, instead of following instructions to play as a part of a team.

On another occasion when I discussed with Akwe the spiritual aspects of football, he was explicit that Pentecostal practices directly replaced *jars*. The use of material objects was the central aspect to this transition that had supposedly taken place with the proliferation of Pentecostal denominations in the region. As Akwe explained:

In earlier times, there were not so many churches like today. Christianity was there, but not so many churches like now. At the time when I was small, when I would play interquarter, somebody might give you some small thing to put in your boot. We didn't even know what that was. . . . But not so long ago, after the 1990s, when I was older and started playing more, churches were around everywhere. It became easy to find anointed stickers, oil, holy water. So now you could take a sticker and press it to your leg.

According to Akwe, Pentecostal tools directly replaced *jars*. In his interpretation, the proliferation of Pentecostal materials pushed out *jars* from the "spiritual battle" of football. As previously mentioned, the point is not to show beyond doubt whether Pentecostal tools have replaced *jars*. Rather, the point is that the two occupied the same space in many athletes' imagination and in their construction of the spiritual world and that the athletes sought similar effects from both. This complicates Pentecostals' emphasis on radical rupture: people also engage with Pentecostalism because of the possibility of continuity with other forms of magico-religious practices.

Prophecy, Star, and Spiritual Eyes: Tackling Uncertainty

For Pentecostal Christians, the "gift of prophecy" is the ability that some have to look into the spiritual world and see not only the future but also past events that were invisible to common people. Moreover, through dedicated prayers, those with this valuable gift can attempt to affect change in the physical world and reverse undesirable outcomes. Pentecostal notions such as "prophesy," "star," and "spiritual eyes," and how they are deployed in everyday life in the context of football, can further demonstrate how novel cultural forms emerge from blending between Christianity and practices akin to *jars* despite the claims of radical rupture.

Emil often spoke about his ability to see the future and the past during deep prayers. He was able to see the entire team of Buea Young Star FC laid out in a formation on a football field, each member with his own "star" above his head. This is how he explained the notion of a "star":

> Your star is what you are supposed to be, how great you are supposed to be. The brighter the star, the brighter your destiny. . . . When I talk about a star, I talk about what you can do and be great, who you can become.

The "star" invokes images of possibility of a brighter future. It also invokes the idea of fulfilling destiny, understood as an active and agentive notion rather than predetermination. For example, as I already noted in the introduction, Emil identified our teammate Ayuk as having the "brightest star" on the entire team. Before Ayuk's departure for Europe, his "star" was not shining as brightly as it could, as it was covered by malevolent forces in the spiritual world. If he was to allow his star to shine, Ayuk had to begin "serving God." The ability to see into the spiritual world allows gifted Pentecostals like Emil to not only predict the future but also imagine possibilities that seem absent from the immediate environment.

Prophecies are indications not only of the course of future events but also of the need to effect change. In late 2014, when Buea Young Star FC competed in the regional cup competition and played important matches twice a week, Emil claimed to be able to foresee his teammates' injuries and the outcomes of upcoming matches. In the quarterfinal, he predicted that the team was going to lose. He mobilized one of his best friends on the team, also a dedicated Pentecostal Christian, and they fervently prayed together for several days in an attempt to reverse the outcome. In the quarterfinal, it worked: Buea Young Star FC won, despite Emil's visions. Prior to the subsequent semifinal, Emil had a similar prophetic vision. This time, however, he lacked time to "reverse" the prophecy through prayers, and his vision came to pass: the team lost the match and was eliminated. Prophecies reflect uncertainty that is part and parcel of competitive football, a social activity fraught with unpredictable results and injuries. Prayers that attempt to affect the outcomes of prophecies suggest the possibility to bring about change.

Some Cameroonians are skeptical of prophecies and question whether spiritual figures' access to the spiritual world is genuine. How do Pentecostal men of God come to terms with failures to correctly predict match outcomes? Saint Collins recounted once being accused of false prophecy. On one occasion, a football team of University of Buea students was preparing for a national interuniversity competition in Ngaoundéré in the Adamawa Region of Francophone Cameroon. Before leaving, they visited Saint Collins in search of prayers and prophecies to help them win. The man of God delivered as expected: in his own words, "God opened his spiritual eyes," and he prophesied that the team would reach the finals. However, the footballers returned to Buea sooner than expected, having been eliminated early. They accused Saint Collins of being a "fake prophet."

Saint Collins defended himself by claiming that the players did not follow his instructions. They were supposed to pray together at exactly midnight before the match, but they had disregarded this instruction. More important, Saint Collins instructed them to use a "mantle" that he had provided. Mantles were pieces of cloth (handkerchiefs, headgear, dresses, shirts, or socks) anointed by men of God. If these items came in physical contact with a prophet, they would carry his spirit. Saint Collins anointed one of his shirts and gave clear instructions to the footballers: before leaving their dressing rooms, each one of them was to wear the anointed shirt for a few minutes, pray with it, and then hand it over to his teammate, until the shirt circulated among all of them. However, the footballers were careless and left Buea without the anointed shirt. According to Saint Collins, this disregard for instructions was the reason behind their failure in the tournament. Thus strict instructions and a material object could make or break a prophecy—not unlike the prohibitions and instructions commonly given by a *jars man*. In addition, Saint Collins acknowledged the volatile nature of a prophecy and spiritual battle:

> It is normal that those things happen. But it does not mean that I am a fake prophet or a fake man of God. At times, you see what God is showing you, but later on things can change. Maybe the other people that played there were praying harder.

His interpretation shows that a match is a spiritual battle not only for "pragmatic" footballers like Akwe, who use Pentecostal prayers to win matches and score goals, but also for Pentecostal men of God well versed in Christianity.

On the surface, "prophecy" and "star" seemed to be Christian practices and concepts: certainly Pentecostal Christians framed them as such. However, this was far from clear, as these notions had a long history in the region. The notion of a "star" was documented in the Southwest Region by Edwin and Shirley Ardener in the 1950s, decades before the proliferation of Pentecostal churches (Ardener 1956). Edwin Ardener briefly discussed the case of a young man who believed his "star" to be "blindfolded" by a jealous person, which made him continually lose jobs. The problem was solved by a combination of rites, *medicine*, and amulets (Ardener 1956: 105).[8] From Edwin Ardener's account it was unclear whether the "star" emerged from Christian missionaries and mainline churches present in the region since the 1840s or rather belonged to an older belief system. Moreover, footballers always linked the "star" to the spiritual world but not always to Christian practices. I was told that one may make a spiritual sacrifice of one of his kin in order to "polish his star," i.e., to have his kin killed or abducted by spiritual forces in order to achieve success, in football or elsewhere. This was an idea that clearly pointed to accusations of witchcraft, specifically *nyongo*, by which one could obtain supernatural powers and lavish wealth by sacrificing a family member (Ardener and Ardener 1960: 339; Ardener 1996: 248–50). The "star" is thus not so clearly Christian or novel as it may appear. Practices that resemble "prophesying" are also far from novel. Saint Collins's evocation of "spiritual eyes" is especially reminiscent of the practice of traditional healers to use a "second pair of eyes" (Geschiere 2013: 71–73). Both "prophecy" and "star" are most likely products of a long period of borrowing and appropriation of practices between different traditions of spirituality, in a similar way that, as Joseph Tonda (2002) suggests, both Christianity and "traditional" spirituality participate (and have long participated) in an ongoing process of mutual constitution and entanglement.

Finally, as demonstrated in previous sections, Pentecostal practices and ideologies deployed in football—spiritual eyes, material objects, the idea of a spiritual battle on the field, tapping the power of the supernatural, clear instructions and prohibitions of spiritual advisors, bodily consequences of supernatural powers—all have striking parallels in different iterations of *jars*. The practices of *jars* and of Pentecostal Christianity outlined above do not constitute exhaustive lists, but the similarities are striking. This is not to argue that Pentecostalism is *jars* dressed up in Christianity (although, as suggested in the example of the Winners Chapel controversy, some Cameroonians may interpret it as such) but to suggest that both are a part of a process of continuous blending with and borrowing from each other, despite Pentecostals' claims of a rupture.

Rupture and Continuity: Beyond the Opposition

As Haynes (2017) has convincingly argued for the case of Pentecostal Christians on the Zambian Copperbelt, the balance between continuity and change, between "accommodation and critique" (2017: 162), is central to Pentecostalism.[9] This spiritual movement "both resonates with local concerns and, at least sometimes, serves as a framework for calling local models into question" (Haynes 2017: 161). The discourse and claim of rupture is important to understanding the appeal of Pentecostal Christianity for young Cameroonian men in general and aspiring footballers in particular: it provides an ideological framework for self-fashioning through rejection of other spiritual and social forms. Understanding that it is a moral statement is equally important: it provides Pentecostal Christians with a claim to moral high ground and constructs non-Christian practices as immoral, making them easier to reject. But rupture coexists with continuities. For many footballers, the Holy Spirit inhabits the same space in the spiritual world as the other spirits that Pentecostals distance themselves from and work to cast out. Claiming rupture from discursively constructed "tradition" and framing the rupture as a moral statement is a key element of the appeal of Pentecostal Christianity, but it is also one that generates overlaps. These overlaps are important: they are part of the reason why Pentecostal practices are attractive to young footballers. Footballers engage with the Holy Spirit as a source of power, and some perceive Pentecostal objects as direct replacements for *jars*, that is, as objects that have the potential to reward them with the "instant efficacy" (Comaroff and Comaroff 2000: 314–15) they usually associate with sorcery. Given the importance of both radically breaking away from the past and the overlaps of new forms of spirituality with older ones, it is not very useful to consider rupture and continuity as opposing forces. Instead, one process enables the other, and both are central to understanding the appeal of Pentecostalism, for footballers and beyond.

Perhaps most importantly, spirituality has physical consequences for many footballers and can provide a framework for moral and gendered self-transformation. I continue to explore this in the next chapter, where I turn to issues of spirituality, athletic performance, and sex.

Notes

1. The purchase of spiritual practices was not unusual in the Southwest Region, especially in the Manyu Division (and in Cross River State in neighboring Nigeria), where people frequently exchanged associations and their knowledge (Röschenthaler 2004).
2. There were many more examples of the variety of practices and rumors of *jars* in football: a team spending a night on a particular ancestor's grave before a crucial match; sacrificing animals and smearing their blood on the walls of the opposing team's dressing room; planting objects with spiritual powers at stadium entrances in order to sabotage the visiting team. I focused here only on examples relevant to this chapter and on those I could substantiate with a fair amount of detail.
3. See Janson (2016) for a notable exception of Chrislam in Nigeria.
4. For a similar account of conversion to Christianity in search of an alternative source of power, spiritual and otherwise, see Peel (2000).
5. See Tapang Ivo Tanku, "Cameroon's President Orders Pentecostal Churches Closed," CNN, updated 15 August 2013, retrieved 13 January 2018 from edition.cnn.com/2013/08/14/world/africa/cameroon-churches/; Andres Caballero, "Pray or Prey? Cameroon's Pentecostal Churches Face Crackdown," NPR, 13 April 2014, retrieved 13 January 2018 from https://www.npr.org/2014/04/13/300975474/pray-or-prey-cameroons-

pentecostal-churches-face-crackdown; Moki Edwin Kindzeka, "Reopened Cameroon Churches Fear Criticizing Government," VOA, 30 October 2015, retrieved 13 January 2018 from http://www.voanews.com/a/reopened-churches-in-camroon-not-critizing-biya-government/3029686.html.
6. "And when he had called unto him his twelve disciples, he gave them power against unclean spirits, to cast them out, and to heal all manner of sickness and all manner of disease" (Matthew 10:1, King James Bible).
7. In Cameroonian Pidgin, *skin* refers to the body. Having something *for ma skin* translates roughly to having it "on me."
8. Edwin Ardener limited these findings to the Bakweri, people indigenous to the Southwest Region's coast. Only one of my interlocutors whose accounts I used for this chapter was Bakweri; however, the region has long been a destination for migrants from different parts of Cameroon, and with the mixing of people came also the mixing of ideas, beliefs, and practices.
9. The question however remains whether it is *specific* to Pentecostalism.

CHAPTER 5

Anxious Athletes, Spiritual Wives
Football, Pentecostalism, and the Body

When in August 2014 I met Derrick, a teammate at the Buea Young Star FC football academy, his zeal for training was particularly intense. At twenty years old, he was proud of being the youngest member of the team's starting lineup. His hopes of a contract abroad were fueled by his kinship networks that stretched to Europe: his father was an entrepreneur living in Sweden and was very supportive of his athletic endeavors. He was on his way to establishing himself as a powerful midfielder.

In October 2014, Derrick's performances visibly deteriorated. In regional league matches his passes were not going through, his short sprints slowed down considerably, and his intimidating defensive technique was absent. He was often substituted before halftime and soon lost his position in the starting eleven. The cause was not clear, and Derrick himself, although visibly irritated, avoided complaining and making excuses.

It soon became clear that he was suffering from a stubborn injury. He tried his best to hide the pain from the coach. He resisted being relegated to the bench and insisted that he was fit to train and play. When questions about his performance mounted, he finally confided to a few of our teammates that he had strained his adductor muscles. Commonly known as a "groin pull," this injury among footballers occurs when the muscles of the upper and inner thigh are strained.

Why would Derrick hide his affliction from the coaches? During one training session, Derrick failed to continue hiding his increasing pain. Pointing toward his groin area, he complained to the coach that the pain was unbearable. The coach was not surprised and showed little sympathy in his initial response: "This is because you are working on the other side!" "Working" pointed to a physically straining activity, and "the other side" referred to the bedroom. The accusation, which Derrick clearly expected, meant that his injury was caused by too much sex. The coach immediately offered a solution: a visit to a medical clinic, five days of injections, some prescribed medications, and one week of rest. It went without saying that Derrick had to suspend his sexual activities.

Derrick's recovery, however, was slow. Several months passed until he started training full-time. Plans for his preparation for trials abroad were put on hold. Over time, he became the butt of jokes: "Derrick likes women too much!" some of his teammates laughed during friendly banters after training sessions.

While continuing to taunt him, some offered an alternative explanation for his predicament. The team captain, Emil, the dedicated Pentecostal Christian I wrote about in previous chapters, hinted to me that Derrick had been affected by what Pentecostals called a "spiritual wife": an evil spirit in the form of an attractive woman who haunted men's dreams and seduced them into intercourse. The spirit operated in the "spiritual world" (see chapter 4) but provoked a "physical" reaction: men would ejaculate in their sleep and wake up in wet bedsheets. This was frequently happening to Derrick, the team captain contended, and the frequent ejaculations, coupled with intensive training, caused him to strain his adductor muscles and consequently skip trainings and miss opportunities for trials abroad.

For many months Derrick was hesitant to openly talk to me about his injury. In August 2015 he finally shared with me the details of the story. He described his injury as having been caused by wet dreams. He had responded quickly by visiting a well-respected health center in Buea, where he consulted a doctor and spent a substantial amount of money on tests and medications. The problem persisted, which suggested that it was beyond physical. Searching for a fuller explanation for his predicament, he turned to his uncle, a pastor at the Full Gospel Mission, one of the largest Pentecostal churches in the Southwest Region, who confirmed that his problem was a "spiritual wife."

At the time of our last conversation, Derrick was again fit and back in the starting eleven in Buea Young Star FC. He seemed to have recovered, at least for the time being. His recovery included prayers and medications:

> I would pray, I would pray, I would pray. I don't go to these traditional healers, I don't believe in that. . . . For this, you only have to pray, and also take medicines. I took different injections and drank medicines. . . . So yes, I had that problem, and that caused my injury, but now I am praying, and I am playing well, and it is better.

Finally, he said he was disturbed by unfounded accusations from his teammates, coaches, and the club manager that he had too much sex. Quite the contrary, he emphasized his dedication to being faithful to his girlfriend, whom he had decided to marry, and boasted of his ability to avoid sexual temptations.

Derrick's problems highlight tensions in performing a particular masculine role produced by two separate but interrelated processes: his years of training with Buea Young Star FC, where the manager awarded young footballers who "behaved well" with the possibility of mobility; and his consultation with a Pentecostal pastor, who provided a solution to his struggles with involuntary nightly ejaculation. His story illustrates how football training, sexual morality, and what Pentecostal Christians in Cameroon call the spiritual world become entangled in the body of an aspiring athlete. For young athletes, sexual practices are a cause of frequent anxiety, not least because of their alleged effects on the body. Footballers, together with their coaches and managers, subscribe to the long-standing myth in international sports that sex hampers their athletic performances, and they struggle to control their sexual practices as part of their future life project, which involves their bodily capital. Pentecostal Christianity is one way of dealing with this embodied anxiety. This chapter focuses on young footballers' efforts to control and maintain their athletic bodies—negotiating sexual practices, training effectively, and eating regularly—and the difficulties they have in doing so, in order to reveal how spirituality, morality, and aspirations of social mobility come together to make gendered (masculine) subjects.

Sporting endeavors in general are clear examples of how bodies can be centers of action and possibility, tools for engaging with the world, but also of how they need to be subjected to disciplinary regimes. As scholars have recognized for a long time, the body is a primary instrument for action, and it serves as both technical object and technical means (Mauss 1935). Through socialization and education, bodies become "socially informed" (Bourdieu 1977: 124) and repositories for social norms, class identities, or gender identities (Bourdieu 2004). In addition, more than simply repositories, bodies can be an "existential ground of culture" (Csordas 1990: 5), i.e., a site where cultures become materialized and real. At the same time, athletic bodies need to be subjected to manipulation, training, and disciplining regimes. Athletic bodies need to be "docile" (Foucault 1995) to become useful: "The body becomes a useful force only if it is both a productive body and a subjected body" (Foucault 1995: 26).

Young Cameroonian footballers are subjected to disciplining regimes of coaches at football clubs and academies whose ideas about training are grounded in professionalized sports and technical knowledge that was mainly formulated in the West. Footballers are also influenced by indigenous ideas about the body and its role in physical activities. This raises the question of whether it is useful to consider bodies clear products of one or the other "culture" or "social structure." It is an accepted idea in anthropology that techniques of the body are not universal but instead vary among societies (Mauss 1935) and are said to reflect a particular social structure (Bourdieu 1977). Yet the case of athletes who are influenced by both Western discourses of professional sports and local discourses about the body and gendered morality show that, as Besnier (2012) suggests, bodies are not products of clearly outlined and separated "societies," "cultures," or "social structures" (the term depends on the theoretical current) but of an amalgam of global and local discourses and practices. In addition, the case of footballers suggests that it is probably not too useful to see bodies as expressions of "culture" conceived as a composite of past experiences, given that footballers aspire to use their bodies as tools for social and geographical mobility—clearly part of a future-oriented project.

Pentecostal Christianity also plays an important role in young footballers' body regimes. As I have shown in chapter 4, Pentecostal Christians emphatically prioritize the spiritual over the physical, and Pentecostal footballers in Cameroon maintain this idea. At first glance, this seems to be in conflict with a sports industry that prioritizes control over the physical body in order to enhance its performance. For much of my fieldwork, I took it for granted that such a tension existed, only to discover that for most of the Pentecostal footballers I met the spiritual and the material did not clash but instead converged in the process of training and maintaining an athletic body. Exploring this convergence but also the ways athletes negotiate and resolve tensions between the materiality of sports and the pervasiveness of spirituality shows how the process of molding effective, athletic bodies that perform well involves spiritual work and forces beyond the physical.

Pentecostal Christianity is a fertile domain for rethinking the entrenched oppositions between spirit and matter, belief and ritual, content and form, and mind and body. The material approach to Pentecostalism (Meyer and Houtman 2012; Vásquez 2011) in anthropology convincingly criticizes two entrenched modes of thinking about Christian spirituality: one, anthropologists' focus on meaning and belief as privileged domains of inquiry, and two, Protestant Christians' claims that their faith moves beyond reliance on concrete material forms and regards matter as secondary and signification as primary. A focus on the materiality of Pentecostalism means moving away from ideas, concepts, and ideologies as immaterial abstractions and toward ways that ideas operate in and construct a tangible, material, concrete reality.

Marked as it is in different parts of the world by vigorous prayers and passionate dancing, Pentecostal Christianity demonstrates the power of bodily engagement in spiritual practices. Even though Pentecostal Christianity nominally follows the Protestant ideology that privileges immaterial abstractions over material things, one reason for Pentecostalism's massive worldwide appeal is its ability to animate the senses and the bodily experience of the Holy Spirit among its believers. Pentecostal Christianity mobilizes and authorizes the body as the "harbinger of ultimate truth and authenticity" (Meyer 2010: 756). The believer's material body, bodily senses, and experiences are central to understanding Pentecostal Christianity's appeal.

The theoretical current that focuses on material aspects of Pentecostalism, especially the body, is useful when considering the experiences of young Cameroonian athletes, but it requires a slight shift in focus. Studying Pentecostal Christianity outside its most obvious spaces—such as churches, congregations, and religious schools—and locating it in other social spaces—such as football fields and athletes' interactions with spiritual leaders in the context of sports—reveals that the disciplining regimes of Pentecostalism and sports intersect in athletes' potent yet vulnerable bodies. Here I am not so much concerned with sensations and bodily experience as with young men's efforts to cultivate and maintain control over their bodies as part of their future life projects. Focusing on how young athletes engage with Pentecostal denominations demonstrates how Pentecostal Christianity operates not only by engaging believers' bodily senses (Meyer 2010; Vásquez 2011) but also by providing resources for the discipline, control, and care of the body, which are crucial aspects of athletic endeavors.

My choice to focus on the body is grounded in ethnography: as will become clear in the sections below, young athletes emphasize that they need to pay much more attention to maintaining their bodies than "common" Cameroonians, "ordinary" men, or *waytman* researchers. But close attention reveals that the body is inseparable from issues such as gendered morality, spirituality, and aspirations for a future abroad.

Football and the Dangers of Sex

On Buea's football fields, footballers frequently debated how sex affected their performances. In May 2015 I joined two of my friends, Tabe and Iroko, in their early morning training sessions at the Molyko Omnisport Stadium. Our goal was to improve endurance, so we focused on running, rope skipping, and abdominal exercises rather than technique with the ball or tactics. Tabe, whom I already mentioned in chapter 3, was a significantly more experienced footballer than Iroko. After having played a few seasons with a club in Douala and competing in the Cameroonian first division, he spent two years of his early twenties playing on second- and third-division clubs in the United Arab Emirates, where he was well paid. Upon the end of his contract he returned to Cameroon, but his family members quickly "ate" most of his savings. Looking for opportunities in Europe, he tried his luck with a first-division club in a southeast European country, only to return to Cameroon, disappointed and with no money. In 2015 he tried again to migrate to the Emirates. He was a member of Christ Embassy International, a well-known international Pentecostal church with headquarters in Nigeria, and regularly attended their youth congregation in Buea.

Iroko trained at Buea's stadium regularly with teams competing on different levels (from regional to national). "Iroko" was his nickname, which in Bakweri mythology refers to an extraordinarily resilient and tough tree with mystical powers. He had never left Cameroon. In the apartment complex where he lived, he was considered a troublemaker, inviting complaints from residents about noise well into the small hours of the night. He was a frequent butt of Tabe's jokes about his propensity for *mimbo* (alcoholic drinks) and nightlife.

At one point during our morning training session, Tabe brought up the topic of activities harmful to athletes' bodies:

> Drinking is not good for you. When you drink beer, you need to train more, so that it can come out of your body [*komot for yu skin*]. It will come out, but you must work more to make it so [*makes a waving gesture with his hand above his right arm, suggesting it evaporates out of the body*]. . . . Also, you cannot have sex with a woman. The water that comes out [*wata weh deh komot lek piss*], that is not a small thing. When that happens, you need seventy-two hours to recuperate. And you must run a lot, like two hundred kilometers. When you have sex, the next morning you will have pain in your joints. If you do not do too much sports, you can do it, you will not feel it too much. But if you want to do sports, you cannot! It will affect you too much.

Iroko did not immediately respond to Tabe, and we all continued with our exercises. A while later, as we walked back from the training session, I asked him to comment on what Tabe had said:

> Tabe is a crazy man [*kres-man*]. What will happen if you drink a small beer? On the contrary, if you have too much power in your body, you need to relax. For me, I have too much power [*flexes his arm muscles*], and beer will make you relax. I don't fear drinking beer. But I fear having sex with a woman. That will make you lose power.

While footballers' views on consuming alcohol could differ, ranging from complete abstinence to occasional avoidance to recreational use, I was somewhat surprised to learn that footballers had an almost unanimous opinion about sexual acts. All seemed to agree that ejaculation resulted in a loss of physical energy that somehow needed to be replenished. Uncontrolled sexual activity could also lead to injuries. Replenishing the lost energy took time and returning to previous fitness levels required significant additional training, so sex was to be avoided, especially immediately before important matches. Thus controlling sex, most specifically ejaculation, was a primary concern for young footballers, who needed to deal with the tensions between, on the one hand, desire and desirability and, on the other, physically demanding training.

Anxiety over ejaculation at times led footballers to make the conscious decision to refrain from having multiple sexual partners. However, what was more important were their partners' sexual demands. Consider the following. In March 2015 Emil and I were returning from a Buea Young Star FC training session when we came across our teammate Franklin. A tall and skillful attacker ("number nine") in his mid-twenties, he had transferred from Unisport Limbe FC, hoping that the new club president in Buea would arrange trials abroad for him. On that particular day, he did not show up for the morning training session. When we encountered him on the street in Molyko near his rental, he used his current girlfriend as an excuse. Apparently, her sexual appetite was harmful to his performance. The following exchange between Franklin, Emil, and me ensued:

> **Emil:** That girl will ruin your career.
>
> **Uroš:** Which girl?
>
> **Emil:** He has some girl, she keeps him in the house all the time.
>
> **Franklin:** That one is a bad girl. But I will stop seeing her. Woman is a bad thing, it distracts you from football.
>
> **Emil** [*speaking to Uroš*]: Sometimes she keeps him inside the house the whole day, when he comes to train he has no power.
>
> **Franklin:** Sometimes I'm in the house with her, I don't want to go anywhere, I don't even want to go to trainings. And she knows me well, for a long time now, so she knows my weaknesses. I cannot resist her. When she is there, I have to do it.
>
> **Uroš:** But this is fine, you only cannot do it before a match, no?
>
> **Franklin:** Uroš, you know ejaculation is a waste of energy.
>
> **Emil:** Yes, and players here do not eat well [*no di chop fayn*], so they cannot recuperate, meaning sometimes even after a week it will still affect you in the field. And especially if she holds you the whole day! Some women don't even know that this is a bad thing.

My goal here is not to establish whether footballers' athletic aspirations were indeed threatened by the sexual demands of their girlfriends. Rather, this exchange reiterates that the body is central for young footballers' choices of sexual partners. There were no indications that Franklin led a particularly promiscuous lifestyle—even if he did, the problem was not whether he had many sexual partners or one regular partner. Rather, the problem was the waste of physical energy through ejaculation.

In some cases, women, particularly girlfriends, were central figures for applying the regimes of sexual disciplining. According to some, this was not an easy task, considering that the young men had serious sexual appetites and were prone to "chasing" women and having many sexual partners, and, as athletes and young men, they were sexually attractive to young women. In previous chapters I wrote about Ayuk, the exceptionally quick winger for Buea Young Star FC. When I met him in late 2014, he was renting a room in a small, simple wooden house, with no toilet or running water, in Campaign Street, a quarter in Great Soppo considered tough and dodgy by some.[1] He had a six-year-old daughter with Katie, a young Bamileke woman who resided in the same quarter.[2] Eighteen years old when she delivered her daughter, she followed her father's instructions and quit school to take care of the child.

Katie felt she had to work hard to "keep" Ayuk. She did not like the way he attracted the attention of young women, both around the football field and in the quarter. She admired his clothing style and comportment, which she referred to as "clean": he dropped his pants below his waistline, revealing the top of his clean, shiny white boxer briefs. She found his style particularly attractive, but, as she was aware, so did many other young women, and she was determined to keep them away.

Ayuk was born in the Manyu Division among a Banyangi ethnic group. One prominent stereotype held that Banyangi men were prone to seeking many sexual partners. Both men and women, and both Grassfielders and coastal people in Buea, considered Banyangi men as *nyanga boy-dem*: young men who paid particular attention to their appearance and style.[3] Banyangi men, the stereotype went, had a *woman-eye*: they "liked women" and were particularly skilled at gaining their attention. People often linked the promiscuity of Banyangi men to the reputation of Banyangi women, who supposedly were inclined to become sex workers. According to rumors, the larger towns of the Southwest Region, such as Kumba and Limbe, had entire quarters known for places where women originating from the Manyu Division sold sex. Even though the stereotype about Banyangi women was likely inflated by colonial administrators, who in their reports tended to label all unmarried migrant women as prostitutes (Walter Gam Nkwi, personal communication), there are records of young women from the Manyu Division migrating to Nigeria and other parts of Cameroon to sell sex (Niger-Thomas 2001). Katie was conscious of the reputation of Banyangi men, although she saw it as a wider trend that included Cameroonian men in general. She argued that almost every *boy-pikin* (young man or child) was promiscuous when they were young. Ayuk was a case in point—although he had recently "calmed down," not least because of Katie's continual efforts to ward off female contenders and because of their daughter, who demanded attention and responsibility.

Katie was particularly offended by allegations that she was responsible for Ayuk's bad stints on the field. These allegations implied that she was luring him into having sex before crucial matches. She contended, however, that she played an important role in controlling Ayuk's sexual practices:

> He [the manager] would call me, and all the others [teammates] would talk, "Ayuk is not fit, Ayuk cannot run," and say that I caused it! I would tell them, "What do you mean I caused it, I would always refuse him." Sometimes he wants to do it, but he has a match the next day. I refuse him, and he gets *veks* [angry]! But the next day

he goes to the field, comes back, and tells me, "I played such good football, people swamped to *dash* [give] me money!" I tell him, "You see?!"

Katie was well informed regarding the "common knowledge" among footballers about the detrimental effects of sex on physical performance and deemed herself to be part of this disciplining regime. Considering her fierce insistence on Ayuk being faithful—in her eyes, not an easy task—she arguably played a significant role in this disciplining.

In practice, Katie's role as Ayuk's long-term girlfriend was ambiguous. One time she recalled how Ayuk was taken to a week-long training camp where female visitors were not allowed. One night, however, she managed to sneak into Ayuk's room and spend a few hours with him before leaving the camp unnoticed. She did not explain her transgression further, except for a playful smile. But the story shows how young footballers in Buea needed to deal with tension between youthful desirability and sexual restraint. The coaches and managers were not the only ones who exercised control over young men's bodies: women who were either their long- or short-term girlfriends played a crucial role in this precarious regime of managing sexual desire.

Finally, despite footballers' and their girlfriends' evocation of the body as a source of anxiety, sex was not simply harmful because of its effect on the body. Sex, or rather, women, were part of a wider corpus that footballers referred to as "distractions." Footballers, and to an even greater degree their coaches, saw their girlfriends as the most harmful of distractions that included gambling, drinking alcohol, and night life. When young footballers took part in training camps, such as the one mentioned above, coaches forbade footballers from using mobile phones. One of the reasons they gave me was that it sheltered footballers from problems that distracted from training or matches—such as a girlfriend informing them she had become pregnant. In other examples, the women could inform them that they had to go to the hospital and needed money to pay the bills. In this sense, even family members were seen as potential distractions, especially when they asked for money. Thus young men had to be isolated from falling for masculine vices, such as drinking and womanizing, as well as from masculine obligations, especially providing money. Coaches and footballers cited effects on the athletic body as the main problem, but these were clearly an expression of a wider range of vices that men could fall for, or numerous demands they were asked to meet.

Traditional Bakweri Wrestling: A Comparison

The injunction to avoid sex before competitions is a common one for male athletes in many parts of the world, a myth reproduced by many, from football coaches to superstar athletes like Muhammad Ali. In Cameroon, the idea that sexual intercourse has detrimental effects on one's body may have roots in indigenous perspectives on sex and physical strength. There are examples throughout the African continent to suggest this. For instance, for the ba-Sakata of the Democratic Republic of Congo, heterosexual activity leads to the loss of *makasi* ("force" or "power" in Lingala) for men and its gain for women (Bekaert 2000). In urban Kinshasa, young men fear that they might lose their "star," a spiritual entity that stands for success and good luck, in sexual intercourse (Pype 2012: 266). Cameroonians have also long employed the notion of a "star" to refer to success (see chapter 4). In this case, avoiding sexual encounters with women has less to do with the material body and more to do with concerns over elusive success and bad luck.

In the Southwest Region, indigenous perspectives were never clear-cut, not least because of the tremendous mixing of different ethnic groups, traditions, and beliefs in the region. One parallel could be found in another competitive physical activity popular among young men—*wesua* or *pala-pala*, Bakweri traditional wrestling (figure 5.1).[4] Proponents of *wesua* spoke about tensions around sex in similar terms. In Bokwai, a Bakweri village ten minutes by road from Buea, old and retired wrestling *ngumu* ("champions" or "heroes" in Mokpe, the language of the Bakweri) were generally happy about the recent surge in popularity of traditional wrestling, with Sunday bouts between wrestlers from eight Bakweri villages increasingly attracting Cameroonians' attention. Even though *wesua* has probably never disappeared from Bakweri villages, it seemed to be revived by significant support from senior civil servants. Known for its long history of producing wrestling champions, Bokwai was particularly successful in reviving the tradition: in 2015 the village won the annual tournament for the fifth time in a row. But while old *ngumu* from Bokwai welcomed this surge in popularity, they also felt that some of the rituals and practices that used to be central to wrestlers' regimens were no longer being followed. One of these was celibacy during the week prior to Sunday wrestling bouts. According to Samba Esowe, a *ngumu* whose success as a wrestler peaked in the 1980s, serious wrestlers had to take "precautions" before important bouts, one of which was abstention from sexual intercourse for a week. When I interviewed him in May 2015, in the midst of the wrestling season, he offered that the main reason for celibacy was the belief, handed down from parents to younger generations, that women were detrimental to male athletes' success and brought bad luck. In the week prior to an important Sunday bout, a serious wrestler needed to avoid sleeping with women. If he had a wife and could not avoid sleeping in the same bedroom, he had to resist having sex, and the wife was tasked with refusing his advances. The *ngumu* also emphasized the need to avoid consuming food prepared by menstruating women, including cousins and sisters. The wrestler had several options: consuming simple

Figure 5.1. Whoever forces his opponent to touch the ground with his back or belly wins. The *sanja* or "wrapper" that one of the wrestlers is wearing around his waist indicates that he is representing his village Bokwai, the standing champions. Bova, Cameroon, May 2015. Photo by the author.

bread from small shops, preparing his own food, or having his food prepared by "not-yet-matured" (premenstrual) women, such as his younger sisters.

The idea that men need to avoid contact with menstruating women is, of course, not exclusive to the Bakweri or to the wrestlers, but it is a fairly common notion in many places around the world. For instance, in Kinshasa, semen or menstrual blood are believed to be capable of transmitting evil spirits (Pype 2012: 266). Classic ethnographic accounts of Highland Papua New Guinea societies detail how menstrual blood is seen as polluting and dangerous for men (Herdt 1981). In addition, the idea that men need to maintain control over the loss of semen is observed among wrestlers in North India (Alter 1995) and Hindu men in general (Alter 1997). However, in both wrestling and football in Cameroon, the belief that sexual intercourse needed to be avoided prior to physically straining endeavors did not squarely originate in "tradition." On the contrary, it was often couched in terms of a "modern" and "scientific" knowledge associated with regulated sports competition on a national and international level. Another notable *ngumu* from Bokwai argued that sexual intercourse, along with a few other practices such as drinking alcohol and staying up late in nightclubs, made the wrestler "lose weight," meaning that he was more exposed to being taken down by an opponent. The *ngumu* traced back this knowledge to Bakweri customs, but also to his preparations for a competition in Olympic freestyle wrestling (what Cameroonians called "carpet wrestling") in Yaoundé, where he won the 1979 championship awarded by the Fédération Camerounaise de Lutte. Similarly, one of the region's most celebrated wrestlers, Tonga Nganda, who represented Cameroon in several international freestyle wrestling competitions in Egypt and Russia and trained his sons and other young wrestlers to compete in international competitions, was fairly dismissive of Bakweri customs in wrestling. Yet he claimed that during the season wrestlers can have sex only on Mondays, because they need ample time to recuperate for their Sunday performance. But, according to him, refusing food from menstruating women was a superstitious belief and a remnant of the past. It seems that the particular focus on the bodily consequences of sexual intercourse had more to do with regulations of international sports competitions than with Bakweri customs and beliefs.

In football, the case was similar. John Mayebi, the region's celebrated coach whom I wrote about in previous chapters, argued from the point of view of a "professional" coach that sexual intercourse involves the tensing of muscles and tendons and leads to a loss of energy. He was slightly more forgiving than other football coaches: he allowed forty-eight hours for recuperation. Another coach—formerly of Unisport Limbe FC, who transferred to Buea Young Star FC for a better salary—prided himself on being the only expert in the Southwest Region who had spent five months in the renowned International Coaching Course at the University of Leipzig in Germany. He nominally forbade sexual intercourse after Tuesday, four days before Sunday matches. Other coaches made similar prohibitions, citing their education and knowledge of science as a source while dismissing the avoidance of menstruating women as a superstitious tradition of the countryside.

It seems that both in football and wrestling the particular emphasis on the material body, and the bodily consequences of sexual intercourse, were strikingly more pronounced in "technical" and "scientific" discourses of global sports. On a global scale, sports in general has frequently been the point of tension between different conceptions of the body and its place in society, the environment, and cosmology. For instance, Brownell (1995) recounts how her and other athletes' bodies were measured and tested at the U.S. Olympic Training Center in Colorado Springs and how disciplinary regimes of science were applied: "Science is such an ultimate voice of authority that one feels absolutely defenseless under its gaze" (1995: 167). There are also parallels with professionalized rugby clubs, in which medical examiners analyze players' blood and urine samples and test their muscles and joints for flexibility, then guide athletes' careers based on the results (Guinness 2014). At the same time, the "scientific" approach to athletes' bodies grounded in Western biomedicine and the Cartesian separation between mind and body has frequently been met with resistance, for example, when athletes in the West tried to recover the holistic approach to the body by seeking knowledge of Eastern medicine (Besnier, Brownell, and Carter 2018: 89–90). So, on the one hand, athletes sought to recover the holistic approach to the body that included lifestyle and moral development; on the other hand, professionalized sport demanded more from athletes' bodies and sought to alienate the athletic body from its environment and treat it as a tool (Besnier, Brownell, and Carter 2018: 94).

In the Southwest Region of Cameroon, the origins of prohibitions on sexual intercourse before athletic performance could be traced to different sources of knowledge, some profiled as traditional, immemorial, and couched in terms of culture and heritage, others in terms of scientific and technical knowledge. The prohibitions and rules in Cameroon were amalgams of these different forms of knowledge. In practice, both wrestlers and footballers were anxious about the presence and dangers of women. The young Bakweri wrestlers I followed considered the norm of avoiding menstruating women as an "old belief" but still attempted to follow it, because, as one of them said, "It is true that a woman makes a man weak." Footballers seemed obsessed with the dangers of ejaculation but also saw women more generally as distractions that ought to be avoided. Thus, in both football and wrestling, the material body is a central source of power and anxiety, but it cannot be separated from gendered morality—norms, expectations, and vices.

Pentecostal Christianity and the Control of Sexuality

Pentecostal Christianity was another moral and bodily regime that focused on young people's sexual practices. Consider the following. In December 2014, I accompanied one of my friends to the most prominent nightclub in Buea, aptly named "Las Vegas," packed with mirrors and leather seats and booming with the latest *Naija* (Nigerian) hits. This was a rare occasion: throughout my fieldwork, I felt I needed to refrain from late nights to avoid being judged by my Pentecostal friends and hampering my relationships with them. On this particular evening, during our third round of drinks, my thirty-year-old friend, formerly a respectable midfielder but with no "career" ambitions, shared with me his girlfriend troubles. They had been together for more than four years, yet three months prior to our conversation they started having issues. Her mother had become a born-again Christian and insisted that her daughter should follow. Most frustratingly for my friend, she insisted that they were not allowed to have sex before getting married, or at least before my friend showed serious intent to tie the knot. According to my friend, the girl obeyed her mother: she visited him in his rental on a daily basis, but at around 6:30 P.M., when it got dark, she left with no explanation. Stricken by this development, my friend went to visit the Pentecostal church that the girl's mother attended, a tiny makeshift wooden house similar to many ad hoc churches in the region. "When I saw that small church, I said no, they cannot control me like that!" he angrily told me. There were other concerns in their relationship: considering marriage after four years was not unexpected, and he was not stable enough financially to pay the bride price, an unavoidable obligation. Yet he was particularly unhappy about the sexual disciplining by a Pentecostal denomination (and a Pentecostal mother) that, in his view, had little authority to police his sexual practices. Less than a month later, their relationship ended.

My friend was not happy with the Pentecostal policing of sex, but many other young footballers I interacted with looked for exactly this kind of romantic relationship. Pentecostal denominations preach abstention from sex before marriage because they consider premarital sex a defilement of one's body and a sin against God. Christians, especially Pentecostals, refer to sexual intercourse outside of marriage as "fornication," a word with a strong moralizing tone. It appears frequently in the King James Version of the Bible that many of my Pentecostal friends consulted. For example: "Flee fornication. Every sin that a man doeth is without the body; but he that committeth fornication sinneth against his own body. What? Know ye not that your body is the temple of the Holy Ghost which is in you, which ye have of God, and ye are not your own?" (1 Corinthians 6:18–19). In the Good News Bible, another common version that my friend Emil (see chapter 4) gave me, hoping that I would discover Jesus Christ as Lord and Savior, "flee fornication" is replaced by "avoid immorality." For Cameroonian Pentecostals, when one commits the sin of fornication, one becomes exposed to evil spirits (such as "spirits of youthful lust"), which can have detrimental effects in other areas of social life or in the future (e.g., in marriage or bearing children). One then needs to be delivered from such spirits by a "man of God" (Pentecostal prophet or pastor). This message to abstain from sex is a common Christian and Pentecostal message around the continent (see, e.g., Pype 2012; Burchardt 2011).[5]

For young footballers, Pentecostal Christianity was a social space to challenge the supposed norm of promiscuous practices associated with them. The challenge was posed discursively, in daily moralizing conversations and interactions, but also materially, through the control of sexuality and the discipline of the body. Young footballers, whom many Cameroonians consider especially prone to a lifestyle that involves permissive sexuality, and yet for whom the athletic body is a central source of capital and an instrument for pursuing a brighter future, were in an especially appropriate position to pose these challenges by disciplining their bodies.

Despite church teachings, most young unmarried Pentecostal couples I met were not celibate. Pentecostal couples interpreted Christian moral codes about sexual practices as a guiding principle, not a strict rule (see also Burchardt

2011). As Maribel, a long-term girlfriend of one of my football friends and a member of the Apostolic Church, briefly explained, "The church can only advise, it cannot command." In most cases, young Pentecostal Christians looked for long-term partners, ideally Pentecostals or those open to the faith. They emphasized their plan for a monogamous and long-term relationship, with a clear prospect of marriage. Some of my football friends told me they felt obliged to break up with their girlfriends when they became born again because they had no intention of proposing to them. While young Pentecostal couples were not celibate before marriage, they were committed to monogamy and controlling sexuality. I spoke to Maribel about her sexual activity with her partner, my friend from Unisport Limbe FC. She said, "Our relationship is not based on sex. . . . Even if we see each other for a short time, like just after the match when he has free time, we just sit like this and discuss, we don't need to have sex. . . . And he cannot have so much sex, it takes him so much time to recuperate after that." What young footballers increasingly seemed to cherish was a long-term relationship that would allow them to, among other things, maintain control over their sexual activity. Pentecostal Christianity, with its emphasis on the supposed dangers of "free" sexual activity and insistence on monogamy, seemed to be an appropriate place to look. In their preaching of monogamy and control of sexual practices, Pentecostals were in tune with football coaches, who also argued that monogamy was beneficial to footballers' performances.

Marine Spirits and Overcoming Immobility

For young Cameroonian footballers, sexuality can become entangled with aspirations for mobility. The example of Derrick from the beginning of this chapter showed how female evil spirits can meddle with young athletes' training regimes. Not surprisingly, they can also disrupt their migration projects. One solution was to consult with Pentecostal men of God.

Consider this story, told to me by Akwe, my Buea Young Star FC teammate (see chapter 3), and Saint Collins Aliche, the young charismatic man of God (see chapter 4). In 2013, a year before falling out with his manager (see chapter 3), Akwe had an opportunity to travel abroad for trials but could not get a visa to travel to Europe. His manager was eager to send him abroad, but embassies of European countries in Cameroon and Nigeria turned down his applications. His brother, a born-again Christian, advised him to consult his man of God, Saint Collins, who had already helped him sign a contract with a football club in Bamenda (Akwe's brother was also a talented footballer).

During Akwe's visit, the young prophet had a revelation that the cause of the visa applications being rejected was a woman who was possessed by an evil spirit from the "marine kingdom," the "kingdom of darkness." The man of God described the woman's appearance in detail, confirming the accuracy of his prophecy.[6] I asked Saint Collins for more details about the woman in question and the evil spirit:

> **Saint Collins:** She is a real lady, a normal human being like you, but the lady is possessed by an evil spirit from the marine kingdom. The spirit is passing through that lady to do evil things to youths.
>
> **Uroš:** Okay, and the lady was his girlfriend, or, I don't know, his sister . . . ?
>
> **Saint Collins:** No, his girlfriend! One of his girlfriends. You know, footballers have so many girlfriends. So it was one of the girlfriends he once dated, but they are no longer together.

Once the root of the problem was established, Saint Collins prayed with Akwe to deliver him from the evil spirit. He prophesied for the last time: he pointed out the signs Akwe would encounter before traveling, the clothes he was going to wear, the bag he was going to carry, the items he was going to pack. Reportedly, everything happened as expected. Akwe obtained a visa and traveled to Europe for trials. After his first trip, he returned to Cameroon—this was considered a failure. But when he applied for a visa a second time, he was allowed to travel again. His trials were successful, and he reported that a club in Eastern Europe was interested in keeping him on their team. Notably, following Saint Collins's instructions, Akwe stopped dating the lady in question.

The diagnosis of a "female spirit from the marine world," a trope that Pentecostal Christians use interchangeably with that of a "spiritual wife" (as in the example from the beginning of this chapter), refers to the marine spirits, such as *mami wata*, that are common in West and Central Africa and in the West African diaspora (Drewal 2008). *Mami wata*, what in Europe would be called a "mermaid," is usually a beautiful female figure who can deliver extraordinary riches but can also threaten people's relationships.[7] *Mami wata* has frequently been interpreted as a metaphor for Africans' ambiguous experience of modernity and commodity fetishism, replete with attractions and possibilities, but also dangers (Argenti 2010; Masquelier 1992; Bastian 1997).

Mami wata is not a straightforward evil figure for all Cameroonians (see, e.g., Lammers 2004: 214–15; 224–26). For Pentecostal Christians, however, she is clearly a demon. As a seductress, *mami wata* uses her sexual appeal to lure human beings into a relationship with a "spiritual spouse" that eventually leads to their destruction (Masquelier 1992; Meyer 1998; Pype 2011). She provides otherworldly sexual experiences (Bastian 1997: 126; Pype 2011: 290–91; Meyer 2008) but is capricious in her relationships and refuses to enter into real marriage and motherhood (Bastian 1997: 124–25). Most interpretations of *mami wata*'s seductions conjure the danger of transgressive female sexuality and its meanings in patriarchal societies. She embodies sexuality disconnected from fertility, unbounded from the constraints of marriage and maternity, and men fear it as dangerous and disruptive (Masquelier 1992: 62–64). She is men's expression of disruptive qualities of unbounded female sexuality that is immoral and needs to be placed under control.

Cameroonian footballers' encounters with seductive marine spirits and spiritual wives suggest that these interpretations are correct, but they also suggest more. In the context of young footballers' supposed promiscuity, of the Pentecostal belief that premarital sex is sinful, and of young footballers' belief that sex affects their performance, the images of spiritual wives and seductive female spirits are comments on the immoral sexuality of young men. When Derrick's Pentecostal friends talked about him and his problems with a spiritual wife, they also commented on his "love of women" that was holding him back. It was even somewhat contradictory to make such a claim, since *mami wata* is said to deplete her victim's sexual appetite. In any case, a spiritual "diagnosis" was also a judgment on the immorality of his acts. When Akwe was said to be affected by marine spirits, the main reason was his promiscuous lifestyle, supposedly characteristic of him and many other footballers. As Saint Collins opined while talking about Akwe, "[The footballers] like this enjoyment, good life, girls love them, but it is destruction." The seductive marine spirits are then also metaphors for the dangers of men's transgressive sexual acts. Judging by these encounters, it is young men who need to transform themselves by changing their sexual practices in order to avoid "contracting" evil spirits through transgressive sex.

In addition, marine spirits are not simply metaphors. They also serve as catalysts for long-term effects in real life. The goal of Christian deliverance from a marine spirit is not to absolve a young man from guilt and allow him to continue without the burden of the spirits but to change him. As the material approach to Pentecostalism would suggest (Meyer 2010; Vásquez 2011), marine spirits and spiritual wives are not only a diagnosis of a problem, immaterial abstractions that serve as a secondary level of commentary on the world, but also active attempts to transform practices and moral attitudes and trigger change. The perceived dangers of female spirits are not only commentaries on immoral practices but also attempts at long-term transformation, a form of Pentecostal disciplining of sexuality.

Finally, one of the key appeals of Saint Collins Aliche to young footballers was his record of helping young people leave the country. The young man of God frequently bragged about his "spiritual sons and daughters" who were scattered all over the world: Germany, Poland, the United States, China, Angola (figure 5.2). He claimed to have helped them obtain their visas and large sums of money for their airfares. Saint Collins was himself transnationally ori-

Figure 5.2. A Cameroonian footballer, one of Saint Aliche's "spiritual sons," in deep prayer before a training session with his new team in Southern Poland. May 2016. Photo by the author.

ented: several times he expressed an interest in continuing with university education and founding a Pentecostal church in Europe or the United States. He helped footballers' mobility both spiritually, by leading them through prayers, and materially, by providing them with personal contacts and financial assistance to obtain passports and visas—highly valued commodities for young footballers keen to leave the country.

This begins to explain why the footballers gravitated to Pentecostal Christianity for moral guidance about sexuality. Pentecostalism and Christianity were not the only institutions in Cameroon that aimed to control young men's sexuality. As shown above, retired Bakweri wrestling champions maintained ideas of controlling sexual practices. However, these ideas were inseparable from the moral training that bound young men to village social structures. According to wrestling *ngumu*, a good wrestler was respectful of the village, and, most important, family and elders. Without this respect, *ngumu* maintained, they could not wrestle. In the Grassfields societies of the Northwest Region, *fondoms* (kingdoms) also have prominent norms that seek to control young men's sexual encounters, as Grassfields elders have long instructed young men to remain celibate until marriage. The morality of *fondoms* that forbids young bachelors to have sexual intercourse was the norm in Grassfields villages until the late 1970s. Since then, the older generation has been complaining that youths have become sexually permissive, and notables surrounding the *fon* (king) have struggled to reclaim control over young men's sexuality (Warnier 2007: 233–66). But these norms bind young men to the hierarchical structures of *fondoms* in the Grassfields. In contrast, Pentecostal Christians distance themselves from these "traditional" institutions that anchor young men in local hierarchies, supporting instead dreams of mobility and efforts to travel abroad. Pentecostalism is attractive for the young footballers because it is a disciplining regime that not only protects them from local imaginaries like *mami wata* but also promises engagement with transnational circuits.

Eating and Fasting

Sex was not the only source of anxiety for footballers who struggled to maintain their bodies. Another was eating: having an adequate diet was a challenge. Emil emphasized this point in the previously quoted exchange between him, Franklin, and me when he claimed that young footballers in Buea "do not eat well" (*no di chop fayn*). Buea Young Star FC players often complained to their coaches about the difficulties of maintaining a regular diet appropriate for a daily training regimen. Occasionally, during training sessions, when coaches pushed the footballers beyond their limits and the footballers had difficulties keeping up, they gestured with their hands toward their mouth, indicating that they were hungry and had no money to eat well. This was a particular difficulty for footballers who had migrated to Buea from elsewhere in Cameroon. They lived far away from their family compounds and from the women who bore most of the burden of preparing food. Emil and Franklin were cases in point: Emil migrated from Fundong in the Grassfields, an eight-hour bus ride from Buea, while Franklin's family household was in Tiko, about one hour away. Like many other footballers in Buea Young Star FC, they lived in cheap rentals, for which they paid between CFA 7,000 (US$12.25) and 15,000 (US$26.25) per month, which was a challenge for them to afford. The cheapest meals in Buea eateries cost between CFA 300 (US$0.5) and 500 (US$0.9). Migrant footballers had no regular source of income (almost none of them worked), and they usually received only minimal amounts from their families. As I showed in chapter 3, footballers frequently complained to coaches about the irregularity of "training bonuses," i.e., small daily allowances of around CFA 500 (US$0.9), which coaches commonly gave to footballers to pay for meals. The bonuses were, however, notoriously irregular, and at times footballers did not receive any for several months. Short on cash, they often mobilized their social networks for their daily meals—relatives who resided in Buea, family friends, pastors, coaches, or friends like me who were better off. This made for an irregular diet that hampered the footballers' attempts to maintain their bodies.

At the same time, footballers regularly scrutinized each other's bodies for signs of too much "enjoyment," i.e., excessive eating and drinking. A corpulent male body can be an idiom of prosperity and powerful masculinity in many settings in Cameroon, while on other occasions people invoke it as a way to ridicule the powerful (Mbembe 2001: chapter 3). For footballers, quite unsurprisingly, a growing belly was a sign that a footballer was enjoying too much good food (and perhaps beer and whiskey) and was becoming lazy with his training. In particular, footballers were wary of kinds of food deemed harmful to their bodies. Traditional dishes that originated from the countryside were key points of contention. Some footballers claimed that their physical strength originated from the traditional diets of their ethnic groups on which they had grown up. This was most commonly expressed by the Banyangi, who proudly claimed that their traditional diet of water-fufu and eru, a dish based on cassava's starchy tuberous root, provided them with superior strength. However, most footballers disregarded such claims as outdated beliefs, as they learned from their coaches to avoid food that was marked as "heavy." Coaches insisted footballers eat food that was "light"—a plate of spaghetti or rice with tomato sauce and occasionally a small piece of fish or chicken (red meat was to be avoided). It is perhaps significant that many of the cocoyam-based dishes deemed harmful to the athletic body, such as *kwacoco* with *banga soup* prepared by the Bakweri or *achu* prepared by Northwesterners, were traditional delicacies that invoked the Cameroonian countryside. Just like the structured training deemed necessary to discipline the powerful bodies of *kontri nayn* footballers who only knew how to use their physical strength to play the game (see chapter 3), dieting regimes effectively taught the footballers that their countryside bodies needed to be disciplined to fit the demands of the sport and the transnational market.

In addition, unlike Unisport Limbe FC footballers, Buea Young Star FC footballers did not have a formidable training infrastructure available to them. As I have shown in chapter 2, football clubs ideally had an extensive infrastructure that included dormitories, separate kitchens, and private training fields, but these were rare. Clubs such as Unisport Limbe FC used such infrastructure to isolate footballers from their social surroundings and control their activities and bodies. They would prepare meals three times per day in order to ensure that footballers ate regularly and appropriately (meaning only rice or spaghetti). Buea Young Star FC footballers and those of almost all other clubs and academies were left to take care of their bodies and diets in their usual social surroundings in their neighborhoods. Most footballers were therefore expected to learn to discipline their bodies themselves.

Pentecostalism, again, played a role in dieting. While the imperatives of football coaches converged with Pentecostalism in matters of disciplining sexual practices, the two at first sight seemed to be in conflict when it came to matters of diet. Pentecostal denominations and men of God prescribed periods of "dry fasting," avoiding all food and water between 6:00 A.M. and 6:00 P.M., and often longer. For example, the Christ Embassy International Church would encourage their followers to fast for one week, telling them to break the fast only after the Friday evening church service. These were not obligations but rather encouragements, and dedicated Pentecostal footballers occasionally fasted on their own initiative. On the surface, "dry fasting" clashed with footballers' demanding training schedules. Both footballers and coaches recognized that fasting, like sex, led to a loss of physical energy, which was detrimental to training and performance, and prescribed ways of managing fasting and training. For example, Paul Ashu, a goalkeeper coach at Unisport Limbe FC and a well-known physical education teacher as well as a dedicated Pentecostal Christian, developed a three-day fasting program for football players who wanted to fast in the middle of a football season. After the Sunday football match, a player could fast for one full day on Monday but still drink water ("wet fasting"). On Tuesday, the player should break the fast at 12:00 A.M. and on Wednesday fast between 6:00 A.M. and 12:00 A.M. He should stop fasting on Thursday and focus on training for the Sunday match. Another method, the one most preferred by the Pentecostal coach, was to endure a weeklong period of dry fasting to allow the player to "feed in the word of God," but only during preseason preparations, i.e., before the season's intensely competitive period. According to the coach, this resulted in a solid spiritual "foundation" and spiritual "strength," after which the footballer could easily "regenerate power from God" during the competitive season by fasting for only three to six hours. Thus fasting, when properly planned, was advisable despite the immediate physical difficulties, because it gave one strength for the long term.

For Pentecostal footballers, fasting was a physical challenge, but an important and necessary one. They were not obliged by men of God or coaches to fast but chose to do it on their own. My Pentecostal interlocutors insisted on instructions that had to be followed. First, fasting was not simply "not eating." As I have shown above, footballers frequently did not "eat well" because of their economic hardships, but Pentecostal footballers did not consider this fasting. Rather, fasting was a deliberate decision and a conscious effort to avoid food, which also involved praying and reading the Bible. Second, one was not supposed to communicate to anyone in one's social surroundings that one was fasting, as this could invite pity and admiration that could lead to gratification. Pentecostal footballers insisted that their teammates and coaches were oblivious to their fasting, in part because they trained extra hard to compensate. Third, one could have prophetic visions as a result of fasting and praying, i.e., insights into the spiritual world, but that should not be the motivation for fasting. Instead, the motivation should be to become "spiritually strong" in the long term. So, despite the immediate effect on the body, fasting for Pentecostal footballers was not antithetical to training and performing. Instead, when properly managed, it was part of a long-term spiritual preparation that eventually translated into a better performance, winning matches, and success in general.

Spirituality, Morality, and the Athletic Body

Spirituality, in this case Pentecostalism, is a method for disciplining the body that is increasingly attractive for the footballers, despite tensions between the material and the spiritual. And while many of its directives are reminiscent of prohibitions that traditional healers might enforce (see chapter 4), the emphasis on long-term development and moral transformation is crucial. Pentecostalism is also appealing as a disciplinary regime that supports young men's aspirations to move abroad and desires to break away from local hierarchies. It is also relevant that Pentecostal disciplining of the body is not directly enforced. Footballers choose whether and when to fast, and they can negotiate sexual practices. Pentecostalism then emerges as a disciplining regime that is at once strict and unambiguous—there are clear directives about what is morally acceptable and what is not—while at the same time leaves room for interpretation and negotiation to individuals. This dual quality is another reason why Pentecostalism appeals to footballers.

As the above cases show, the athletic body is hardly simply a result (or an expression) of a particular society, culture, or social structure. It is rather an amalgam of different discourses and practices, some termed as technical and originating from the West, others termed as traditional. In practice, it is often not possible to differentiate the two, although attempting to find the sources of practices and discourses is useful to showing how blurred the boundaries are between them. Moreover, considering footballers' bodies as expressions of a tradition does no justice to the fact that they struggle to train and maintain their bodies as part of a future-oriented project of social and geographical mobility. Finally, as the body is the most obvious center of attention for athletes, it emerges as a site in which gendered morality—norms, judgments, and demands—and gendered aspirations become materialized in a very urgent way. Pentecostalism shapes masculinities, as it appears as a solution to athletes who deal with unpredictable flows and closures of transnational circuits.

Notes

1. I often felt this was an unfair characterization of Campaign Street, a somewhat run-down quarter but populated by people from all walks of life: teachers, civil servants, small business owners, footballers, university students. It seemed like it was mostly my Pentecostal friends who regarded it as a "bad" neighborhood.
2. Bamileke is an ethnic group native to the West Region, in Francophone Cameroon. They are known for their "entrepreneurial spirit" (Warnier 1993) and their propensity to migrate, both within Cameroon and overseas (Ndjio 2009).
3. *Nyanga*, a Cameroonian Pidgin English term, can loosely be translated as "style," although much of the meaning is lost in translation. *Nyanga* can refer to the ostentatious display of stylish jewelry, such as shiny earrings, bracelets, or necklaces. It can refer to a particularly well-done hairstyle or clothes of the latest fashion. It can also refer to an attitude, urban and stylish. In addition, *nyanga* can refer to a playful pretense. For example, a footballer might wear a bandage over his injury. The bandage might be caused by a legitimate injury, but it could also be a *nyanga*—harmless and aimed at attracting attention. The term applies to both men and women.
4. *Wesua* is a Bakweri tradition, but traditional wrestling is not exclusive to this ethnic group. A similar version of wrestling (*lutte traditionnelle*) is practiced in the Littoral Region.
5. A notable exception is a recent Pentecostal movement in Zimbabwe that, surprisingly, finds inspiration to encourage polygyny and sexual prowess in the Bible (Jeater 2016).
6. As I have shown in chapter 4, when the Pentecostal men of God "prophesy," they do not necessarily predict future events. Rather, a "prophecy" is a verbalized revelation about events and details that could not otherwise have been known by the prophet.
7. Even though marine spirits are common in indigenous cosmologies, such as *liengu* among the Bakweri (Ardener 1975) and *miengu* among the Duala (Wilcox 2008), it is not unreasonable to compare them to European "mermaids," given that *mami wata* is likely a product of colonial encounter (Drewal 2008).

Conclusion

Masculinities, Faith, and the Production of Aspiration

In May 2016, eight months after my departure from Cameroon, I arranged a meeting with Eyong Enoh, one of the most successful international footballers to emerge from Cameroon's Anglophone regions. We met in his house in Amsterdam—Enoh spent much of his illustrious career playing for AFC Ajax, historically the most successful football club in the Netherlands and one of the most successful clubs in the world. I was admittedly starstruck, as opportunities to meet elite athletes are rare. I thought of my Cameroonian friends who considered him their idol and flaunted my "selfie" with the famous footballer on social media for them to see. The charisma and attraction of success in elite sports is indeed powerful (figure 6.1).

Besides his football skills, Enoh is well-known for being a dedicated Pentecostal Christian. Photographs from his matches with the Cameroonian na-

Figure 6.1. Taking a selfie: the author with the famous Cameroonian midfielder Eyong Enoh. Amsterdam, the Netherlands, June 2016. Photo by the author.

tional football team show him wearing a shirt with an inscription "Jesus is Lord" underneath his regular team jersey. When his busy schedule of professional football would allow him to visit the Southwest Region (he was born in Kumba and grew up between Buea, Limbe, and Tiko), he would not miss the opportunity to visit the Apostolic Church, one of the largest Pentecostal denominations in Anglophone Cameroon, which was attended by several of my friends who figured in the preceding chapters.

Naturally, we began talking about his life-changing event of becoming a born-again Christian when he was a teenager. His story was not surprising:

> When I became born again, my lifestyle changed.... There are many ways you are led to sin. I stopped drinking alcohol and going to nightclubs.... I also stopped spending time with many of my friends.... I would still visit them and their families, but I would not spend so much time with the people that would not contribute to my future. So I decided that I needed to be very focused and that I needed to be very disciplined.

This was a narrative I came to expect from Cameroonian Pentecostals, footballers or others. It was common for young footballers to formulate an ideology of focus and discipline—one that trickles down from elite athletes to a growing number of young men who aspire to sign contracts with small regional clubs—in terms of becoming a born-again Christian and avoiding sinful practices. Note also that the future emerges as central in Enoh's decision-making about his lifestyle and socializing, another common theme that I frequently heard from my Pentecostal friends in Buea and Limbe.

But to my surprise, when I told Enoh that many young footballers in Cameroon see him as an idol and inspiration both for playing football and becoming born again, he quickly shifted his tone of initial approval into one quite critical of the young men:

> **Enoh:** There are many Pentecostal churches in Cameroon, but many young people don't take the church and the word of God in the right way. Most of them pray to have success in life, to leave the country, to play football, to become rich. Maybe they know that Eyong Enoh is a success, and he is following the word of God, so if they follow it, they will achieve that success. But this is a wrong way to go about it. They think if they pray, maybe they will have success, but having success in football is most of all about hard work. Of course then, there is the question of opportunity. Some people get an opportunity, others do not. There are many talented people that never got an opportunity. But you only need to find your place somewhere.
>
> **Uroš:** Some people would say that is unfair.
>
> **Enoh:** But who is to say what is fair and what is not?

Eyong Enoh emerges here as a reluctant idol for young Cameroonian men. His advice to young footballers seems to be that they should not consider Pentecostalism a magical method of achieving success quickly but as a source of deeper self-transformation. At the same time, Pentecostalism clearly can be helpful in instilling a moral and bodily regime of self-discipline and focus that the competitive world of professional sports demands.

On the one hand, Enoh's perspective is quite different from that of many aspiring footballers I worked with in Cameroon, who fervently prayed to perform better on the field, to be selected among the many, and to harness the power of the Holy Spirit to successfully play professionally abroad. On the other hand, his message resembles that of my dedicated Pentecostal friends in Buea and Limbe who insisted on the importance of humility and focus. These two aspects, taken together, are central to understanding the intersection of football aspirations and Pentecostalism in contemporary Cameroon, which is characterized by the attraction of enticing opportunities of miraculous success, but also by an ideology of self-discipline, hard work, and focus. It is this dual nature that is crucial in shaping young men as gendered subjects in the Southwest Region of Cameroon and arguably also elsewhere in post-structural-adjustment West Africa where young men are captivated by the attractive possibilities of globalized industries and the promises of contemporary spiritual movements.

Football aspirations and Pentecostalism in Cameroon thus invite more general conclusions. Firstly, the focus on Cameroonian footballers reflects the nature of aspirations for social mobility in the context of globalized neoliberal capitalism. Secondly, convergence between Pentecostal morality and the demands of football coaches and managers demonstrates the central role of spirituality in contemporary conditions of precarity. Finally, a focus on athletic aspirations shows how future-making projects shape gendered (in this case, masculine) subjects and allows us to move beyond limited approaches to men as either victims of contemporary transnational processes or powerful agents who reproduce the hegemony of masculinity. Here I offer concluding words on these issues, first mentioned in the introduction of this book.

Neoliberalism, "Suffering," and the Production of Aspiration

Some anthropologists have recently argued that the word "neoliberalism" has become such an overused term in anthropological writing that it has lost most of its meaning and analytical purchase. For instance, in a recent debate on the subject published in the *Journal of the Royal Anthropological Institute*, James Laidlaw called it "a slur for all seasons" (2015: 912), Jonathan Mair argued that "neoliberalism-ism leads to poor ethnography" (2015: 917), and both argued that anthropologists should entirely abandon "neoliberalism" as a concept.

Such criticism has merit. However, policies grounded in neoliberal economic theory profoundly affect people's lives around the world. Anthropologists can rather do better by being more specific about the "uses of neoliberalism" (Ferguson 2010). Mine are anchored in three specific processes described in detail in chapters 1 and 2. The first is the structural adjustment programs imposed by the World Bank, International Monetary Fund, and Western donors throughout the countries of the global South in the 1980s and 1990s, in Cameroon specifically since 1989. These programs in Cameroon, as elsewhere in Africa (Ferguson 2006; Harrison 2010), have failed to bring the economic prosperity and political change they promised: the national currency was devalued, the economy plummeted, unemployment increased, and young people from poor backgrounds suffered. The second important process is the globalization and commercialization of football, which accelerated in the 1990s. The infusion of television and sponsorship deals in the sport and the spread of satellite television throughout African countries resulted in the proliferation of images of superstar athletes, the expansion of the transnational market for football players, the proliferation of football academies, and new possibilities for young men to become mobile (socially and geographically) by playing football. The third process, described in detail in chapter 2, is the commodification of young men as football players. Managers in football academies such as Buea Young Star FC assign a market value to young men's athletic bodies and skills, invest in them, and make predictions about the return on their investment. These three processes—structural adjustments, commercialization of football, and commodification of players—are separate processes, but they are connected, and they represent a break with the practices of the past.

The young aspiring footballers whose stories appear in this book are exemplars of the orientation toward the future that has recently become a point of interest for anthropologists. In particular, young men show an incredible "capacity to aspire" (Appadurai 2013: 179–96), i.e., an ability to imagine an alternative future that social theorists such as Appadurai celebrate as a resource for progress. They cultivate a kind of "ethics of possibility," creative and optimistic thinking and acting, a positive force that Appadurai contrasts with the negative "ethics of probability" that he locates in "amoral forms of global capital" and "private adventurism" (Appadurai 2013: 295). But before we start celebrating the potential of young men's aspirations and their orientation to possibilities despite unlikely odds, we need to assess the larger context of their dreams. Football dreams in West Africa are a product of large-scale socioeconomic transformations grounded in ideas of economic liberalization and global circulation of capital. And while "global capital" and "private adventurism" in football appear to offer the young men new ways to aspire to become mobile and overcome economic uncertainty, they also introduce new forms of precarity.

Importantly, what emerges from the stories in this book is the value of suffering for the sake of an uncertain future. As demonstrated in detail in chapter 2, while young footballers in Cameroon routinely, as they say, "suffer" on the football fields, especially when they need to train and play without compensation, their academy managers insist that they need to be taught a new form of "suffering," one that asks them to forego present needs and orient themselves to future success in the globalized market. In this way, academies teach young men to embrace the precarity that the globalized market brings. The ethnography of Buea Young Star FC shows that the propensity to engage precarity is not simply "there" among young men but needs to be produced and cultivated. Whether it is a Cameroonian football manager who needs to instill the young men with a notion that they need to "suffer" now in order to qualify for a better future abroad (chapter 2), a European football coach who complains that African footballers need to learn focus and discipline (chapter 3), a manager convincing the young men's relatives that they should invest money so the young men feel obliged to work hard abroad (chapter 3), or a coach regulating young men's sexual habits and eating practices (chapter 5), this is a process of disciplining young men to take part in the globalized market and the neoliberal economy.

This corresponds to the idea that neoliberalism differs from classical economic liberalism. While classical economic liberalism rests on the faith in free markets, neoliberalism needs to be actively constructed (Mirowski 2009: 434–35)—nation-states need to take active steps to introduce market dynamics to fields that were previously run otherwise (such as healthcare and education). As a result of neoliberal structural adjustments, the sovereignty of many nation-states (especially in West Africa) has become fragmented, and the work of governmentality is being increasingly undertaken by transnationally oriented non-state actors (Piot 2010: chapter 5)—in the case of this book's topic, by private football academies and Pentecostal denominations. It is even more striking that this is taking place in Cameroon, where the institutions of the nation-state are still very much present in the organization of social and economic life.[1] Even here, as shown in chapter 2, the trend is that the organization of football is moving away from elite figures intertwined with the nation-state and parastatal companies, and small ad hoc academies appear to be more adaptable to changes in the transnational market. Thus the context (structural adjustment programs and globalization of football) is grounded in ideas of opening countries to free markets, and the subjects that are able to take part in these markets are not a given but need to be produced and cultivated.

This is also important when we consider young footballers as transnational migrants. The ethnography of football academies and young footballers offers a new perspective on migrants and complicates common preconceptions—which saturate European media—of African migrants as people willing to endure an enormous amount of suffering for the sake of a better future. The young men I worked with are indeed driven to undertake migration projects, mostly due to economic hardships and lack of jobs. In fact, as shown throughout the book, the young men who are flocking to football academies like Buea Young Star FC and who engage with Pentecostal "men of God" (prophets and pastors) willingly submit themselves to disciplinary regimes that promise them participation in transnational circuits. But football academies that consider young athletes as sellable commodities play a crucial active role. The academies do not simply find and "harvest" desperate young men willing to suffer abroad. Instead, they seek to cultivate migrants willing to embrace the precarity characteristic of globalized neoliberal capitalism.

Spirituality—Between Instant Efficacy and Faith in Humility

One of the striking findings of this book is that the morality prescribed by Pentecostal churches and men of God resembles quite closely the demands that football managers and coaches make on young athletes. While young men used to deal with uncertainties inherent to the sport by using sorcery and consulting traditional healers (and many still do, albeit less frequently and more secretively), a growing number of young men are turning instead to Pentecostal men of God for solutions to old and new forms of uncertainty in football.

Whether it is the marine spirits that cause unforeseen injuries (chapter 5) or the interpretations of volatile decision-making by football managers as the workings of the devil (introduction), spirituality provides imagery to account for the uncertainty that permeates football. Spirituality is also an attempt to achieve concrete and immediate goals—to win matches, score goals, experience a physical boost and increased stamina (chapter 4), and have a better chance when applying for visas and looking for scarce opportunities to migrate abroad (chapter 5). In these instances, Pentecostalism and sorcery are similar, and young men use them with similar intentions.

In other instances, Pentecostalism seems to demand more from its followers. Pentecostal footballers preach for a long-term commitment and alignment with Christian tradition and insist on a radical break with other forms of spirituality (chapter 4). Men of God promote a substantial transformation of gendered morality and especially focus on controlling sexual practices and extolling the values of monogamous relationships (chapter 5). They argue for a need to produce new forms of masculinity, equally opposed to masculinities that rely on traditional structures and those grounded in urban "vices." Finally, Pentecostal footballers and the men of God who guide them preach that focusing on the sport, pursuing a proactive approach to life, valuing hard work, and cultivating humility will bring better results, despite the odds being stacked against them (chapter 3). These seem to be new ideas and demands.

Despite the convergence of men of God and football coaches and managers, following the word of God and the moral and body regimes of Pentecostal churches does not guarantee mobility or football success. Recall Emil, the charismatic team captain and man of God who figured prominently in this book. Despite his unwavering faith, disciplined lifestyle, commitment to training, and unrelenting efforts to obtain travel documents, he never left Cameroon. More generally, uncertainty frequently suffuses footballers' interactions with men of God and the Holy Spirit: Will they be selected among the many? Can they persevere despite hardships? Can they overcome the disadvantages of poverty and marginality? Faith offers footballers a way of dealing with the "cruel optimism" (Berlant 2011) that transnational professional football produces and feeds on. The Pentecostal emphasis on self-discipline, humility, and faith that God provides for the faithful gives young players the tools to deal with the millenarian promises, temptations, and opportunities to fail that are part and parcel of sports careers. In this way, Pentecostal morality becomes a form of self-making that prepares one for participation in the neoliberal economy.

In that sense, Pentecostalism is not simply a reflection of economic processes of millennial capitalism anchored in magical practice and the allure of accruing wealth from nothing. Even though Pentecostal practices are clearly grafted onto other forms of spirituality, and in football in particular on practices of *jars*, it would be reductive to consider them "holy-owned subsidiaries" (Comaroff and Comaroff 2000: 314) of occult economies. Perhaps in the 1990s, during the explosion of the Charismatic prosperity gospel in West Africa, the particular "name it and claim it" ideology stood out as a Christian movement that resembled occult engagements and responded to the "mercenary desires" (Comaroff and Comaroff 2000: 314) of the new age of millennial capitalism (chapter 1). This intertwining of occultism and Pentecostalism is still present for many Cameroonians, as shown by the example of the moral outrage surrounding the pastor of the Winners Chapel in Bamenda, who was accused of dabbling in witchcraft (chapter 4). But the ethnography of young aspiring football migrants and their relationships with men of God demonstrates that the ideology of immediate efficacy cannot be separated from the moral demands of self-discipline and the production of an alternative form of masculinity.

Here the notion of suffering for the sake of success in the future is again useful—without it, there can be no success in football. This does not square so easily with the "instant efficacy of the magical and the millennial" (Comaroff and Comaroff 2000: 314–15) purported to characterize the contemporary prosperity gospel. Added to the desire for instant results is the emphasis on self-discipline and belief in the future despite unlikely odds. Pentecostalism makes this explicit: prayer is central to making the leap of faith that miracles will happen despite the odds. But Pentecostal efforts also need to incorporate the faith in focus and hard work; the transformation of gendered morality, away from "sinful" practices; and tools to deal with individual failures. Pentecostalism is attractive precisely because it articulates both the possibility of immediate efficacy and the ideology of long-term self-discipline and self-transformation.

Analyses of African young men are often based on concepts such as "social navigation" (Vigh 2006; 2009) or "zigzagging" (Jones 2010; Masquelier 2019) that emphasize how young people, forced to deal with unstable economic conditions and uncertainty of outcomes, make multiple investments in their future and maneuver ever-changing conditions. This is certainly applicable to Cameroonian footballers who attempt to maneuver their way out of the country, one example being the group of footballers who used a trip to a youth tournament in Italy to defect and search for employment in Europe (chapter 1). But how do we square this with footballers' ideas, those that trickle down from the heights of elite sports, that one needs absolute focus on the sport in order to succeed in it, and with Pentecostals' ideas that dedication to Christianity and avoiding "sin" is the only right path to success? This is a call for stability in the face of precarity, or even more accurately, a call to have faith despite ever-changing and uncertain conditions. The convergence of Pentecostalism's moral and bodily regimes with football training suggests the making of stability in an unstable world and the need for having faith that stability will bring results despite the uncertainty and unlikely odds. Note here that this is arguably a much bigger leap of faith than the hope that using *jars* will allow one to score goals and avoid injuries. Thus neoliberal capitalism is not only about the magical "ability to deliver in the here and now" (Comaroff and Comaroff 2000: 314) but also about the precarious promise that faith, focus, humility, and self-discipline will bring social mobility.

Masculinities—Between Economy, Morality, and the Body

This book sought to show that aspirations for mobility through football are central to the analysis of masculinities in post-structural-adjustment West Africa and globalized neoliberal capitalism. The struggles and aspirations of young Cameroonian footballers demonstrate that representations of men from the global South either as powerful and hegemonic agents who reproduce patriarchal norms or as passive victims of transnational processes are inadequate and reductive. As a growing body of literature suggests (see, e.g., Miescher

2005; Ouzgane and Morrell 2005; Smith 2017; Spronk 2012), research on masculinities, especially on African men, does not have to concern "problematic" masculinities grounded in illegality, violence, or "predatory" sexual practices to generate new insights. Rather, throughout this book, I sought to show the roles of economy and morality in the making of masculinities and how the two materialize through young men's bodies.

As it is in almost any other professional sport, success in football is elusive, even unlikely. It requires an enormous amount of talent, dedication, labor, and luck. Young men in the global South experience even more obstacles than their counterparts in richer countries, as they train on neglected fields and see their visa and passport applications routinely rejected. Only few can succeed to "reap the fruits of their labor," to paraphrase the words—Ayuk's—that opened this book. Even then they can only hope for a stint of a few years, perhaps a decade, the best hope in a sport that pays for young bodies. Why, then, is football so attractive to so many young Cameroonians? More precisely, why do so many young Cameroonians put an enormous amount of time and work into an activity that they realize is not likely to pay them back?

One answer to this question is masculinity. Football captures the minds and animates the bodies of young Cameroonian men because it caters to their key masculine aspirations. It offers them a possibility to travel abroad and play the beautiful game that they have played and watched on television since childhood. Thus it allows them to participate in the transnational imagery of masculine success, as exemplified by elite athletes and their international stardom. At the same time, football, at least on the surface, offers young men an opportunity to avoid becoming "useless" and begin earning money and providing for their families. Despite the cultivation of dreams of individual glory abroad, and despite young men's rejection of the "African tradition" and countryside (chapter 3), strong emphasis on the morality of social responsibilities, especially toward kin, remains (figure 6.2). Football appears to allow young men to live up to their elders' demand to financially contribute to their households, a key marker of their transition to social adulthood, one that has become increasingly unattainable since the neoliberal austerity measures.

Thus the promise of football speaks to masculine aspirations grounded both in individual ambitions and collective demands and promises participation in both local and global regimes of valuation. As the football manager demands young men to begin suffering for the sake of a supposedly brighter future (chapter 2) and asks their families to invest in their travels to make them more "serious" (chapter 3), local demands of adult masculinity are increasingly grounded in transnational processes that on the surface seem to provide social mobility but also come with new forms of uncertainty and new ways of failing.

Masculinity is also central in the way people invoke it as a problem and an obstacle, a reason for a lack of progress. Taking part in overly physical in-

152 | *The Precarity of Masculinity*

Figure 6.2. Three generations of family members gathered in a kitchen around a three-stone cooking fire. Fundong, Cameroon, January 2015. Photo by the author.

terquarter matches, spending too much time socializing with young men in the quarters, having a lack of focus due to "distractions" such as drinking and gambling (chapter 3), or having too many sexual partners or too much sex, all of these, for many Cameroonians, diminish one's possibilities to not only perform well on the field but also take advantage of the scarce opportunities to obtain visas and passports (chapter 5). Cameroonians also discuss how problems of uncertainty will be solved only after men manage to change: if they would only avoid distractions and women and stay away from friends in the quarters, they would manage to avoid becoming "useless men." Thus young men are navigating a range of moral judgments and evaluations, and their practices cannot be reduced to individually motivated actions or fulfillments of social demands; they are moral practices and constitute gendered morality.

Pentecostal men of God who advise footballers are central in making the connections between gendered morality and success. Pentecostalism claims to offer a solution to the precarity of masculinity and to the difficulties of achieving masculine aspirations. It provides the young men with ideological resources for self-transformation and emerges as a site of production of an alternative form of masculinity that should have a better chance of overcoming local challenges and becoming transnationally mobile. Yet even this form of "Pentecostal masculinity" cannot be considered clearly "hegemonic": it cannot guarantee success in the fickle football industry and in reaching a meaningful adulthood by providing for the family. Rather, Pentecostalism becomes a space to express and negotiate masculine aspirations, discipline problematic masculine subjects, and prepare young men for new forms of precarity. Thus the convergence of football dreams and Pentecostal faith shows how transnational aspirations and precarity profoundly shape young men in Cameroon, but also far beyond, wherever the "global production of desire" (Trouillot 2001: 129) meets young men's fears of becoming superfluous in the eyes of those closest to them.

Note

1. Since 2016 the Cameroonian government's presence in the Anglophone Southwest and Northwest Regions has acquired a particularly sinister tone, forcefully reminding Anglophone Cameroonians who protested against the increasing Francophone influence that they need to submit to the power of the centralized Cameroonian state (Kewir et al. 2021; Willis et al. 2019).

References

Abu-Lughod, Lila. 1986. *Veiled Sentiments: Honor and Poetry in a Bedouin Society*. Berkeley: University of California Press.

Adebanwi, Wale. 2017. "Approaching the Political Economy of Everyday Life: An Introduction." In *The Political Economy of Everyday Life in Africa: Beyond the Margins*, edited by Wale Adebanwi, 1–32. Woodbridge: Boydell and Brewer.

Agergaard, Sine, and Christian Ungruhe. 2016. "Ambivalent Precarity: Career Trajectories and Temporalities in Highly Skilled Sports Labor Migration from West Africa to Northern Europe." *Anthropology of Work Review* 37(2): 67–78.

Akindes, Gerard A. 2011. "Football Bars: Urban Sub-Saharan Africa's Trans-local 'Stadiums.'" *International Journal of the History of Sport* 28: 2176–90.

Akoko, Robert Mbe. 2007a. "'Ask and You Shall Be Given': Pentecostalism and the Economic Crisis in Cameroon." Doctoral thesis, African Studies Centre, Leiden.

———. 2007b. "'You Must Be Born-Again': The Pentecostalisation of the Presbyterian Church in Cameroon." *Journal of Contemporary African Studies* 25(2): 299–315.

Akyeampong, Emmanuel, and Charles Ambler. 2002. "Leisure in African History: An Introduction." *International Journal of African Historical Studies* 35(1): 1–16.

Alberti, Benjamin, Severin Fowles, Martin Holbraad, Yvonne Marshall, and Christopher Witmore. 2011. "'Worlds Otherwise': Archaeology, Anthropology, and Ontological Difference." *Current Anthropology* 52(6): 896–912.

Alegi, Peter. 2010. *African Soccerscapes: How a Continent Changed the World's Game*. Athens: Ohio University Press.

Allison, Anne. 2013. *Precarious Japan*. Durham, NC: Duke University Press.

Alpes, Maybritt Jill. 2012. "Bushfalling at All Cost: The Economy of Migratory Knowledge in Anglophone Cameroon." *African Diaspora* 5: 90–115.

———. 2017. "Why Aspiring Migrants Trust Migration Brokers: the Moral Economy of Departure in Anglophone Cameroon." *Africa: The Journal of the International African Institute* 87(2): 304–21.

Alter, Joseph S. 1992. *The Wrestler's Body: Identity and Ideology in North India*. Berkeley: University of California Press.

———. 1995. "The Celibate Wrestler: Sexual Chaos, Embodied Balance and Competitive Politics in North India." *Contributions to Indian Sociology* 29: 109–31.

———. 1997. "Seminal Truth: A Modern Science of Male Celibacy in North India." *Medical Anthropology Quarterly* 11(3): 275–98.

Ammann, Carole, and Sandra Staudacher. 2021. "Masculinities in Africa Beyond Crisis: Complexity, Fluidity, and Intersectionality." *Gender, Place & Culture* 28(6): 759–68.

Andersson, Ruben. 2014. "Hunter and Prey: Patrolling Clandestine Migration in the Euro-African Borderlands." *Anthropological Quarterly* 87(1): 119–49.

Andrews, David L., and Michael L. Silk, eds. 2012. *Sport and Neoliberalism: Politics, Consumption, and Culture*. Philadelphia: Temple University Press.

Appadurai, Arjun. 1986. "Introduction: Commodities and the Politics of Value." In *The Social Life of Things: Commodities in Cultural Perspective*, edited by Arjun Appadurai, 3–63. Cambridge: Cambridge University Press.

———. 2013. *The Future as a Cultural Fact: Essays on the Global Condition*. London: Verso.

Archambault, Caroline S. 2011. "Ethnographic Empathy and the Social Context of Rights: 'Rescuing' Maasai Girls from Early Marriage." *American Anthropologist* 113(4): 632–43.

Ardener, Edwin. 1956. *Coastal Bantu of the Cameroons: The Kpe-Mboko, Duala-Limba and Tanga-Yasa Groups of the British and French Trusteeship Territories of the Cameroons*. London: International African Institute.

———. 1975. "Belief and the Problem of Women." In *Perceiving Women*, edited by Shirley Ardener, 1–27. London: Malaby Press.

———. 1996. "Witchcraft, Economics, and the Continuity of Belief." In *Kingdom on Mount Cameroon: Studies in the History of the Cameroon Coast, 1500–1970*, edited by Shirley Ardener, 243–60. Providence, RI: Berghahn Books. First published in 1970.

Ardener, Edwin, and Shirley Ardener. 1960. "Motives for Migration to Work: General Conclusions." In *Plantation and Village in the Cameroons: Some Economic and Social Studies*, edited by Edwin Ardener, Shirley Ardener, and W. A. Warmington, 248–63. London: Oxford University Press.

Argenti, Nicolas. 2007. *The Intestines of the State: Youth, Violence, and Belated Histories in the Cameroon Grassfields*. Chicago: University of Chicago Press.

———. 2010. "Things That Don't Come by the Road: Folktales, Fosterage, and Memories of Slavery in the Cameroon Grassfields." *Comparative Studies in Society and History* 52(2): 224–54.

Asad, Talal. 1993. "The Construction of Religion as an Anthropological Category." In *Genealogies of Religion: Discipline and Reasons of Power in Christianity and Islam*, edited by Talal Asad, 27–54. Baltimore: John Hopkins University Press.

Astuti, Rita. 2017. "On Keeping Up the Tension between Fieldwork and Ethnography." *HAU: Journal of Ethnographic Theory* 7(1): 9–14.

Atekmangoh, Christina. 2017. *"Les Mbengis"—Migration, Gender, and Family: The Moral Economy of Transnational Cameroonian Migrants' Remittances*. Bamenda: Langaa RPCIG.

Aterianus-Owanga, Alice. 2013. "A Rap Music 'Based on Strength': The Construction of Masculinity on the Libreville Rap Scene." *Cahiers d'études africaines* 209–10: 143–72.

Baller, Susann. 2014. "Urban Football Performances: Playing for the Neighbourhood in Senegal, 1950s–2000s." *Africa: The Journal of the International African Institute* 84(1): 17–35.

Banaś, Paweł. 2016. "For Every Drogba There Are Hundreds of West African Football Hopefuls Who Struggle." *The Conversation Africa*, 13 October 2016, retrieved 13 October 2016 from https://theconversation.com/for-every-drogba-there-are-hundreds-of-west-african-football-hopefuls-who-struggle-66533.

Baral, Anna. 2016. "Beyond Unrest: Changing Masculinities and Moral Becoming in an African Urban Market." *Etnofoor* 28(2): 33–53.

Bastian, Misty L. 1997. "Married in the Water: Spirit Kin and other Afflictions of Modernity in Southeastern Nigeria." *Journal of Religion in Africa* 27(2): 116–34.

Bawak, Jessie. 2012. "Mr. Henry Njalla Quan on STV Straight Talk with Jessie Bawak." YouTube, 18 May 2012, retrieved 18 December 2017 from https://www.youtube.com/watch?v=RC2VrBEhwNY.

Bayart, Jean-François. 1979. *L'État au Cameroun*. Paris: Presses de la Fondation Nationale des Sciences Politiques.
———. 2000. "Africa in the World: A History of Extraversion." *African Affairs* 99: 217–67.
Bekaert, Stefan. 2000. *System and Repertoire in Sakata Medicine (Democratic Republic of Congo)*. Uppsala: Uppsala University Press.
Berlant, Lauren. 2011. *Cruel Optimism*. Durham, NC: Duke University Press.
Besnier, Niko. 1996. "Heteroglossic Discourses on Nukulaelae Spirits." In *Spirits in Culture, History, and Mind*, edited by Jeannette Marie Mageo and Alan Howard, 75–97. London: Routledge.
———. 2012. "The Athlete's Body and the Global Condition: Tongan Rugby Players in Japan." *American Ethnologist* 39(3): 491–510.
———. 2015. "Sports Mobilities across Borders: Postcolonial Perspectives." *International Journal of the History of Sport* 32(7): 849–61.
———. 2018. "Globalization, Sport, and the Precarity of Masculinity." Last updated 31 January 2018, retrieved 7 September 2018 from http://www.global-sport.eu/.
Besnier, Niko, Susan Brownell, and Thomas F. Carter. 2018. *The Anthropology of Sport: Bodies, Borders, Biopolitics*. Oakland: University of California Press.
Besnier, Niko, Domenica Gisella Calabrò, and Daniel Guinness, eds. 2021. *Sport, Migration, and Gender in the Neoliberal Age*. London: Routledge.
Besnier, Niko, Daniel Guinness, Mark Hann, and Uroš Kovač. 2018. "Rethinking Masculinity in the Neoliberal Order: Cameroonian Footballers, Fijian Rugby Players, and Senegalese Wrestlers." *Comparative Studies in Society and History* 60(4): 839–72.
Bourdieu, Pierre. 1977. *Outline of a Theory of Practice*. Cambridge: Cambridge University Press.
———. 2004. "The Peasant and his Body." *Ethnography* 5(4): 579–99.
Brownell, Susan. 1995. *Training the Body for China: Sports in the Moral Order of People's Republic*. Chicago: University of Chicago Press.
Brusco, Elizabeth E. 1995. *The Reformation of Machismo: Evangelical Conversion and Gender in Colombia*. Austin: University of Texas Press.
Burchardt, Marian. 2011. "Challenging Pentecostal Moralism: Erotic Geographies, Religion, and Sexual Practices among Township Youth in Cape Town." *Culture, Health & Sexuality* 13(6): 669–83.
Burnton, Simon. 2018. "World Cup Stunning Moments: Cameroon Shock Argentina in 1990." *The Guardian*, 13 March 2018, retrieved 23 December 2018 from https://www.theguardian.com/football/ blog/2014/feb/12/world-cup-25-stunning-moments-cameroon-argentina.
Business in Cameroon. 2014. "Cameroon to Increase Minimum Wage from 28,000 to 36,270 FCFA." *Business in Cameroon*, 22 July 2014, retrieved 6 December 2017 from http://www.businessincameroon.com/public-management/2207-4959-cameroon-to-increase-minimum-wage-from-de-28-000-to-36-270-fcfa.
Caballero, Andrés. 2014. "Pray or Prey? Cameroon's Pentecostal Churches Face Crackdown." NPR, 13 April 2014, retrieved 13 January 2018 from http://www.npr.org/2014/04/13/300975474/pray-or-prey-cameroons-pentecostal-churches-face-crackdown.
Cepek, Michael L. 2016. "There Might Be Blood: Oil, Humility, and the Cosmopolitics of a Cof'an Petro-being." *American Ethnologist* 43(4): 623–35.
Clignet, Remi, and Maureen Stark. 1974. "Modernisation and Football in Camerouon." *Journal of Modern African Studies* 12(3): 409–21.
Cole, Jennifer. 2010. *Sex and Salvation: Imagining the Future in Madagascar*. Chicago: University of Chicago Press.

Cole, Jennifer, and Deborah Durham. 2007. "Introduction: Age, Regeneration, and the Intimate Politics of Globalization." In *Generations and Globalization: Youth, Age, and Family in New World Economy*, edited by Jennifer Cole and Deborah Durham, 1–28. Bloomington: Indiana University Press.

Cole, Jennifer and Christian Groes. 2016. "Introduction: Affective Circuits and Social Regeneration in African Migration." In *Affective Circuits: African Migrations to Europe and the Pursuit of Social Regeneration*, edited by Jennifer Cole and Christian Groes, 1–26. Chicago: University of Chicago Press.

Comaroff, Jean. 2009. "The Politics of Conviction: Faith on the Neoliberal Frontier." *Social Analysis* 53(1): 17–38.

Comaroff, Jean, and John L. Comaroff. 2000. "Millennial Capitalism: First Thoughts on a Second Coming." *Public Culture* 12(2): 291–343.

Connell, R. W. 1987. *Gender and Power*. Sydney: Allen and Unwin.

Connell, R. W., and J. W. Messerschmidt. 2005. "Hegemonic Masculinity: Rethinking the Concept." *Gender and Society* 19: 829–59.

Cornwall, Andrea. 2002. "Spending Power: Love, Money, and the Reconfiguration of Gender Relations in Ado-Odo, Southwestern Nigeria." *American Ethnologist* 29(4): 963–80.

Cornwall Andrea, and Nancy Lindisfarne, eds. 1994. *Dislocating Masculinity: Comparative Ethnographies*. London: Routledge.

Cornwall, Andrea, Frank Karioris, and Nancy Lindisfarne, eds. 2016. *Masculinities under Neoliberalism*. London: Zed.

Crawley, Michael. 2019. "'Condition': Energy, Time and Success amongst Ethiopian Runners." Doctoral thesis, University of Edinburgh.

———. 2021. "'This Is Business!': Ethiopian Runners in a Global Marketplace." In *Sport, Migration, and Gender in the Neoliberal Age*, edited by N. Besnier, D. G. Calabrò, and D. Guinness, 47–64. London: Routledge.

Csordas, Thomas J. 1990. "Embodiment as a Paradigm for Anthropology." *Ethos* 18(1): 5–47.

Darby, Paul. 2000. "The New Scramble for Africa: African Football Labour Migration to Europe." *European Sports History Review* 3: 217–44.

———. 2013. "Moving Players, Traversing Perspectives: Global Value Chains, Production Networks and Ghanaian Football Labour Migration." *Geoforum* 50: 43–53.

Darby, Paul, Gerard Akindes, and Matthew Kirwin. 2007. "Football Academies and the Migration of African Football Labor to Europe." *Journal of Sport & Social Issues* 31(2): 143–61.

Daswani, Girish. 2013. "On Christianity and Ethics: Rupture as Ethical Practice in Ghanaian Pentecostalism." *American Ethnologist* 40(3): 467–79.

———. 2015. *Looking Back, Moving Forward: Transformation and Ethical Practice in the Ghanaian Church of Pentecost*. Toronto: University of Toronto Press.

Dawley, William, and Brendan Jamal Thornton. 2018. "New Directions in the Anthropology of Religion and Gender: Faith and Emergent Masculinities." *Anthropological Quarterly* 91(1): 5–23.

de Genova, Nicholas. 2002. "Migrant Illegality and Deportability in Everyday Life." *Annual Review of Anthropology* 31: 419–47.

de la Cadena, Marisol. 2010. "Indigenous Cosmopolitics: Conceptual Reflections beyond 'Politics.'" *Cultural Anthropology* 25(2): 334–70.

de Witte, Marleen. 2012. "Buy the Future, Now! Charismatic Chronotypes in Neoliberal Ghana." *Etnofoor* 24(1): 80–104.

Donnelly, Peter, and Leanne Petherick. 2004. "Workers' Playtime? Child Labour at the Extremes of the Sporting Spectrum." *Sport in Society* 7(3): 301–21.

Drewal, Henry John, ed. 2008. *Sacred Waters: Arts for Mami Wata and Other Divinities in Africa and the Diaspora*. Bloomington: Indiana University Press.
Engelke, Matthew. 2004. "Discontinuity and the Discourse of Conversion." *Journal of Religion in Africa* 34(1–2): 82–109.
———. 2007. *A Problem of Presence: Beyond Scripture in an African Church*. Berkeley: University of California Press.
———. 2010. "Past Pentecostalism: Notes on Rupture, Realignment, and Everyday Life in Pentecostal and African Independent Churches." *Africa* 80(2): 177–99.
———. 2012. "Dangerous Things: One African Genealogy." In Dick Houtman and Birgit Meyer, eds. *Things: Religion and the Question of Materiality*: 40–61. New York: Fordham University Press.
Enria, Luisa. 2016. "'I Must Stand like a Man': Masculinity in Crisis in Post-war Sierra Leone." In *Masculinities under Neoliberalism*, edited by Andrea Cornwall, Frank Karioris, and Nancy Lindisfarne, 136–50. London: Zed.
Eriksen, Annelin, Ruy Llera Blanes, and Michelle MacCarthy. 2019. *Going to Pentecost: An Experimental Approach to Studies in Pentecostalism*. New York: Berghahn Books.
Esson, James. 2013. "A Body and a Dream at a Vital Conjuncture: Ghanaian Youth, Uncertainty and the Allure of Football." *Geoforum* 47: 84–92.
———. 2015a. "Better off at Home? Rethinking Responses to Trafficked West African Footballers in Europe." *Journal of Ethnic and Migration Studies* 41(3): 512–30.
———. 2015b. "Escape to Victory: Development, Youth Entrepreneurship and the Migration of Ghanaian Footballers." *Geoforum* 64: 47–55.
———. 2020. "Playing the Victim? Human Trafficking, African Youth, and Geographies of Structural Inequality." *Popul Space Place* 26: e2309.
Esson, James, and Eleanor Drywood. 2018. "Challenging Popular Representations of Child Trafficking in Football." *Journal of Criminological Research, Policy, and Practice* 4(1): 60–72.
Evans-Pritchard, Edward Evan. 1976. *Witchcraft, Oracles, and Magic among the Azande*. Oxford: Clarendon Press. Originally published in 1937.
Farquhar, Judith, and Margaret Lock. 2007. "Introduction." In *Beyond the Body Proper: Reading the Anthropology of Material Life*, edited by Margaret Lock and Judith Farquhar, 1–16. Durham, NC: Duke University Press.
Fassin, Didier. 2009. "Les économies morales revisitées." *Annales: Histoire, Sciences Sociales* 6: 1237–66.
Ferguson, James. 2006. *Global Shadows: Africa in the Neoliberal World Order*. Durham, NC: Duke University Press.
———. 2010. "The Uses of Neoliberalism." *Antipode* 41(S1): 166–84.
Fioratta, Susanna. 2015. "Beyond Remittance: Evading Uselessness and Seeking Personhood in Fouta Djallon, Guinea." *American Ethnologist* 42(2): 295–308.
Fokwang, Jude. 2008. "Being Young in Old Town: Youth Subjectivities and Associational Life in Old Town." Doctoral thesis, University of Toronto.
———. 2009. "Southern Perspective on Sport-in-Development: A Case Study of Football in Bamenda, Cameroon." In *Sport and International Development*, edited by Roger Levermore and Aaron Beacom, 198–218. Basingstoke: Palgrave Macmillan.
Foot Solidaire. 2017. "Qui Sommes Nous." Retrieved 1 February 2017 from http://www.footsolidaire.org/association-foot-solidaire/qui-sommes-nous.
Foucault, Michel. 1995. *Discipline and Punish: the Birth of the Prison*. New York: Vintage Books. First published in 1979.
———. 2008. *The Birth of Biopolitics: Lectures at the College de France 1978–1979*. Basingstoke: Palgrave Macmillan.

Freeman, Carla. 2014. *Entrepreneurial Selves: Neoliberal Respectability and the Making of a Caribbean Middle Class*. Durham, NC: Duke University Press.
Fuh, Divine. 2012. "The Prestige Economy: Veteran Clubs and Youngmen's Competition in Bamenda, Cameroon." *Urban Forum* 23: 501–26.
Gaibazzi, Paolo. 2012. "Cultivating Hustlers: The Agrarian Ethos of Soninke Migration." *Journal of Ethnic and Migration Studies* 39(2): 259–75.
———. 2014. "Visa Problem: Certification, Kinship, and the Production of 'Ineligibility' in the Gambia." *Journal of the Royal Anthropological Institute* 20: 38–55.
———. 2015. *Bush Bound: Young Men and Rural Permanence in Migrant West Africa*. New York: Berghahn Books.
Gershon, Ilana. 2011. "Neoliberal Agency." *Current Anthropology* 52(4): 537–55.
Geschiere, Peter. 1997. *The Modernity of Witchcraft. Politics and the Occult in Postcolonial Africa*. Charlottesville: University of Virginia Press.
———. 2009. *The Perils of Belonging: Autochthony, Citizenship, and Exclusion in Africa and Europe*. Chicago: University of Chicago Press.
———. 2013. *Witchcraft, Intimacy, and Trust: Africa in Comparison*. Chicago: University of Chicago Press.
Geschiere, Peter, and Francis B. Nyamnjoh. 2000. "Capitalism and Autochthony: The Seesaw of Mobility and Belonging." *Public Culture* 12(2): 423–52.
Gibson, Owen. 2015. "Sky and BT Retain Premier League TV Rights for Record £5.14bn." *The Guardian*, 10 February 2015, retrieved 17 December 2017 from https://www.theguardian.com/ football/2015/feb/10/premier-league-tv-rights-sky-bt.
Gifford, Paul. 2004. *Ghana's New Christianity: Pentecostalism in a Globalizing African Economy*. London: Hurst.
Gilbert, Juliet. 2015. "The Heart as a Compass: Preaching Self-Worth and Success to Single Young Women in a Nigerian Pentecostal Church." *Journal of Religion in Africa* 45: 307–33.
Graeber, David. 2015. "Radical Alterity Is Just Another Way of Saying 'Reality': A Reply to Eduardo Viveiros de Castro." *HAU: Journal of Ethnographic Theory* 5(2): 1–41.
Guilbert, Kieran. 2015. "Chasing Dreams: Young African Footballers Duped, Dumped by Traffickers." *Reuters*, 7 December 2015, retrieved 15 May 2021 from https://www.reuters.com/article/africa-soccer-trafficking/chasing-dreams-young-african-footballers-duped-dumped-by-traffickers-idINL8N13R3V920151207.
Guinness, Daniel. 2014. "Being Fijian in the Global System of Professional Rugby Union." Doctoral thesis, University of Oxford.
———. 2018. "Corporal Destinies: Faith, Ethno-nationalism, and Raw Talent in Fijian Professional Rugby Aspirations." *HAU: Journal of Ethnographic Theory* 8(1/2): 314–28.
Gutmann, Matthew C. 1996. *The Meaning of Macho: Being a Man in Mexico City*. Berkeley: University of California Press.
Guyer, Jane. 2004. *Marginal Gains: Monetary Transactions in Atlantic Africa*. Chicago: University of Chicago Press.
Hann, Mark. 2018. "Sporting Aspirations: Football, Wrestling, and Neoliberal Subjectivity in Urban Senegal." Doctoral thesis, University of Amsterdam.
———. 2021. "The Dream Is to Leave: Imagining Migration and Mobility through Sport in Senegal." In *Sport, Migration, and Gender in the Neoliberal Age*, edited by N. Besnier, D. G. Calabrò, and D. Guinness, 195–212. London: Routledge.
Harrison, Graham. 2010. *Neoliberal Africa: The Impact of Global Social Engineering*. London: Zed Books.
Haynes, Naomi. 2012. "Pentecostalism and the Morality of Money: Prosperity, Inequality,

and Religious Sociality on the Zambian Copperbelt." *Journal of the Royal Anthropological Institute (N.S.)* 18: 123–39.

———. 2013. "On the Potential and Problems of Pentecostal Exchange." *American Anthropologist* 115(1): 85–95.

———. 2017. *Moving by the Spirit: Pentecostal Social Life on the Zambian Copperbelt*. Oakland: University of California Press.

Hawkins, Ed. 2015a. *The Lost Boys: Inside Football's Slave Trade*. London: Bloomsbury.

———. 2015b. "Victims or Fraudsters? The World of Football Trafficking Laid Bare." *The Independent*, 22 December 2015, retrieved 15 May 2021 from https://www.independent.co.uk/sport/football/news-and-comment/victims-or-fraudsters-the-world-of-football-trafficking-a6783421.html.

Herdt, Gilbert. 1981. *Guardians of the Flutes*. Vol. 1: *Idioms of Masculinity*. Chicago: University of Chicago Press.

Hodgson, Dorothy L. 1999. "'Once Intrepid Warriors': Modernity and the Production of Maasai Masculinities." *Ethnology* 38(2): 121–50.

Holbraad, Martin. 2010. "Against the Motion." In "Ontology Is Just Another Word for Culture: Motion Tabled at the 2008 Meeting of the Group for Debates in Anthropological Theory, University of Manchester." Debate edited by Soumhya Venkatesan. *Critique of Anthropology* 30(2): 152–200.

Holbraad, Martin, and Morten Axel Pedersen. 2017. *The Ontological Turn: An Anthropological Exposition*. Cambridge: Cambridge University Press.

Honwana, Alcinda Manuel. 2012. *The Time of Youth: Work, Social Change, and Politics in Africa*. Sterling: Kumarian Press.

Hopkinson, Leo. 2019. "Hit and Move: Boxing and Belonging in Accra, Ghana." Doctoral thesis, University of Edinburgh.

———. 2021. "Being 'the Best Ever': Contradictions of Immobility and Aspiration for Boxers in Accra, Ghana." In *Sport, Migration, and Gender in the Neoliberal Age*, edited by N. Besnier, D. G. Calabrò, and D. Guinness, 176–94. London: Routledge.

Hossain, Adnan. 2021. "From Liberation to Neoliberalism: Race, Mobility, and Masculinity in Caribbean Cricket." In *Sport, Migration, and Gender in the Neoliberal Age*, edited by N. Besnier, D. G. Calabrò, and D. Guinness, 83–100. London: Routledge.

Igonya, Emmy Kageha, and Eileen Moyer. 2013. "Putting Sex on the Table: Sex, Sexuality and Masculinity among HIV-Positive Men in Nairobi, Kenya." *Culture, Health & Sexuality* sup4: S567–80.

Inhorn, Marcia C., and Emily A. Wentzell 2011. "Embodying Emergent Masculinities: Men Engaging with Reproductive and Sexual Health Technologies in the Middle East and Mexico." *American Ethnologist* 38(4): 801–15.

James, C. L. R. 2005. *Beyond a Boundary*. London: Yellow Jersey Press. First published in 1963.

Janson, Marloes. 2016. "Unity through Diversity: A Case Study of Chrislam in Lagos." *Africa: The Journal of the International African Institute* 86(4): 646–72.

Jeater, Diana. 2016. "Masculinity, Marriage and the Bible: New Pentecostalist Masculinities in Zimbabwe." In *Masculinities Under Neoliberalism*, edited by Andrea Cornwall, Frank Karioris, and Nancy Lindisfarne, 165–82. London: Zed Books.

Jeffrey, Craig. 2010. "Timepass: Youth, Class, and Time among Unemployed Young Men in India." *American Ethnologist* 37(3): 465–81.

Johnson-Hanks, Jennifer. 2005. "When the Future Decides: Uncertainty and Intentional Action in Contemporary Cameroon." *Current Anthropology* 46(3): 363–85.

Jones, Jeremy L. 2010. "'Nothing Is Straight in Zimbabwe:' The Rise of the *Kukiya-kiya* Economy 2000–2008." *Journal of Southern African Studies* 36(2): 285–99.

Jua, Nantang. 2004. "'Spatialization' and Valorization of Identities in Contemporary Cameroon." In *The Leadership Challenge in Africa: Cameroon Under Paul Biya*, edited by John Mukum Mbaku and Joseph Takougang, 299–334. Trenton: Africa World Press.

Kalir, Barak. 2005. "The Development of a Migratory Disposition: Explaining a 'New Emigration.'" *International Migration* 43(4): 167–96.

Kewir, James Kiven, Gordon Crawford, Maurice Beseng, and Nancy Annan. 2021. *Shrinking Civic Space and the Role of Civil Society in Resolution of Conflict in Anglophone Cameroon*. Retrieved 1 June 2021 from https://www.coventry.ac.uk/globalassets/media/global/08-new-research-section/ctpsr/civic_space_cameroon-web-report-jan-2021.pdf.

Kindzeka, Moki Edwin. 2015. "Reopened Cameroon Churches Fear Criticizing Government." *VOA*, 30 October 2015, retrieved 13 January 2018 from http://www.voanews.com/a/reopened-churches-in-camroon-not-critizing-biya-government/3029686.html.

Khan, Arsalan. 2018. "Pious Masculinity, Ethical Reflexivity, and Moral Order in an Islamic Piety Movement in Pakistan." *Anthropological Quarterly* 91(1): 53–77.

Klein, Alan M. 1991. *Sugarball: The American Game, the Dominican Dream*. New Haven, CT: Yale University Press.

———. 1993. *Little Big Men: Bodybuilding Subculture and Gender Construction*. Albany: State University of New York Press.

———. 2008. "Progressive Ethnocentrism: Ideology and Understanding in Dominican Baseball." *Journal of Sport and Social Issues* 32(2): 121–38.

Kleinman, Julie. 2016. "From Little Brother to Big Somebody: Coming of Age at the Gare du Nord." In *Affective Circuits: African Migrations to Europe and the Pursuit of Social Regeneration*, edited by Jennifer Cole and Christian Groes, 245–68. Chicago: University of Chicago Press.

Konings, Piet. 2006. "Solving Transportation Problems in African Cities: Innovative Responses by the Youth in Douala, Cameroon." *Africa Today* 53(1): 35–50.

———. 2011. *The Politics of Neoliberal Reforms in Africa: State and Civil Society in Cameroon*. Leiden: African Studies Centre.

Konings, Piet, and Francis Nyamnjoh. 2003. *Negotiating an Anglophone Identity: A Study of the Politics of Recognition and Representation in Cameroon*. Leiden: Brill.

Kovač, Uroš. 2016. "'Juju' and 'Jars': How African Athletes Challenge Western Notions of Doping." *The Conversation*, 28 October 2016, retrieved 13 January 2018 from https://theconversation.com/juju-and-jars-how-african-athletes-challenge-western-notions-of-doping-67567.

Laderman, Scott. 2014. *Empire in Waves: A Political History of Surfing*. Berkeley: University of California Press.

Laidlaw, James. 2015. "Proposing the Motion: A Slur for All Seasons." In "Debate: 'The Concept of Neoliberalism Has Become an Obstacle to the Anthropological Understanding of the Twenty-First Century.'" Debate edited by Soumhya Venkatesan. *Journal of the Royal Anthropological Institute (N.S.)* 21: 911–23.

Lambek, Michael. 2006. "Body and Mind in Mind, Body and Mind in Body: Some Anthropological Interventions in a Long Conversation." In *Anthropology in Theory: Issues in Epistemology*, edited by Henrietta L. Moore and Todd Sanders, 424–36. Oxford: Blackwell Publishing. Originally published in 1998.

———. 2010. "Toward an Ethics of the Act." In *Ordinary Ethics: Anthropology, Language, and Action*, edited by Michael Lambek, 39–63. New York: Fordham University Press.

———. 2012. "Religion and Morality." In *A Companion to Moral Anthropology*, edited by Didier Fassin, 341–58. New York: Fordham University Press.

———. 2014. "What Is 'Religion' for Anthropology? And What Has Anthropology Brought to 'Religion'?" In *A Companion to the Anthropology of Religion*, edited by Janice Boddy and Michael Lambek, 1–32. Malden: Wiley Blackwell.

Lammers, Marie-Christine. 2004. "Snakes and Sirens: An Anthropological Journey along the Plural Pathways to Experience Mystery, Interpret Suffering and Restore Health in contemporary Douala (Cameroon)." Doctoral thesis, University of Turin.

Lanfranchi, Pierre, and Matthew Taylor. 2001. *Moving with the Ball: The Migration of Professional Footballers*. Oxford: Berg.

Larkin, Brian. 2017. "The Form of Crisis and the Affect of Modernization." In *African Futures: Essays on Crisis, Emergence, and Possibility*, edited by Brian Goldstone and Juan Obarrio, 39–50. Chicago: University of Chicago Press.

Larkin, Brian, and Birgit Meyer. 2006. "Pentecostalism, Islam, and Culture: New Religious Movements in West Africa." In *Themes in West Africa's History*, edited by Emmanuel Kwaku Akyeampong, 286–312. Oxford: James Currey.

Law, Alan, Jean Harvey, and Stuart Kemp. 2002. "The Global Sport Mass Media Oligopoly: The Three Usual Suspects and More." *International Review for the Sociology of Sport* 37(3–4): 279–302.

Leseth, Anne. 1997. "The Use of Juju in Football: Sport and Witchcraft in Tanzania." In *Entering the Field: New Perspectives on World Football*, edited by Gary Armstrong and Richard Giulianotti, 159–74. Oxford: Berg.

Lima, Diana. 2012. "Prosperity and Masculinity: Neopentecostal Men in Rio de Janeiro." *Ethnos* 77(3): 372–99.

Lin, Xiaodong. 2016. "'Filial Son,' Dislocated Masculinity and the Making of Male Migrant Workers in Urban China." In *Masculinities under Neoliberalism*, edited by Andrea Cornwall, Frank Karioris, and Nancy Lindisfarne, 66–79. London: Zed.

Lindhardt, Martin. 2015. "Men of God: Neo-Pentecostalism and Masculinities in Urban Tanzania." *Religion* 45(2): 252–72.

Lindley, Anna. 2009. "The Early-Morning Phonecall: Remittances from a Refugee Diaspora Perspective." *Journal of Ethnic and Migration Studies* 35(8): 1315–34.

Lindsay, Lisa A., and Stephan F. Miescher, eds. 2003. *Men and Masculinities in Modern Africa*. Portsmouth: Heinemann.

Little, Christopher. 2016. "The Precarity of Men: Youth, Masculinity, and Money in a Papua New Guinean Town." Doctoral thesis, University of Toronto.

Mahmood, Saba. 2005. *Politics of Piety: The Islamic Revival and the Feminist Subject*. Princeton, NJ: Princeton University Press.

Mains, Daniel. 2007. "Neoliberal Times: Progress, Boredom, and Shame among Young Men in Urban Ethiopia." *American Ethnologist* 34(4): 659–73.

Mair, Jonathan. 2015. "Proposing the Motion. The Concept of Neoliberalism as a Moral Schema." In "Debate: 'The Concept of Neoliberalism Has Become an Obstacle to the Anthropological Understanding of the Twenty-First Century.'" Debate edited by Soumhya Venkatesan. *Journal of the Royal Anthropological Institute (N.S.)* 21: 911–23.

Mangan, James Anthony. 1998. *The Games Ethic and Imperialism: Aspects of the Diffusion of an Ideal*. London: Frank Cass. First published 1986.

Marshall, Ruth. 2009. *Political Spiritualities: The Pentecostal Revolution in Nigeria*. Chicago: University of Chicago Press.

Masquelier, Adeline. 1992. "Encounter With a Road Siren: Machines, Bodies and Commodities In the Imagination of a Mawri Healer." *Visual Anthropology Review* 8(1): 56–69.

———. 2013. "Teatime: Boredom and the Temporalities of Young Men in Niger." *Africa: The Journal of the International African Institute* 83(3): 385–402.

———. 2019. *Fada: Boredom and Belonging in Niger*. Chicago: Chicago University Press.

Mauss, Marcel. 1935. "Les Techniques du Corps." *Journal de psychologie* 32: 271–93.
Mbembe, Achille. 2001. *On the Postcolony*. Berkeley: University of California Press.
———. 2017. *Critique of Black Reason*. Durham, NC: Duke University Press.
Mbembe, Achille, and Janet Roitman. 1995. "Figures of the Subject in Times of Crisis." *Public Culture* 7(2): 323–52.
McGuigan, Jim. 2014. "The Neoliberal Self." *Culture Unbound* 6: 223–40.
McLean, Kristen E. 2021. "'Post-crisis Masculinities' in Sierra Leone: Revisiting Masculinity Theory." *Gender, Place & Culture* 28(6): 786–805.
Meiu, George Paul. 2009. "'Mombasa Morans': Embodiment, Sexual Morality, and Samburu Men in Kenya." *Canadian Journal of African Studies* 43(1):105–28.
Melly, Caroline M. 2011. "Titanic Tales of Missing Men: Reconfigurations of National Identity and Gendered Presence in Dakar, Senegal." *American Ethnologist* 38(2): 361–76.
Meyer, Birgit. 1998. "'Make a Complete Break with the Past': Memory and Postcolonial Modernity in Ghanaian Pentecostalist Discourse." *Journal of Religion in Africa* 28(3): 316–349.
———. 1999. *Translating the Devil: Religion and Modernity among the Ewe in Ghana*. Edinburgh: Edinburgh University Press.
———. 2004. "Christianity in Africa: from African Independent to Pentecostal-Charismatic Churches." *Annual Review of Anthropology* 33: 447–74.
———. 2008. "Mami Water as a Christian Demon: The Eroticism of Forbidden Pleasures in Southern Ghana." In *Sacred Waters: Arts for Mami Wata and Other Divinities in Africa and the Diaspora*, edited by Henry John Drewal, 383–98. Bloomington: Indiana University Press.
———. 2010. "Aesthetics of Persuasion: Global Christianity and Pentecostalism's Sensational Forms." *South Atlantic Quarterly* 109(4): 741–63.
———. 2014. "Mediation and Immediacy: Sensational Forms, Semiotic Ideologies, and the Question of the Medium." In *A Companion to the Anthropology of Religion*, edited by Janice Boddy and Michael Lambek, 309–26. Malden: Wiley Blackwell.
———. 2016. "How to Capture the 'Wow': R. R. Marett's Notion of Awe and the Study of Religion." *Journal of the Royal Anthropological Institute* 22: 7–26.
Meyer, Birgit, and Dick Houtman. 2012. "Introduction: Material Religion—How Things Matter." In *Things: Religion and the Question of Materiality*, edited by Dick Houtman and Birgit Meyer, 1–26. New York: Fordham University Press.
Miescher, Stephan F. 2005. *Making Men in Ghana*. Bloomington: Indiana University Press.
Millar, Kathleen M. 2018. *Reclaiming the Discarded: Life and Labor on Rio's Garbage Dump*. Durham, NC: Duke University Press.
Mirowski, Philip. 2009. "Defining Neoliberalism." In *The Road from Mont Pèlerin: The Making of the Neoliberal Thought Collective*, edited by Philip Mirowski and Dieter Plehwe, 417–55. Cambridge, MA: Harvard University Press.
Morrell, Robert. 2002. "Men, Movements, and Gender Transformation in South Africa." *Journal of Men's Studies* 10(3): 309–27.
Morrell, Robert, and Lahoucine Ouzgane. 2005. "African Masculinities: An Introduction." In *African Masculinities: Men in Africa from the Late Nineteenth Century to the Present*, edited by Lahoucine Ouzgane and Robert Morrell, 1–20. New York: Palgrave Macmillan.
Musariri, Linda, and Eileen Moyer. 2021. "A Black Man Is a Cornered Man: Migration, Precarity and Masculinities in Johannesburg." *Gender, Place & Culture* 28(6): 888–905.
Ndjio, Basile. 2008a. "Millennial Democracy and Spectral Reality in Post-colonial Africa." *African Journal of International Affairs* 11(2): 115–56.
———. 2008b. "Mokoagne Moni: Sorcery and New Forms of Wealth in Cameroon." *Past and Present* 200: 271–89.

———. 2009. "Migration, Architecture, and the Transformation of the Landscape in the Bamileke Grassfields of West Cameroon." *African Diaspora* 2: 73–100.

———. 2012. "Postcolonial Histories of Sexuality: The Political Invention of a Libidinal African Straight." *Africa: The Journal of the International African Institute* 82(4): 609–31.

Newell, Sasha. 2007. "Pentecostal Witchcraft: Neoliberal Possession and Demonic Discourse in Ivoirian Pentecostal Churches." *Journal of Religion in Africa* 37: 461–90.

———. 2012. *The Modernity Bluff: Crime, Consumption, and Citizenship in Côte d'Ivoire*. Chicago: University of Chicago Press.

Niehaus, Isak. 2015. "Moralising Magic? A Brief History of Football Potions in a South African Homeland Area, 1958–2010." *Journal of Southern African Studies* 41(5): 1053–66.

Niger-Thomas, Margaret. 2000. "'Buying Futures': The Upsurge of Female Entrepreneurship Crossing the Formal/Informal Divide in Southwest Cameroon." Doctoral thesis, African Studies Centre, Leiden.

———. 2001. "Women and the Arts of Smuggling." *African Studies Review* 44(2): 43–70.

Noddings, Nel. 1984. *Caring: A Feminine Approach to Ethics and Moral Education*. Berkeley: University of California Press.

Nonos, Frédéric. 2015. "Coupe Top 2015: 18 jeunes intègrent l'Efbc." Camfoot.com, 9 August 2015, retrieved 7 September 2017 from https://www.camfoot.com/actualites/coupe-top-2015-18-jeunes-integrent,21958.html.

Nyamnjoh, Francis. 2005. "Images of Nyongo amongst Bamenda Grassfielders in Whiteman Kontri." *Citizenship Studies* 9(3): 241–69.

———. 2011. "Cameroonian Bushfalling: Negotiation of Identity and Belonging in Fiction and Ethnography." *American Ethnologist* 38(4): 701–13.

Nyamnjoh, Francis B., and Ben Page. 2002. "Whiteman Kontri and the Enduring Allure of Modernity among Cameroonian Youth." *African Affairs* 101: 607–34.

Ocobock, Paul. 2017. *An Uncertain Age: The Politics of Manhood in Kenya*. Athens: Ohio University Press.

Okeowo, Alexis. 2016. "The Soccer-Star Refugees of Eritrea." *New Yorker*, 12 December 2016, retrieved 7 September 2017 from https://www.newyorker.com/magazine/2016/12/12/the-soccer-star-refugees-of-eritrea.

O'Neill, Bruce. 2014. "Cast Aside: Boredom, Downward Mobility, and Homelessness in Post-Communist Bucharest." *Cultural Anthropology* 29(1): 8–31.

Orock, Rogers Tabe Egbe. 2015. "Elites, Culture, and Power: The Moral Politics of 'Development' in Cameroon." *Anthropological Quarterly* 88(2): 533–68.

Osella, Caroline, and Filippo Osella. 2006. *Men and Masculinities in South India*. London: Anthem.

Ouzgane, Lahoucine, and Robert Morrell, eds. 2005. *African Masculinities: Men in Africa from the Late Nineteenth Century to the Present*. New York: Palgrave Macmillan.

Oyakhilome, Chris. 2016. *The Power of Your Mind: Walk in Divine Excellence through the Power of a Renewed Mind*. Abuja: LoveWorld Publishing.

Pannenborg, Arnold. 2008. "How to Win a Football Match in Cameroon: An Anthropological Study of Africa's Most Popular Sport." MA thesis, African Studies Centre, Leiden.

———. 2012. "Big Men Playing Football: Money, Politics and Foul Play in the African Game." Doctoral thesis, African Studies Centre, Leiden.

Parish, Jane. 2015. "Beyond Occult Economies: Akan Spirits, New York Idols, and Detroit Automobiles." *HAU: Journal of Ethnographic Theory* 5(2): 101–20.

Pearce, Tola Olu. 2012. "Reconstructing Sexuality in the Shadow of Neoliberal Globalization: Investigating the Approach of Charismatic Churches in Southwestern Nigeria." *Journal of Religion in Africa* 42: 345–68.
Peel, J. D. Y. 2000. *Religious Encounter and the Making of the Yoruba*. Bloomington: Indiana University Press.
———. 2016. "Similarity and Difference, Context and Tradition, in Contemporary Religious Movements in West Africa." *Africa: The Journal of the International African Institute* 86(4): 620–27.
Pelican, Michaela. 2013. "International Migration: Virtue or Vice? Perspectives from Cameroon." *Journal of Ethnic and Migration Studies* 39(2): 237–58.
Perry, Donna L. 2005. "Wolof Women, Economic Liberalization, and the Crisis of Masculinity in Rural Senegal." *Ethnography* 44(3): 207–26.
Piot, Charles. 2010. *Nostalgia for the Future: West Africa after the Cold War*. Chicago: University of Chicago Press.
Piot, Charles, with Kodjo Nicolas Batema. 2019. *The Fixer: Visa Lottery Chronicles*. Durham, NC: Duke University Press.
Poli, Raffaele. 2006. "Migration and Trade of African Football Players: Historic, Geographical, and Cultural Aspects." *Africa Spectrum* 41(3): 393–414.
Poli, Raffaele. 2010. "Understanding Globalization through Football: The New International Division of Labour, Migratory Channels and Transnational Trade Circuits." *International Review for the Sociology of Sport* 45(4): 491–506.
Poli, Raffaele, Loïc Ravenel, and Roger Besson. 2015. "Exporting Countries in World Football." *CIES Football Observatory Monthly Report* 8.
———. 2021. "Expatriate Footballers Worldwide: Global 2021 Study." *CIES Football Observatory Monthly Report* 65.
Pool, Robert. 1994. *Dialogue and the Interpretation of Illness: Conversations in a Cameroon Village*. Oxford: Berg.
Pype, Katrien. 2007. "Fighting Boys, Strong Men and Gorillas: Notes on the Imagination of Masculinities in Kinshasa." *Africa: The Journal of the International African Institute* 77(2): 250–71.
———. 2011. "Confession cum Deliverance: In/Dividuality of the Subject among Kinshasa's Born-Again Christians." *Journal of Religion in Africa* 41: 280–310.
———. 2012. *The Making of the Pentecostal Melodrama: Religion, Media, and Gender in Kinshasa*. New York: Berghahn Books.
Ralph, Michael. 2007. "Prototype: In Search of the Perfect Senegalese Basketball Physique." *International Journal of the History of Sport* 24(2): 238–63.
Ratele, Kopano. 2016. *Liberating Masculinities*. Cape Town: HSRC Press.
Rial, Carmen. 2012. "Banal Religiosity: Brazilian Athletes as New Missionaries of the Neo-Pentecostal Diaspora." *Vibrant* 9(2): 130–59.
Rio, Knut, Michelle MacCarthy, and Ruy Blanes. 2017. "Introduction to Pentecostal Witchcraft and Spiritual Politics in Africa and Melanesia." In *Pentecostalism and Witchcraft: Spiritual Warfare in Africa and Melanesia*, edited by Knut Rio, Michelle MacCarthy, and Ruy Blanes, 1–36. Basingstoke: Palgrave Macmillan.
Robbins, Joel. 2004. "The Globalization of Pentecostal and Charismatic Christianity." *Annual Review of Anthropology* 33: 117–43.
———. 2007. "Continuity Thinking and the Problem of Christian Culture: Belief, Time, and the Anthropology of Christianity." *Current Anthropology* 48(1): 5–38.
———. 2009. "Pentecostal Networks and the Spirit of Globalization: On the Social Productivity of Ritual Forms." *Social Analysis* 53(1): 55–66.

———. 2013. "Beyond the Suffering Subject: Toward an Anthropology of the Good." *Journal of the Royal Anthropological Institute* 19(3): 447–62.
Roitman, Janet. 2017. "Africa Otherwise." In *African Futures: Essays on Crisis, Emergence, and Possibility*, edited by Brian Goldstone and Juan Obarrio, 23–38. Chicago: University of Chicago Press.
Röschenthaler, Ute. 2004. "Transacting Obasinjom: The Dissemination of a Cult Agency in the Cross River Area." *Africa: The Journal of the International African Institute* 74(2): 241–76.
Ruel, Malcolm. 1982. "Christians as Believers." In *Religious Organization and Religious Experience*, edited by John Davis, 9–31. London: Academic Press.
Sabar, Galia. 2010. "Witchcraft and Concepts of Evil amongst African Migrant Workers in Israel." *Canadian Journal of African Studies/La Revue canadienne des études africaines* 44(1): 110–41.
Schatzberg, Michael G. 2006. "Soccer, Science and Sorcery: Causation and African Football." *Africa Spectrum* 41(2): 35–69.
Schultz, Susanne U. 2021. "'It's Not Easy.' Everyday Suffering, Hard Work and Courage. Navigating Masculinities Post Deportation in Mali." *Gender, Place & Culture* 28(6): 870–87.
Scotch, N. A. 1961. "Magic, Sorcery, and Football among Urban Zulu: A Case of Reinterpretation under Acculturation." *Journal of Conflict Resolution* 5(1): 70–74.
Scott, James C. 1976. *The Moral Economy of the Peasant: Rebellion and Subsistence in Southeast Asia*. New Haven, CT: Yale University Press.
Shaw, Rosalind. 2002. *Memories of the Slave Trade: Ritual and the Historical Imagination in Sierra Leone*. Chicago: University of Chicago Press.
Silberschmidt, Margrethe. 2001. "Disempowerment of Men in Rural and Urban East Africa: Implications for Male Identity and Sexual Behavior." *World Development* 29(4): 657–71.
Simoni, Valerio. 2015. "Breadwinners, Sex Machines and Romantic Lovers: Entangling Masculinities, Moralities, and Pragmatic Concerns in Touristic Cuba." *Etnográfica* 19(2): 389–411.
Smith, Daniel Jordan. 2004. "Youth, Sin and Sex in Nigeria: Christianity and HIV/AIDS-Related Beliefs and Behaviour among Rural-Urban Migrants." *Culture, Health & Sexuality* 6(5): 425–37.
———. 2009. "Managing Men, Marriage, and Modern Love: Women's Perspectives on Intimacy and Male Infidelity in Southeastern Nigeria." In *Love in Africa*, edited by Jennifer Cole and Lynn M. Thomas, 157–80. Chicago: University of Chicago Press.
———. 2017. *To Be a Man is Not a One-Day Job: Masculinity, Money, and Intimacy in Nigeria*. Chicago: University of Chicago Press.
Soothill, Jane E. 2007. *Gender, Social Change and Spiritual Power: Charismatic Christianity in Ghana*. Leiden: Brill.
Spall, John. 2020. *Manhood, Morality & the Transformation of Angolan Society: MPLA Veterans & Post-war Dynamics*. Rochester, NY: James Currey.
Spronk, Rachel. 2012. *Ambiguous Pleasures: Sexuality and Middle Class Self-Perceptions in Nairobi*. New York: Berghahn Books.
———. 2014. "The Idea of African Men: Dealing with the Cultural Contradictions of Sex in Academia and in Kenya." *Culture, Health & Sexuality* 16(5): 504–17.
Tanku, Tapang Ivo. 2013. "Cameroon's President Orders Pentecostal Churches Closed." CNN, 15 August 2013, retrieved 13 January 2018 from http://edition.cnn.com/2013/08/14/world/africa/cameroon-churches.
Thompson, Edward P. 1971. "The Moral Economy of the English Crowd in the Eighteenth Century." *Past & Present* 50: 76–136.

Thornton, Jamal. 2016. *Negotiating Respect: Pentecostalism, Masculinity, and the Politics of Spiritual Authority in the Dominican Republic*. Gainesville: University Press of Florida.
Thornton, Brendan Jamal. 2018. "Victims of Illicit Desire: Pentecostal Men of God and the Specter of Sexual Temptation." *Anthropological Quarterly* 91(1):133–71.
Tonda, Joseph. 2002. *La guérison divine en Afrique Central (Congo, Gabon)*. Paris: Karthala.
Trouillot, Michel Rolph. 2001. "The Anthropology of the State in the Age of Globalization: Close Encounters of the Deceptive Kind." *Current Anthropology* 42(1): 125–38.
Tsing, Anna Lowehaupt. 2015. *The Mushroom at the End of the World: On the Possibility of Life in Capitalist Ruins*. Princeton, NJ: Princeton University Press.
Ungruhe, Christian, and James Esson. 2017. "A Social Negotiation of Hope: Male West African Youth." *Boyhood Studies* 10(1): 22–43.
van de Kamp, Linda. 2011. "Converting the Spirit Spouse: The Violent Transformation of the Pentecostal Female Body in Maputo, Mozambique." *Ethnos* 76(4): 510–33.
van der Meij, Nienke, and Paul Darby. 2014. "No One Would Burden the Sea and Then Never Get Any Benefit: Family Involvement in Players' Migration to Football Academies in Ghana." In *Football and Migration: Perspectives, Places, Players*, edited by Richard Elliott and John Harris, 159–79. London: Routledge.
van Dijk, Rijk. 1998. "Pentecostalism, Cultural Memory and the State: Contested Representations of Time in Postcolonial Malawi." In *Memory and the Postcolony: African Anthropology and the Critique of Power*, edited by Richard Werbner, 155–81. London: Zed Books.
van Klinken, Adriaan S. 2012. "Men in the Remaking: Conversion Narratives and Born-Again Masculinity in Zambia." *Journal of Religion in Africa* 42: 215–39.
———. 2016. "Pentecostalism, Political Masculinity and Citizenship: The Born-Again Male Subject as Key to Zambia's National Redemption." *Journal of Religion in Africa* 46: 129–57.
van Stapele, Naomi. 2021. "Providing to Belong: Masculinities, Hustling and Economic Uncertainty in Nairobi 'Ghettos.'" *Africa: The Journal of the International African Institute* 91(1): 57–76.
Vásquez, Manuel A. 2011. *More Than Belief: A Materialist Theory of Religion*. Oxford: Oxford University Press.
Vidacs, Bea. 2010. *Visions of a Better World: Football in the Cameroonian Social Imagination*. Münster: Lit Verlag.
Vigh, Henrik. 2006. *Navigating Terrains of War: Youth and Soldiering in Guinea-Bissau*. New York: Berghahn Books.
———. 2009. "Motion Squared: A Second Look at the Concept of Social Navigation." *Anthropological Theory* 9(4): 419–38.
———. 2015. "Militantly Well." *HAU: Journal of Ethnographic Theory* 5(3): 93–110.
———. 2016. "Life's Trampoline: On Nullification and Cocaine Migration in Bissau." In *Affective Circuits: African Migrations to Europe and the Pursuit of Social Regeneration*, edited by Jennifer Cole and Christian Groes, 223–44. Chicago: University of Chicago Press.
———. 2017. "Caring through Crime: Ethical Ambivalence and the Cocaine Trade in Bissau." *Africa: The Journal of the International African Institute* 87(3): 479–95.
Vigh, Henrik Erdman, and David Brehm Sausdal. 2014. "From Essence Back to Existence: Anthropology beyond the Ontological Turn." *Anthropological Theory* 14(1): 49–73.
Viveiros de Castro, Eduardo. 2011. "Zeno and the Art of Anthropology: Of Lies, Beliefs, Paradoxes, and Other Truths." *Common Knowledge* 17(1): 128–45.
———. 2015. "Who Is Afraid of the Ontological Wolf? Some Comments on an Ongoing Anthropological Debate." *Cambridge Journal of Anthropology* 33(1): 2–17.

Warnier, Jean-Pierre. 1993. *L'esprit d'entreprise au Cameroun*. Paris: Karthala.
———. 2007. *The Pot King: The Body and Technologies of Power*. Leiden: Brill.
Weiss, Brad. 2009. *Street Dreams and Hip Hop Barbershops: Global Fantasy in Urban Tanzania*. Bloomington: Indiana University Press.
West, Harry G. 2005. *Kupilikula, Governance, and the Invisible Realm in Mozambique*. Chicago: University of Chicago Press.
Wignall, Ross. 2016. "From Swagger to Serious: Managing Young Masculinities between Faiths at a Young Men's Christian Association Centre in The Gambia." *Journal of Religion in Africa* 46: 288–323.
Wilcox, Rosalinde G. 2008. "Mami Watas, Miengu, and Mermaids: Water Spirits of Coastal Cameroon." In *Sacred Waters: Arts for Mami Wata and Other Divinities in Africa and the Diaspora*, edited by Henry John Drewal, 293–302. Bloomington: Indiana University Press.
Williams, John. 1994. "The Local and the Global in English Soccer and the Rise of Satellite Television." *Sociology of Sport Journal* 11(4): 376–97.
Willis, Roxana, Joseph McAulay, Ndjodi Ndeunyema, and James Angove. 2019. *Human Rights Abuses in the Cameroon Anglophone Crisis: A Submission of Evidence to UK Parliament*. Report from the University of Oxford Faculty of Law. Retrieved 1 June 2021 from https://ohrh.law.ox.ac.uk/wordpress/wp-content/uploads/2019/11/Cameroon-Anglophone-Crisis-Report-online.pdf.
Yang, Jie. 2010. "The Crisis of Masculinity: Class, Gender, and Kindly Power in Post-Mao China." *American Ethnologist* 37(3): 550–62.
Zigon, Jarrett. 2011. *"HIV Is God's Blessing": Rehabilitating Morality in Neoliberal Russia*. Berkeley: University of California Press.

Index

academy/ies, 2, 6, 7, 16, 39, 41, 43, 49–59, 68, 74
adulthood, 3, 5, 7, 13–15, 51, 63, 67, 68, 83
Africa Cup of Nations, 40, 61
age falsification, 20, 61, 62, 71
agent(s), 2, 40–42, 59
Ahidjo, Ahmadou, 27, 29
alcohol (*mimbo*), 74, 75, 79, 89, 125, 128, 130, 144
Aliche, Saint Collins, 37, 109–12, 116, 117, 134–36
ancestral worship, 38, 70n6, 85, 95n4, 96, 100, 102, 113, 118n2. *See also* traditional spirituality
anointed oil, 3, 98, 111–14
anointed stickers, 98, 110–14
anxiety, 5, 122, 125, 128, 138
Apostolic Church, 34, 35, 78, 99, 107, 134, 144
Appadurai, Arjun, 63, 146
Ardener, Edwin, 116, 117, 119n8
Ardener, Shirley, 116, 117
aspiration(s), 3–5, 45, 50, 72. *See also* dreams
 athletic, 145
 in football, 145, 146
 of mobility, 134, 150, 151
Atem, Valentine, 77, 105, 107
austerity, 5, 9, 11, 12, 21, 44, 65, 151

Bakossi, 74, 95n2
Bakweri, 18, 27, 32, 33, 52, 75, 76, 95n2, 101, 119n8, 128–32
Bamenda, 28, 30, 31, 44, 47n11, 109, 149
Banyangi, 95n2, 101, 127, 139
"big men", 16, 22n6, 29–32, 46, 51, 55, 56, 62, 82, 89

Biya, Paul, viii, 29–33, 44, 109, 110, 118n5. *See also* CPDM
black magic. *See* witchcraft
body/ies, 25, 81, 98, 108, 122–40 *passim*. *See also* capital, bodily
Bonu, Innocent, 33
Buea, 1, 16, 17, 23, 111, 139
Buea Young Star FC, 1, 16–19, 49, 55, 58–62, 65–69, 74, 78, 115
bushfalling, 45. *See also* migration

Cameroon,
 Anglophone, 11, 18, 19, 25–28, 54
 armed conflict in, viii, ix, 11, 12, 26, 47n3
 colonial, ix, 18, 23–28, 32, 90
 Francophone, 25, 26, 39, 54, 106
 independence, 25, 28
 languages of, 18 (*see also* Krio, Mboko Tok, Pidgin)
 national football team, 23, 38, 39, 43, 52, 61, 90
 Northwest Region, 11, 28, 32
 postcolonial, 23, 26–29, 68, 69
 Southwest Region, 11, 16–19, 27, 28, 32, 35, 46, 82, 129, 132
capital,
 bodily, 5, 9, 122, 133
 political, 29–32, 51
 social, 62, 64
 symbolic, 28, 32, 62
capitalism, 8, 9, 13, 21, 145, 148, 150
 millennial, 8, 149 (*see also* neoliberalism)
CDC (Cameroon Development Corporation) 26–29, 33. *See also* parastatal(s)
CDC Tiko, 28, 29, 31, 32, 106

CDC Victoria FC Limbe, 28, 29, 33
Christ Embassy International, 84, 95n3, 124, 140
Christianity, 85, 97, 105, 117
    Baptist Church, 33, 34, 113
    born-again, 34, 96, 97, 99, 132, 134, 144
    Catholicism, 34, 70n6, 99, 110
    history of, in Cameroon, 33, 34
    muscular, 25
    Pentecostal (*see* Pentecostalism)
    Presbyterianism, 34, 57
    Protestantism, 10, 34, 100, 123
club(s). *See* academy/ies
coaches/coaching, 106, 107, 128, 131, 139. *See also* manager(s)
Comaroff, Jean, 5, 8, 10, 118, 149, 150
Comaroff, John L, 5, 8, 10, 118, 149, 150
commercialization of football, 24, 38, 40, 41, 50, 146
commodification of players, 7, 21, 50, 63–65, 67, 146, 148
commodity prices, 29
corporatization, 7
CPDM (Cameroon People's Democratic Movement), 31–33, 44, 47n5, 47n9, 52. *See also* Biya, Paul
crisis,
    economic, 3, 6, 11, 12, 21, 29, 43, 44, 65, 92
    of masculinity (*see* masculinity)
    moral, 92
    political, ix, 11, 12
cruel optimism, 5, 7, 9

dash (to gift), 73, 87, 89, 128
democratization, 29–33, 44, 46
    good governance, 30, 44
demonic forces, 58, 95n4, 96, 97, 108, 109
deregulation, 3, 7
devil, the, 1, 3, 4, 100, 104, 148
"devil league" (regional), 66, 68
diet, 129–30, 138–41. *See also* fasting
Dikongue, Eteki Charles, 31, 32
discipline, 65, 72, 79, 90–93, 122–50 *passim*
disobedient footballers, 72. *See also* masculinity, stereotypes of
don man, 75, 81

Douala, 2, 26, 28, 44, 54, 82, 106
dreams, 5–7, 9, 36, 43–50, 59, 60, 85, 89, 95n5, 146. *See also* aspirations
drinking. *See* alcohol
Drogba, Didier, 6, 80
dualism, 100, 131

Ecole de Football Brasseries du Cameroon, 2, 43, 54, 73. *See also* academy
ejaculation/wet dreams, 121, 122, 125, 126, 132
Elite One (league), 16, 49, 52, 53, 56, 57, 66, 106
elites, ethnic/regional, 27–33, 47n6, 51, 52, 56, 58, 62, 69
English Premier League, 23, 40, 66, 67
Enoh, Eyong, 90, 143–45
entrepreneurs of the self, 5, 70n3
ethics,
    of care, 88
    personal, 34, 35
    of possibility vs. probability, 146 (*see* Appadurai)
ethnicization of politics, 32
ethnography, 10, 16–19, 95n4, 124, 130, 147
Eto'o, Samuel, 6, 82
European football, 2, 3, 18, 19, 23, 24, 39–43, 61, 74, 86
exploitation, 7, 42, 64, 65. *See also* human trafficking

fasting, 34, 138, 140, 141
FECAFOOT (Fédération Camerounaise de Football), 26, 28, 56, 62, 66
fickleness of football industry, 3, 54, 64, 71, 73, 85
FIFA (Fédération Internationale de Football Association), 39, 40, 43, 62, 64
focus, 5, 22, 65, 67, 72, 85, 144, 145, 150
Foot Solidaire, 41
freedom of association, 33, 47n10. *See also* liberty laws
free enterprise, 3, 7, 50
Full Gospel Mission, 34, 35, 121
future thinking/orientation, 49–51, 67–69, 88–92, 122–124, 144–46

gendered
  aspirations, 13, 142
  bodies, 10
  expectations, 86
  identity, 12, 122
  morality, 14–16, 72, 88, 91–94, 122, 124, 132, 142
  subject(s), 5, 8–11, 14, 15, 122, 145
gerontocracy, 6, 89
globalization, 5–9, 13–16, 40, 63, 70n3, 146–50
global production of desire, 10, 153
Grassfields/fielders, 32, 54, 74, 82, 89, 90, 95n2, 138
  fondoms, 138
  See also Northwest Region

hegemonic alliance, 29–31
history of African/Cameroonian football, 24–26, 28, 46
Holy Spirit, 2, 3, 10, 34, 96, 97, 100, 107–9, 113, 118, 123
human trafficking, 41, 42, 48n14, 62–65, 70n11
  Article 19 (recruitment of minors), 62, 63
  International Centre for Sport Security, 41
humility, 14, 72, 88, 90–92, 94, 148–50

ideological resources, 92, 93, 118, 153
idleness, 5, 15, 83, 84
IMF (International Monetary Fund), 7, 29, 30, 44, 146
interquarter tournaments, 23, 73–80, 105
Islam (reformist), 47n11, 92

jars, 37, 38, 47n12, 96–107, 109, 111, 113–118n2, 149, 150. *See also* magico-religious practices, sorcery
jars man, 100–103, 116. *See also* traditional healer
Joshua, T B, 35, 91
juju. *See jars*

kinship, 4, 5, 11, 60, 74, 80–88, 120
kontri-nayn, 79, 80, 140
Krio, 18. *See also* Pidgin English

Léa, Eugène N'Jo, 39
liberalism, classical economic, 147
liberty laws, 33. *See also* freedom of association
Limbe, 16–18, 33, 34, 47n4, 75, 127. *See also* Unisport Limbe FC
Lions Indomptables. *See* Cameroon national football team

magico-religious practices, 21, 22n1, 37, 38, 96–98, 101, 114. *See also jars*, sorcery, witchcraft
manager(s)/management, 30–33, 51–61, 85–94
manhood, tropes of, 13, 72, 92, 94, 97
man of God. *See* men of God
marine spirits, 134–36, 142n7. *See also* spiritual wives
masculinity/ies
  "African", 4, 13
  crisis of, 11, 12
  hegemonic, 4, 12, 15, 80
  moral, 5, 14, 72, 88, 93, 94
  precarity of, defined 12, 13
  stereotypes of, 4, 89, 90, 97, 127
  traditional, 89, 93, 94
Masquelier, Adeline, 15, 136
materiality, 113, 123
Mayebi, John, 106, 107, 131
Mboko Tok, 18, 19, 22n4, 75. *See also* Pidgin English
medicine. *See jars*
medicine man. *See* traditional healer
megachurch, 91, 109, 110, 113
men of God (MOG), 1, 3, 4, 10, 20, 37, 89, 96, 99, 109–11, 116, 134–36, 140–42, 148, 149. *See also* Pentecostal pastors
Merrick, Joseph, 33, 34
Middle Farm, 76, 83
migrants' remittances, 45
migration, 4–6, 19, 39–46, 61–65
  "irregular", 7, 41, 42
migration broker (*doki-man*), 45, 61, 86, 95n6
miracle(s), 34, 35, 84, 89, 91, 109, 110, 114, 145, 150
mobility, 4, 38–46, 63–65, 74, 92, 94, 122
monogamy, 72, 92, 93, 134, 148

moral
 economy, 14, 49, 51, 56–58, 68, 69
 evaluation/judgment, 14, 15, 72, 73, 92, 94
 subject(s), 11, 14, 25, 72, 73, 94
morality, 16, 21, 92, 93, 122, 138, 151. *See also* gendered morality, Pentecostal morality

Ndi, Ni John Fru, 30, 31
neoliberalism, 3, 30, 49, 51, 145–47
 principles of, 3, 7
 uses of, 146
 See also austerity, capitalism, deregulation, free enterprise, political economy, structural adjustment
nightlife (*njoka*), 4, 75, 79, 125, 130, 132, 144
N'Jie, Clinton, 22n5, 23
nyongo, 63, 117. *See also* witchcraft

Obasinjom, 101. *See also* jars, traditional healers
occult, 4, 10, 38, 56–58, 96, 100, 102, 149. *See also* witchcraft
 economies, 8, 149

parastatal(s), 16, 26–29, 33, 52, 56, 62, 69, 147. *See also* CDC
parents, 4, 54, 81–86. *See also* kinship
passport(s), 1, 2, 15, 60–62, 81, 86, 138
patriarchy, 12, 136, 150
patrimony, 29, 30, 44
Pentecostal
 morality, 36, 37, 90, 92, 93, 145, 149
 objects, 98, 109–18 (*see also* anointed oil, anointed stickers)
 pastors, 3, 11, 37, 57, 84, 85, 89, 109, 110, 122 (*see also* men of God)
Pentecostalism,
 break from traditional spirituality (*see* rupture)
 and control of sexuality, 132–38 (*see also* sexual practices)
 and diet, 140, 141
 neo-charismatic, 33–35, 37, 84, 96, 109
 Nigerian, 34, 35, 91, 93, 109, 110, 113, 124
 origins, 10, 33–35
 overlap with traditional spirituality, 107, 113–18
perseverance, 7, 91
Pidgin English (Cameroon), 18, 32, 37, 45, 75, 119n7, 142n3. *See also* Mboko Tok
pikin (young man/child), 13, 74, 81, 127
plantations, 26, 27, 32, 90
political economy, 13, 22, 49, 50, 57, 68, 69. *See also* moral economy
politics of belonging, 32, 33
polygamy/polygyny, 13, 89, 142n5
positive thinking, 84, 95n3
poverty/stagnation, ix, 9, 84, 89, 92, 93, 106, 149
power of God, 105, 107–12
prayer, 36, 37, 57, 58, 99, 109–16
 power house events, 37
precarity,
 delineated, 5, 7, 12, 13
 new forms of, 10, 21, 50, 69, 147, 153
preparation, psychological, 57, 106, 107
president(s), football. *See* manager(s)
Prisons Social Club of Buea, 28, 29
proactive approach. *See* positive thinking
prophecy, 34, 37, 98, 102, 114–17, 135, 141, 142n6
prosperity gospel, 8, 34, 35
 "name it and claim it", 35, 84
 See also Pentecostalism

Quan, Henry Njalla, 33, 47n8

racism, 3, 14, 87, 91
reality of spiritual powers, 98
religion, 10, 72, 92
risk, 6, 8, 49
rituals/rites, 4, 57, 63, 75, 98, 102, 116, 129
rupture, spiritual, 11, 21, 96, 97, 104, 105, 107–9, 113–18

Saint Collins. *See* Aliche
Saker, Alfred, 34
santé (casual football), 23, 75, 76
secret societies, 56–58, 70n6, 76, 102, 104
self-fashioning, 72, 73, 92, 93, 97, 118
sexual activity, 9, 75, 120–31
 policing of, 132–36, 138
slave trade, 63, 64, 65

social navigation, 150
sorcellerie. *See* sorcery
sorcery, 4, 11, 22n1, 22n6, 33, 38, 46, 47n12, 57, 96, 118, 148. *See also* jars, magico-religious practices, witchcraft
spiritual
   attacks, 102–5
   eyes, 98, 102, 114–17
   wives, 121, 135, 136 (*see also* marine spirits)
spirituality,
   delineated, 2–5, 8–11
   Pentecostal (*see* Pentecostalism)
   traditional, 96, 97
"star" (spiritual entity), 3, 114–17, 129
strong-hed (stubborn) man, 65, 81, 86, 88
structural adjustment, ix, 3, 5–7, 11, 12, 29, 30, 46, 146, 147
suffering, 7, 49–51, 67–69, 85–87, 91, 147–49
   subject(s), 49, 50, 68

talent, squandering of, 83, 84
television, 40, 146
   satellite, 40, 41, 146
Tiko United. *See* CDC Tiko
traditional healer(s), 4, 57, 100, 104–6, 110, 117, 121
transfer(s), 39, 60, 61, 64, 125, 131

uncertainty, 2–11, 72, 151, 153
   economic, 5, 6, 8, 13, 45, 73, 147, 150

in football, 29, 67, 91–93, 97, 98, 114, 115, 148, 149
Unisport Limbe FC, 16, 49, 51–61, 78, 140
"useless man", 3–5, 11, 13–15, 72, 80–88, 91, 94, 151

vices,
   masculine, 79–81, 128, 132
   urban, 80, 92, 148
victimhood, 15, 64, 70n11, 73, 145, 150
Victoria. *See* Limbe
Victoria United. *See* CDC Victoria FC Limbe
"village mentality", 89
virility, 4, 9, 13
visa(s), 1, 41, 60, 61, 71, 74, 86, 134–36

waytman, 16, 19, 20, 43, 77, 107
waytman kontri (the West), 19, 45, 74, 75, 81, 90
wesua/pala-pala. *See* wrestling
Winners Chapel, 35, 37, 109, 117, 149. *See also* prosperity gospel
witchcraft, 4, 8, 38, 92, 96, 97, 100–104, 107, 110, 117. *See also* jars, magico-religious practices, occult, sorcery
World Bank, 7, 29, 30, 44, 45, 146
wrestling, 18, 75, 76, 129–32, 138, 142n4

Yaoundé, viii, 26, 28, 54, 106, 109

zigzagging. *See* social navigation